STEP BY STEP

D0431135

STEP BY STEP

Daily Meditations for
Living the Twelve Steps

MURIEL ZINK

Ballantine Books   New York

Sale of this book without a front cover may be unauthorized. If this book is coverless, it may have been reported to the publisher as "unsold or destroyed" and neither the author nor the publisher may have received payment for it.

Copyright © 1991 by Muriel Zink

All rights reserved under International and Pan-American Copyright Conventions. Published in the United States by Ballantine Books, a division of Random House, Inc., New York, and simultaneously in Canada by Random House of Canada Limited, Toronto.

Library of Congress Catalog Card Number: 91-91908
ISBN: 0-345-36759-6

Cover design by James R. Harris
Text design by Holly Johnson

Manufactured in the United States of America

First Edition: November 1991
10 9 8 7 6 5 4 3 2 1

DEDICATION

This book is dedicated to all the beautiful people who, for over thirty years, have inspired me with their wisdom, supported me with their love, and wisely let me make enough mistakes to surrender to a new way of life.

Also, to my husband Russell, my wonderful family, and their wonderful families who—had it not been for my recovery—would have experienced a far different wife, mother, mother-in-law, and grandmother.

ACKNOWLEDGMENTS

I am deeply indebted to my friends Jack Fahey and Claudia Black for their friendship, patience, generosity and unfailing encouragement. Their support and unflagging enthusiasm was, in large measure, the catalyst that kept me going when I thought the well had dried up.

My editor, Cheryl Woodruff, not only proved to be of inestimable sensitivity and patience but somehow also succeeded in being on my same wavelength in both conceptualization and interpretation of the text.

Special thanks go also to Anne Marsin, who weaned me from hand-written copy to the intricacies of computerland and who was always there to assist me when my word processor misbehaved.

THE TWELVE STEPS OF ALCOHOLICS ANONYMOUS

1. We admitted we were powerless over alcohol—that our lives had become unmanageable. **2.** Came to believe that a Power greater than ourselves could restore us to sanity. **3.** Made a decision to turn our will and our lives over to the care of God *as we understood Him*. **4.** Made a searching and fearless moral inventory of ourselves. **5.** Admitted to God, to ourselves and to another human being the exact nature of our wrongs. **6.** Were entirely ready to have God remove all these defects of character. **7.** Humbly asked Him to remove our shortcomings. **8.** Made a list of all persons we had harmed, and became willing to make amends to them all. **9.** Made direct amends to such people wherever possible, except when to do so would injure them or others. **10.** Continued to take personal inventory and when we were wrong promptly admitted it. **11.** Sought through prayer and meditation to improve our conscious contact with God, *as we understood Him*, praying only for knowledge of His will for us and the power to carry that out. **12.** Having had a spiritual awakening as the result of these steps, we tried to carry this message to alcoholics, and to practice these principles in all our affairs.

The Twelve Steps are reprinted and adapted with permission of Alcoholics Anonymous World Services, Inc. Permission to reprint and adapt the Twelve Steps does not mean that AA has reviewed or approved the contents of this publication nor that AA agrees with the views expressed herein. AA is a program of recovery from alcoholism—use of the Twelve Steps in connection with programs and activities which are patterned after AA, but which address other problems, does not imply otherwise.

PREFACE

I had no intention of writing this book until I was approached by some friends, who—like myself—were long-time members of self-help groups and who were intrigued that the same philosophy created by one Twelve Step program could prove to be effective with so many diverse addictions and problems.

The majority of our fellowships—Narcotics Anonymous, Cocaine Anonymous, Gamblers Anonymous, Overeaters Anonymous, Sexual Addicts Anonymous, Divorcees Anonymous, Children of Alcoholics, Adult Children of Alcoholics, Alanon, Alateen, Debtors Anonymous—have all patterned themselves after the Twelve Step program developed by Alcoholics Anonymous.

The undeniable success of AA is such that it would be foolhardy to reinvent the wheel. Therefore, this book is meant to help anyone with an addictive/compulsive problem to avail themselves of AA's surefire formula for recovery.

Each step is assigned a month for consideration and each month has been assigned thirty-one days, so that readers may choose whatever step is the most appropriate to their needs.

For optimum results it is necessary to work through all of the steps, and many of us have found that we continue to revisit one step or another as the events in our lives prescribe.

You will note that only the First and Twelfth Steps use the words *alcohol* or *alcoholics*. Therefore, it is easy to substitute the condition our own problem dictates. The steps, when followed, are powerful, and literally create a blueprint for living that anyone and everyone can find workable.

For purposes of clarity, each time I use the word "disease" in the text, I am using one of the three definitions from the Second College Edition of the American Heritage Dictionary:

> dis ease n. 1. An abnormal condition of an organism or part, esp. as a consequence of infection, inherent weakness, or environmental stress that impairs normal physiological functioning. 2. A condition or tendency, as of society, regarded as abnormal and harmful. 3. Obs. Lack of ease.

It is my hope that by the end of each chapter, you will come to a greater understanding of the import of that step, and will feel a sense of personal accomplishment. The intent of all the steps is simply to uncover, discover, discard and recover—to be able to apply this knowledge in a manner that makes daily living a rewarding and fulfilling experience.

Step One

"We admitted we were powerless over alcohol (our problem) and that our lives had become unmanageable."

Step One is the gateway to the recovery process. Without it, there is very little hope that we can effectively achieve our goal.

In this crucial step we are called upon to admit our personal powerlessness over the dilemma in which we find ourselves. We are called upon to admit that our life has reached a state of such disrepair that we see no possibility of ever setting it right again.

Despite all that we have been taught about never giving up, never yelling "uncle," never admitting defeat, we now find ourselves facing the unrelenting fact that all of our old beliefs have withered and blown away in the reality of our present situation.

We shall learn, as we pursue Step One, that we are facing some puzzling paradoxes: "We have to surrender to win." "To keep what we have, we have to give it away." "Failure is not final—it is actually a stepping stone to success."

Are these contradictory thoughts? We don't think so. They have proven valid for many of us.

Step One

Day 1—ADMISSION

"The journey of a thousand miles begins with a single step."
                                                    LAO-TZU

Today we open the door to a new and positive outlook on life. This "letting in" process expands our horizons and allows us to accept ourselves more fully.

For most of us it is painful to admit our powerlessness. It forces us to confront the fact that our lives are not working as we had hoped, and that in all probability, our own behavior is the cause.

Because each of us is the product of our past, we have been programmed into mind-sets and attitudes we've never thought to question.

We're like the young bride whose husband asked why she cut off the end piece of the ham before she baked it. "Mother taught me to fix it this way," she replied. But, suddenly curious about it, she asked her mother why she made ham this way. "Because," replied her mother, "your granny did hers this way." More determined than ever to get to the bottom of the puzzle, the bride went to her grandmother to solve the mystery. "Well, child," said granny, "I did it because a whole ham wouldn't fit into my oven."

Just like that young bride and her mother, it rarely occurs to us to wonder why we do a thing. We're as conditioned by habit as Pavlov's dog—the bell rings and we perform.

The initial step, then, is for us to admit that it is solely up to us to discover why we have continued to behave in a way that brings up negative feelings and causes us great discomfort.

TODAY'S STEP: *To admit that I am powerless is both a relief and a source of new hope.*

Step One

Day 2—ADMISSION

"Are you part of the problem—or part of the solu-tion?" ANONYMOUS

Did you ever wonder why—although we each have eyes, ears, noses and mouths—we all look so distinctly different? Of course there are family resemblances, and occasionally we'll meet someone who "looks just like cousin Sally." But isn't it incredible that with the billions of people who inhabit this planet, barring identical twins, no two of us look exactly alike?

This is also true of our personalities, our thought pro-cesses, our likes and dislikes, and our beliefs and disbeliefs. We vacillate between wanting to conform and wanting to rebel. Often we view the world with suspicious eyes, feeling we have been treated unfairly. Many of us tend to look at life as a struggle against unreasonable odds.

But there's another way to look at things. We can alter our attitudes and begin to act positively and constructively. We can learn to see value in situations that appear negative, and attempt to come to terms with the world and all its imperfections. These are all worthwhile and attainable goals. But, to achieve them, we must first acknowledge our present dilemma.

It would be handy to have a blueprint for such an undertaking. But because each one of us is unique and special, we can only generalize about the process. We must each plot our own course to fit who we are.

TODAY'S STEP: *I can look at past behavior and past pro-gramming with new eyes.*

Day 3—UNIQUENESS

*"There never were, since the creation of the world,
two cases exactly parallel."* LORD CHESTERFIELD

Whenever we are confronted with a challenge that involves
letting go of our own opinions and being willing to follow
a plan suggested by someone else, we immediately begin to
see all the glitches, all the exceptions we're sure do not
apply to us.

"My case is different!" we cry. It is so necessary for us
to preserve our own uniqueness, our own specialness, that
we're sure that letting go will plunge us into a sea of
nothingness. Right? Wrong.

We are, all of us, unique. We have our own special sense
of identity that has been with us since birth. Some of us
have positive self-images. Others of us suffer from low
self-esteem. However, we are still uniquely "us," and we're
afraid of anything that might take that feeling of "us-ness"
away.

This step, and those that follow, have been carefully
designed to help us get to know the very important and
precious individual we really are. This process scrapes away
the facades and subterfuges we thought were necessary for
our survival. It allows us to see ourselves as free, productive
and worthwhile human beings; to see that while we are
different, we also share many facets of sameness with other
human beings. These similarities allow us not only to profit
by the experience of others, but also to recognize that so
many of our actions have been the result of misguided ideas
and faulty information. We can cherish our uniqueness
while still learning from the experience of others.

TODAY'S STEP: *I know that the path I have chosen is the
right one for me, and I will walk it unafraid.*

Step One

Day 4—WHAT WILL THEY THINK OF ME?

"A life spent in making mistakes is not only more honorable but more useful than a life spent in doing nothing."
GEORGE BERNARD SHAW

Many of us have been so brainwashed by worrying what people will think that we're willing to remain in a state of misery rather than admit we've been going about something the wrong way.

We're afraid of being found out, of showing bad judgment, of being perceived as inept. We are like the near-sighted girl who was invited to dinner by her boyfriend's parents. She mistook a bowl of heavily cinnamoned applesauce for brown gravy and ladled it on her mashed potatoes. "Do you like applesauce on your potatoes, dear?" asked the boy's mother. "Oh, yes," she replied, "I always eat them this way," and then proceeded to finish every bite, afraid they would think she had made a mistake.

People who are late for appointments hate to admit that their own planning was to blame. So they use excuses, such as traffic problems, long-distance phone calls or minor emergencies to explain their tardiness.

Admission comes as a painful step for us because we feel shame and guilt for having been so far off course. It is, however, a liberating step. It opens the door to new possibilities and a much more comfortable existence.

At this point it's good to remember that, if our life isn't working for us, it isn't for lack of trying. It's simply that we haven't yet found the formula that makes it work.

TODAY'S STEP: *In admitting my mistakes, I find the freedom to grow.*

Day 5—CHANGING HABITS

*"The horror of that moment," the King went on,
"I shall never never forget."*

*"You will, though," the Queen said, "if you
don't make a memorandum of it."*   LEWIS CARROLL
ALICE'S ADVENTURES IN WONDERLAND

The First Step establishes guidelines designed to open up
our consciousness, to help us see ourselves more clearly,
and to discover where we have missed the mark. It helps us
gain deeper insight into the "why" of our attitudes.

Behavioral psychologists call this process "successive
approximations." AA refers to it as the Twelve Steps.
The purpose of this process is to help us develop our
desired responses by doing one do-able step at a time.
For instance, when we want to change such behaviors as
drinking alcoholically or using mind-altering chemicals,
binging, purging or overeating, compulsive gambling or
sexual addictions, we can start by tying the proverbial
string around our finger.

By following this process, we can create new patterns
that will focus our thought processes on our specific goal.
For example, most of us have an established morning routine. We go to the bathroom, brush our teeth, comb our
hair, and follow all the habitual practices that ready us for
the day. But what if we change the sequence of these acts?
What if we brush our teeth before we shower, or shave on
the left side first instead of the right? Breaking the routine
reminds us that our goal is to create a lifestyle free from
dependency.

TODAY'S STEP: *I establish sound new habits, one day at a
time.*

Step One

Day 6—ACKNOWLEDGING THE PARENT

"There is no greater bugbear than a strong-willed relative in the circle of his own convictions."

NATHANIEL HAWTHORNE

Eric Berne, founder of transactional analysis, theorized that our inner selves are three distinct and separate entities who vie for control: the parent, the child, and the adult.

This may explain, in part, the confusion that we often feel arise within ourselves as we try to sort out our responses to a situation. Today, let's look at our parent self. How does this entity affect our ability to admit our problem?

Our inner parent is the part of us that was programmed by our own parents, our teachers, our ministers, our guardians or our older siblings. The parent is the critical monitor of our behavior: it acts as taskmaster and guide. The parent burdens us with the tyranny of "shoulds," and it is constantly grading us on our performance, whether this involves work, play or accomplishments. Our inner parent, conditioned by early programming, tries to lead us along the straight and narrow. It continually cautions us against nonconformity.

It is important that we see both the strengths and the weaknesses of our inner parent, for the information stored in that entity is designed to help us plot our journey through life. Although it truly intends to protect us, too often our inner parent controls us in a manner that leads to rigid, stuck behavior.

As we become more familiar with our parent entity, we can readily see its influence on our actions. We begin to realize that we have often restricted ourselves when it was neither necessary nor comfortable to do so.

TODAY'S STEP: *I release the "shoulds" and judgments of my inner critic.*

Day 7—ACKNOWLEDGING THE CHILD

"Mother, may I go out to swim?"
"Yes, my darling daughter.
"Hang your clothes on a hickory limb, but don't go
near the water."   OLD NURSERY RHYME

Since birth, our child entity has recorded all our feelings, emotions, deprivations, misunderstandings, hurts and sorrows, as well as all our pleasures. Our inner child is the adventurer, the explorer, the mischief maker. It is inventive. It can also be stubborn and disobedient. The child rebels at the tyranny of the shoulds; it wants what it wants when it wants it. Instant gratification is its demand. Long-term goals are anathema to this aspect of ourselves.

For many of us, our inner child has long been silenced. From infancy to adulthood, our programming has been one of stifling conformity; of being forced to behave within the prescribed patterns of our families and our communities.

How often have others told us how we feel. "You don't want to play with that nasty little boy." "You're sorry that you hit your sister." "You always feel better after you take your medicine." In reality, we did want to play with that nasty little boy. He was fun! We were not a bit sorry we hit our sister. We would have liked to push her over a cliff. And we hated the medicine. We thought it was yucky, and it made us feel worse than ever.

Now we can recognize that child entity as one to be nurtured, and—within limits—to be granted fulfillment of many of its pleasures.

TODAY'S STEP: *I cherish the beloved child within.*

Day 8—ACKNOWLEDGING THE ADULT

"We are half-ruined by conformity, but we should be totally ruined without it."

CHARLES DUDLEY WARNER

Our adult self is very like the character of Mr. Spock, the alien crew member in "Star Trek." The adult is logical, dispassionate, fair, reasonable and intelligent. He or she does not react emotionally, and can see the sense in the point of view of both our inner parent and child. When conflict arises between the two, the adult attempts to restore order out of chaos. It's as if there were a committee arguing in our heads, churning our emotions into a frenzy.

When communication can be established from child to adult, and from parent to adult, it is possible for the adult to weigh the evidence and translate to each entity the other's point of view. It is at this point that the adult is able to point out viable alternatives.

In other words, our inner conflict, the inability to make comfortable decisions, and our feelings of confusion are somewhat dispelled by our adult voice of reason. It's as if our child is saying, "I want to go to the beach," and our parent fumes, "You can't go. You have to do your homework." The adult says, "Why not go to the beach after your homework is done?"

The child says, "I think I'd like to study law." The parent says, "Better not. It's too tough." The adult says, "What have you got to lose? It might work. If not, you can always try something else."

TODAY'S STEP: *I connect with the dispassionate part of my being and embrace my inner adult.*

Day 9—RELINQUISHING OLD IDEAS

"If at first you don't succeed, chances are you just don't understand the situation."   ANONYMOUS

Suppose you suddenly found yourself transported to an alien land. One where you not only couldn't speak the language of the natives, but where you also were totally unfamiliar with their customs. You'd be hard-pressed to explain your needs. And you'd be fearful that they might interpret some of your actions as hostile. That could create unpleasant consequences.

It's much the same with our recognition and consequent confusion about the fact that we're "out of sync" with the world we live in. We're like the blind men and the elephant: Our impression of the shape of things doesn't gibe with what others perceive. And yet, there is truth and validity in all our perceptions.

This is what makes it doubly hard for us to relinquish our own point of view. We see its validity and cling stubbornly to our position when, clearly, it is not working for us. There is an example in the *Big Book of Alcoholics Anonymous* of a man who persisted in skipping out in front of fast-moving vehicles. First, he had a series of minor accidents. But these were followed by more serious accidents until, finally, he broke both legs. He persisted in this self-defeating behavior the way many of us persist in our determination that, "This time it will be different." So long as we cling to these old ideas, we remain powerless.

TODAY'S STEP: *I readily release ideas that no longer work for me.*

Day 10—SABOTAGE: HOW TO DO IT

"Happiness is not a state to arrive at, but a manner of traveling."
MARGARET LEE RUNBECK

Despite our admission of personal powerlessness, as we work Step One, many of us continue to rebel at the fact that we are unable to effect recovery by our own efforts. We see meetings as unnecessary. We have no intention of affiliating ourselves with a group, and we generally balk at being told what we have to do.

This is when we come face-to-face with the fact that what we *do* have is the power to continue to make ourselves miserable. And here's the way we do it:

• Seeing ourselves as victims of outrageous fortune.
• Feeling we've fallen prey to Murphy's Law: "If anything can possibly go wrong—it will."
• Doing unto others before they do unto us, because we know they're out to get us.
• Denying that any power could be greater than ourselves.
• Living for ourselves alone, because no one else is interested in our well-being.
• Keeping a distance between ourselves and others so they won't find our vulnerable points.
• Taking an inventory of the failings of others, and pointing out their deficiencies to them.
• Refusing help to people, because if we "give them an inch, they'll take a mile."
• Dwelling on the inequities that bestow money and power on those far less deserving than we.
• Feeling sorry for ourselves.

TODAY'S STEP: *I face my current situation squarely and without blame.*

Day 11—THE ENVIRONMENT

"Failure is not final. It is simply missing the mark." ANONYMOUS

Let's take another look at the false evidence that has been influencing us and our thought processes all our lives.

First of all, we had no opportunity to choose our parents. Some of us were fortunate enough to be born into a loving and supportive family unit where we did not experience deprivation of any kind. Others were reared in poverty, on the wrong side of the tracks. Still others grew up in an environment that may have been financially secure, but was also austere or highly critical and disapproving.

We're all products of our environment. But we can no longer continue to blame that environment for the situations in which we find ourselves today.

The overprivileged can say they were never taught self-sufficiency, or how to deal appropriately with life's disappointments. Therefore they've had no experience in coping with negative forces.

Those who have led lives of deprivation blame the absence of nurturing for their dysfunctional behavior and inability to change.

The adults whose childhoods were demanding and critical hold those early imprints responsible for their rebellious behavior.

Although these childhood imprints have certainly influenced us, we cannot blame our behavior solely on them. Yes, we are products of our environment. But we don't have to remain prisoners of it. That's why we call recovery a process.

TODAY'S STEP: *I relinquish the habit of blaming others for my shortcomings.*

Day 12—POWERLESSNESS

"I have the ability to redirect and regulate my thinking, and to establish order and power in my emotions." ANONYMOUS

Admitting personal powerlessness is frightening. All our instincts war against conceding that we have been waging a losing battle against such a powerful foe—ourselves. However, once we're able to admit defeat, we have the opportunity to reverse a process that can only lead to destruction. It is only by admitting our powerlessness that we can redirect our energies toward a more rewarding existence.

Confessing powerlessness doesn't mean humiliating ourselves. Quite the contrary. It is a liberating act. It enables us to see ourselves as being intelligent enough and teachable enough to accept direction from those trailblazers who have proven the effectiveness of this path.

Our innate capabilities continue to exist—and now they can be redirected toward positive goals. Surrender becomes an asset rather than a liability. It is the positive act of letting the unproductive go that enables us to embrace the promise of freedom from bondage.

Only by understanding the elaborate defense system that our addictive behavior has set up are we able to concede our powerlessness and to find the way out of the maze of our honest self-deception. In fact, we will find that "honest self-deception," "failure is not final," and "surrendering to win," will be recurring themes as we pursue our goal of recovery.

TODAY'S STEP: *I fully surrender in order to win.*

Day 13—DENIAL

". . . lest problems of money, property, and prestige divert us from our primary purpose."
FROM THE SIXTH TRADITION OF ALCOHOLICS ANONYMOUS

Our powerlessness is manifested in a continuing pattern of dysfunctional behavior. We fail to see the mounting evidence that is the predominant factor in our addiction. If we examine some of the elaborate rationales that have brought us to this sorry state, we might have a better grasp of how to change things.

We set up intricate defense mechanisms to prevent being exposed as weak and ineffectual. Secretly, though, we fear that we were born with a fatal flaw—and that when they find out, they'll throw us away.

We use denial as a typical defense tactic. We blame other people, places and things for our failures. Often this denial is encouraged by significant others who buy into the myth because it explains why they remain in a relationship that is clearly dysfunctional. As the wife of a prominent and wealthy businessman stated: "Look, I'm not going to rock the boat. I've spent years helping him achieve the success he has today. Now that we have the money and the social standing I've always wanted, I'm not about to leave him and lose all the goodies I really earned. So he's a bastard sometimes. So what? A lot of other women would jump at the chance to snag him."

TODAY'S STEP: *I find the courage and support to let go of denial.*

Day 14—ATTITUDES

"I was a fourteen-year-old boy for thirty years."
                                        MICKEY ROONEY

Our attitudes are threefold: They include beliefs, emotions and actions.

The beliefs that become truth for us are those that French novelist, André Gide, described as allowing us to best use our strength and to find the best means of putting our virtues into action. In other words, if we believe that the unmanageability of our lives is caused by outside circumstances, we see ourselves as innocent victims. This belief blinds us to our own faults.

Emotions are what we feel about things. They are strong, complex, subjective responses, such as love, fear, anger, embarrassment. They do not stem from logic, but rather from instinct. If we are threatened by others, our immediate reaction is "fight or flight."

Actions are what we do. They are the result of behavior prompted by our beliefs and emotions, which often blind us to performing in a more acceptable way. As a result, we tend to feel justified in what we do. For instance, "I have been a truly dependable person (belief), and I resent the fact that my friend sees me as selfish (emotion), therefore I'm going to break our date, and go out with someone else (action)."

TODAY'S STEP: *I reevaluate my attitudes in the light of new evidence.*

Step One

Day 15—FAILURE IS NOT FINAL

"The tragedy in life doesn't lie in not reaching your goal. The tragedy lies in having no goal to reach."
BENJAMIN E. MAYS

At this point we may despair of trying to begin again. Our past efforts seem so fruitless. Our memory tells us that, like the proverbial New Year's Resolutions, we make 'em only to break 'em. This is when we need to remind ourselves over and over again that "failure is not final." It simply means that we've missed the mark and that it's time to reset our direction and take better aim at our objectives.

In his book, *Psycho Cybernetics*, Maxwell Maltz describes this action as one in which we see our object, level our sights, and then—through some maladjustment—swerve slightly. Our target is thereby bypassed and we find ourselves frustrated that we've failed one more time.

When this happens, there's a very strong probability that we've set impossible goals for ourselves, and that the very elaborate mechanisms needed to achieve those goals are beyond our present capacity. This is something we don't like to admit, for we've been inoculated with the serum that demands performance and perfection. We see any deviation from this posture as a form of powerlessness—and God knows, we don't want *them* to see us as wimps.

Accepting ourselves as we are and where we are is a prime requisite of recovery.

TODAY'S STEP: *I examine my mistakes lovingly for what they teach me.*

*"Don't be discouraged. It's often the last key in the
bunch that opens the lock."*   ANONYMOUS

In order to work Step One effectively, we need three
ingredients: Honesty, Open-mindedness and Willingness—H.O.W. These are the crucial components of the
"how" of success, and they are essential to recovery. Without them, our chances of succeeding are negligible. So it is
necessary to admit that the unmanageability of our lives is
directly related to our actions, that like a team of horses
spooked by a mountain lion, we're rushing forward, pell-
mell, with no direction other than escaping from danger.

We have cultivated self-delusion because the pain of
seeing ourselves as solely responsible for our sorry state of
affairs is almost too much to bear. This is the time to
remind ourselves that, in the past, we didn't have the
knowledge or experience to manage our worsening situation. Once we're able to acknowledge this inability, we
open the door to information that helps us eliminate our
feelings of guilt and shame. It's by admitting and owning
these feelings that it becomes possible to rid ourselves of
them.

Our pride has kept us from seeking help from others.
We were afraid of being viewed as stupid or uninformed.
But now we're willing to ask for help. We're willing to
begin to relinquish our old ideas and attitudes so that we
can accept the guidance now being offered to us.

TODAY'S STEP: *I release self-delusion and embrace honesty.*

Day 17—CHANGE

"It isn't important to come out on top. What matters is to be the one who comes out alive."

BERTOLT BRECHT

Everyone has a natural fear of change. We're afraid of the unknown. It's not easy to believe that change might possibly be for the better.

You've heard the term, "She enjoys her misery." Paradoxical as this statement would appear to be, we accept it as a valid statement when we describe someone as "poor pitiful Pearl (or Paul)."

These folks persist in spreading gloom and doom wherever they go. They're like an Al Capp cartoon character in "L'il Abner" who walks around with a black cloud hanging over his head. They are so used to—and even comfortable—in their predicament that they're sure any change would only take them from the frying pan into the fire. They find it almost impossible to risk a leap of faith—even if it promises a better way of life. And yet, in order to recover, we have to change, so we might as well embrace it.

TODAY'S STEP: *I anticipate a change for the better.*

Day 18—SURRENDER

"By nature, men are nearly alike. By practice, they get to be far apart."   CONFUCIUS

By now we have begun to realize that we're confronting a whole new set of possibilities—and they don't necessarily make us feel comfortable.

It's as though we're trapped in an elevator. Our initial reaction is confusion, followed by a wave of fear. We begin to experience mild claustrophobia. Then, feeling angry and frustrated, we jab both the "up" and "down" buttons repeatedly. Nothing happens. We push the alarm button and wait for some response. Nothing happens. We look wildly around to see what other possible recourse we have. It is now—at this point—that we have to admit that our situation is unmanageable. It is now that we must surrender to the fact that we can't get ourselves out of this mess all by ourselves. By the time the voice over the intercom finally assures us that help is forthcoming, we have no problem admitting our personal powerlessness.

Once we can get past our intellectual posturing, we can begin to acknowledge the paralyzing fear that has us locked in a death hold from which we see no escape. But, it's difficult to accept that "the buck stops here," that the decision to make this admission of powerlessness is clearly in our court. Despite the reassurance of others, we don't put much stock in the benefits of surrender. Our entire frame of reference has been: "*They* don't understand. Our case is different."

TODAY'S STEP: *I welcome the clarity to see my powerlessness.*

Step One

Day 19—RIGOROUS HONESTY

"Lying to ourselves is more deeply ingrained than lying to others."
FEODER DOSTOEVSKY

Inherent in the words "had become unmanageable," is the recognition that we got to this stuck place over an extended period of time. There was a point in our lives where we managed very well indeed. However, the euphoric memory of those past successes is now crowding out our ability to surrender; to admit that we are no longer capable of controlling our destiny.

The *Big Book of Alcoholics Anonymous* tells us that they have rarely seen a person fail who has thoroughly followed their path. They further state that those men and women who do not recover have not been able to be completely honest with themselves. They also say that those who succeed seem to have the ability to grasp and develop a program that demands rigorous honesty.

The fact that we've decided to try this program implies that we've chosen to attempt to develop that rigorous honesty. We may well find, though, that the search for such honesty is much more difficult than we had anticipated.

Both honest self-deception and self-delusion have been pervasive stumbling blocks on our path to recovery, because they have been so hard to identify. But, as we progress, we will be better able to recognize them and they'll become valuable tools to help unravel the tangled web of our lives.

TODAY'S STEP: *I have found the courage to face the truth.*

Step One

Day 20—SURRENDER

"The time to repair the roof is when the sun is shining."   JOHN F. KENNEDY

It is indeed paradoxical that in order to win we must surrender, but such is the case in the process of recovery. Perhaps if we look at surrender in the light of a courageous action, rather than viewing it as cowardly, this step may prove more palatable.

People usually view surrender as defeat. On the contrary, it is a clearing of the decks that allows us to make room for all of the positive things that make our lives more satisfying.

We've been told that when Jesus the Carpenter went out into the world, He gathered around Him twelve disciples to help spread His word. These men came from all walks of life. Some came from fine families, were very well off, and were very happy within their own communities. Others were very outgoing and adventurous. Still others were shy and conservative. One was a fisherman, a brawler and a troublemaker. The proposal that the Carpenter laid before each of them was so exciting, so stimulating, so challenging that all of them readily surrendered their lifestyles and their previous philosophies in order to follow His dream. Surrender for them was a letting go in order to let in a whole new challenging concept.

TODAY'S STEP: *I am beginning to understand that surrender is not defeat.*

Day 21—TO GROUP OR NOT TO GROUP

"A good scare is worth more to a man than good advice."
                                                    EDGAR WATSON HOWE

People have asked us about the value of a support group in admitting our powerlessness. We have found that to maximize success, a support group—attended on a regular basis—can be a powerful force. When we hear others sharing their stories of how they dealt with that feeling of powerlessness, it can help pave the way for our own acceptance.

Those of us who have come from very authoritarian backgrounds and have been guided by stringent judgments and biases are going to find it difficult to understand and accept the many differing opinions we find among members of most self-help groups.

However, these differences are very understandable when we realize that everyone simply wants to share their own personal recipes for success in working each step. It is logical for people to feel that what worked for them can work for others.

We'd like to emphasize that in these self-help groups no one person is an absolute authority. Everyone comes to the group with their own individual convictions and biases, and like them, it is up to us to find our own particular path.

And yet, once we recognize that we have a common goal, our differences begin to fade and we start to recognize our similarities. This is when uncertainty and fear give way to purpose and optimism.

TODAY'S STEP: *I wholeheartedly accept the support of my group.*

Day 22—EMOTIONS CAN PRECEDE THOUGHT

"People don't ever seem to realize that doing what's right is no guarantee against misfortune."

WILLIAM McFEE

A study of the way our brains work, conducted at Cornell Medical Center in Manhattan, tells us that key aspects of emotional life, such as deep-seated fears, can operate independently of conscious thought. This might explain why, even though we find our own emotional reactions irritating—because we don't see any reason for them—they still occur. This also might explain why troubling experiences from our earliest years continue, many years later, to have such a powerful effect on us.

The study indicates that many emotional reactions occur before the brain has had time to register fully what is causing the reaction. This might explain why some of the traumas we experienced as infants—such as fear of loud noises, of falling, of abandonment when we're left too long in our crib—continue to produce seemingly groundless emotions today.

Maybe that's why, even when we're grown and our lives are not threatened by illness, economic insecurity, or deprivation of life, we still feel like homeless waifs with our noses pressed against a toy-store window. If emotions can arise before thought, perhaps this clarifies how, despite our best thinking, our actions have led us to our present dilemma.

TODAY'S STEP: *I observe my emotions without judgment.*

Step One

Day 23—QUESTIONS

"Keep a diary and one day it'll keep you."

MAE WEST

This might be an ideal time to pause in our study of the First Step and ask ourselves questions.

Experience has taught us how helpful it is to write down our answers to these queries so our minds don't take side trips when mulling over these queries in our heads.

Many of us have looked at our loss of control and cried out in dismay, "How did I ever get into this situation? Where did I go wrong?"

Later we will do an inventory that will help clarify the answer. But for today, let's start with the following:

• What does the word "control" mean to me?
• What methods have I used to control my life?
• What methods have I used to control the lives of others?

The value of these answers can only be truly experienced when we put pen to paper. Our own truth has a powerful effect on us both visually and emotionally when we see it written out.

Recording our progress in a journal is an invaluable tool for keeping tabs on our habits and behavior. Journaling allows us to see the patterns we have established in our daily lifestyle, and this clear view enables us to think in a more disciplined manner.

TODAY'S STEP: *I release the need to control my life and the lives of others.*

Day 24—MORE QUESTIONS

"True freedom lies in the realization and calm acceptance of the fact that there may very well be no perfect answer." ALLEN REID McGINNIS

Yesterday we asked ourselves about control issues. Today let's ask ourselves a few more questions:
- How do I define "success"?
- How do I define "failure"?
- What do I see as the successes in my life? How do I regard them?
- What do I see as the failures in my life? How do I regard them?
- When someone criticizes me, how do I feel?
- How have those closest to me tried to help me?
- How did I respond to their efforts?
- What's in it for me if I am able to complete this program successfully?

The more explicit we can be in our answers, the more success we will have in continuing our recovery process.

TODAY'S STEP: *Asking and answering questions is a powerful tool for growth.*

Step One

Day 25—CONFUSION

"Things are seldom what they seem,
skim milk masquerades as cream."　　W.S. GILBERT

Did you ever grope for a reason that you hoped would explain some situation in which you found yourself? Did you have the feeling that there was a perfectly plausible answer for why you'd done something but the answer kept escaping you? Many people have experienced such confusion and, despite all their rational evaluations, cannot find truly logical explanations.

For instance, take the CPA who was trying to balance a client's books. He was working without a computer and was constantly brushing away a large fly that persistently kept landing on his ledger. Time after time he tried to reconcile his figures, and time after time they indicated a large discrepancy.

After hours of frustration, this expert in his field, who was called in as a consultant by many large corporations, accidentally dropped his working papers on the floor. As he bent to retrieve them he saw that a figure had been altered. Further examination showed that a fly's leg had dropped on his work, creating the figure "one" where none had belonged.

He had operated with faulty perception—just as we have deceived ourselves many times.

TODAY'S STEP: *As my recovery proceeds, I gain more and more clarity.*

Step One

Day 26—FELLOWSHIPS

"If everyone sweeps in front of his door, the whole city will be clean."   ANONYMOUS

It is not too early in the game to talk about the value of aligning ourselves with one of the various fellowships patterned after the Twelve Steps of Alcoholics Anonymous. The support offered by these groups is not limited simply to meetings. They also teach us to avail ourselves of the proven therapeutic value of telephone contacts. This way we keep in touch with other group members who continue to encourage and support us when we need it most.

All of these Twelve Step fellowships suggest that we find a sponsor as soon as possible. A sponsor acts as a guide to help us through the process of recovery. A sponsor is like a mentor and confidant. Ideally, a sponsor should be someone who has had experience in facing similar problems, who has worked the program, and with whom we feel we can be totally honest. Confidentiality is a hallmark of a good sponsor. This is why we want to feel trusting and comfortable with whomever we choose—or, in some cases, with the person who chooses us!

We can benefit tremendously from the guidance of people who have traveled this route before us. They have helpful techniques to share with us, and we can learn a great deal about ourselves from the experience of others. When we stick to our own recovery program long enough, we often hear what we thought to be our own story told by another. It is always amazing and heartening to find that someone else has had the same feelings and experiences we have had.

TODAY'S STEP: *I profit from the experience of those who've gone before.*

*"Forget your past record. Each moment is a new
beginning."*   ANONYMOUS

No addiction is without its support group of parents,
spouses, relatives and friends. Often, in their desire to
preserve their own image, these are the very people who
support our denial system. They cannot be expected to
offer us authentic feedback.

Let's take the case of the wife whose husband's stature
in the community brings her the reflected glory of being
one of the elite. Despite the fact that her husband is keeping a mistress, the wife doesn't want to rock the boat, or
lose her creature comforts. She doesn't want to disturb the
balance he has established for himself and reasons that as
long as he finds her deficient in certain attributes, he has the
right to seek his pleasure elsewhere.

What about the "perfect" mother who cannot bear to
admit that her teenaged daughter has been behaving in an
antisocial manner?

Or the unloved and neglected child who does everything she can to make people think she has a happy, normal
home with loving and approving parents?

These are the people we call "enablers." Their role is to
put up a smokescreen to hide our addictions from the
world. Most of them see themselves as patient, loving,
helpful persons who stick by us even when we behave in a
most unhealthy manner. Their intent is to help—either us
or themselves. They are totally unaware that what they're
really doing is furthering our progression into disaster.

TODAY'S STEP: *When I listen carefully to others the difference between help and enabling becomes clear.*

Day 28—SECOND THOUGHTS

"If you are distressed by anything external, the pain is not due to the thing itself but to your own estimate of it; and this you have the power to revoke at any moment."
MARCUS AURELIUS

As we near the end of our month-long study of the First Step, we may still be unconvinced about our powerlessness.

Our own plan of action may still feel like the most advisable one to follow. After all, we haven't gone totally under yet, have we? Perhaps we might be wiser to say: "Thanks for all the input. We've really appreciated it, and we're sure it will prove to be of great help."

This is similar to the "buyer's remorse" syndrome so familiar to real estate agents. After they have successfully negotiated for their clients' dream house, the buyers are suddenly overcome with the fear they've made the wrong decision.

At this point, an experienced agent, having gone through this same dynamic many times over, will gently review all the terms and conditions of the clients' purchase, and convince them they've made a splendid decision. The agent is usually right. After the initial fearful plunge into home ownership, most buyers are happy with the outcome.

In essence, we're talking about the same dynamic here. We're negotiating for a new lifestyle. But we're fearful that if we let go of the familiar we'll find ourselves floating aimlessly in a void over which we have no control. We need reassurance that the guidelines and road maps in those steps following this first one will help us chart a new, more productive course.

TODAY'S STEP: *I am beginning to understand that the path of recovery is right for me.*

Step One

Day 29—ADDICTION

"When you try to drown your troubles in drink you just teach them how to swim." ANONYMOUS

When we begin to review our past performances, a pattern starts to emerge. We discover that our problems have caused us pain, and it is simply human nature to want to escape from pain. So, we cast about for methods to do this, or to avoid the situation. We're like Scarlett O'Hara, whose solution was always: "I'll think about it tomorrow." Like the heroine of "Gone With the Wind," we hope the situation will miraculously correct itself, or disappear while we sleep. However, postponing things is not the solution. The problem lurks on the sidelines, ready to pounce on us again at the most inopportune times.

Too often the physicians and therapists to whom we have described our pain and difficulties prescribe medication to alleviate or assuage our feelings of discomfort. Many of us have abused these medications which we defend as legitimate because they were prescribed by a doctor.

In and of themselves—used in moderation—some prescription drugs are very appropriate. We do not deny that there are times when medication is indicated. However, the excessive use of any substance to alleviate stress or to postpone pain indicates addiction.

TODAY'S STEP: *Rather than running from my pain, I now seek out its cause.*

Day 30—RELATIONSHIPS

"It is not true that life is one damn thing after another—it is one damn thing over and over."

EDNA ST. VINCENT MILLAY

The unmanageable state our lives have reached has not only affected us, it has also had a negative effect on everyone with whom we interact.

We do not exist in a vacuum. Like a pebble cast into a still pond, our dysfunction ripples out in concentric circles to interact with many others in many ways.

There are degrees of relationships, which can be described as:

• *Superficial.* These involve casual acquaintances—people with whom we trade, those we employ or are employed by, or serve with on committees.

• *Companionship.* Such relationships are based on shared activities or hobbies—such as tennis, exercise, gardening, adult education classes.

• *Friendship.* These relationships differ from companionship in that the person becomes more important than the activity, and many of our friendships last a lifetime.

• *Romantic:* The romantic relationship encompasses loving and sexual involvement with someone who is also a friend. It is the one that has probably been the most affected by our dysfunction.

• *Parental:* The bond which nurtures, guides, protects, directs, rewards, punishes and ideally encompasses some of the same qualities as those of companionship and friendship.

With even the slightest amount of self-examination, it becomes patently obvious that our use of alcohol, drugs or other compulsive behavior has affected all these relationships.

TODAY'S STEP: *I courageously examine how my compulsions affect my relationships.*

Day 31—WILLING TO BE WILLING

"Even if you're on the right track, you'll get run over if you just sit there."   WILL ROGERS

We have arrived at the last day of our study of the First Step in recovery, so perhaps it would be helpful to remind ourselves of the essence of what we have explored.

We examined the meaning and nuances of the word "admitted," and saw how difficult it was to relinquish our mind-sets and to concede that we are powerless over the dilemma in which we find ourselves mired.

We began to comprehend how, despite our best intentions, we were reduced to a state of uncertainty. This has been wonderfully described by a young woman who said, "I felt like I was confronting a wall of Saran Wrap. There was the world in front of me. I could see it. I wanted to be a part of it. And the wall would give just a little as I pushed on it, but it would never let me in. I was truly on the outside looking in—wanting to belong so badly, yet knowing that my Saran wall muffled my calls for help."

But we are here, on this final day of Step One, because our cry for help was heard. Because we became "willing to be willing" to consider a new way of life, one that just might prove to be the long-sought-after solution to our dilemma.

TODAY'S STEP: *I practice the discipline of H.O.W.— Honesty, Open-mindedness and Willingness every day.*

Step Two

*"Came to believe that a Power greater than our-
selves could restore us to sanity."*

Having completed Step One, we're starting to feel a little
more familiar with how the process of recovery works. But
now that we're facing Step Two, we've begun to have
second thoughts about whether we're willing to proceed.

We're nervous about doing an in-depth analysis of our
own mental health. And we're equally fearful and reluctant
about relinquishing our own self-reliance to a power we
may feel we don't have even a nodding acquaintance with.

This is where we have to experiment a little with faith in
ourselves, and in the process. Because by the time we have
successfully worked through Step Two, we'll very likely
have developed a deeper understanding of why self-will and
self-determination—no matter how much we struggle to
apply them—are simply not powerful enough to effect our
recovery.

Also, by the end of Step Two it should be increasingly
clear how our compulsion/addiction has compelled us to
act in ways that are not indicative of a healthy mind.

Step Two

Day 1—KEEPING AN OPEN MIND

"Nothing is troublesome that we do willingly."
THOMAS JEFFERSON

This step, tends to produce instant denial in most of us. "Restore us to sanity?" we cry. "Are you insinuating that we're crazy?"

Not crazy, perhaps, in the sense that we're certifiable. But we're certainly being asked to look at our behavior, and to see that it has been neither rational nor healthy, and that our own best efforts seem to have failed miserably.

The phrase, "a Power greater than ourselves" may also cause our hackles to rise. Many of us suspect that we're about to be tossed into an "ism" that smacks of religious doctrine. Religion, *per se*, is not a component of the Twelve Steps, although the process may actually strengthen the belief systems of many of us who do follow a formal religious path.

The founders of AA developed the steps on which this program is based. Their book, *Alcoholics Anonymous*, which everyone simply calls the *Big Book*, clearly emphasizes that although their methods have proven successful for hundreds (now millions) of people, the steps they propose are only meant to be helpful suggestions. All they truly hope to do is to show others *precisely* how they can recover from a seemingly hopeless state of mind and body.

When we look at all the missteps we've taken in the past, it's a blessed relief to know that it is possible for us to change our entire direction *today*.

TODAY'S STEP: *I suspend my old beliefs in order to be open to new ones.*

Step Two

Day 2—A POWER GREATER THAN OURSELVES

"One's religion is whatever we are most interested in."
                                                      J.M. BARRIE

More than the other steps, Step Two requires a leap into faith. Any negative responses that may arise are often due to our personal experiences with religion and/or therapy.

This step is not a religious exercise. In the program, we're not focused on any particular deity, but we're not afraid of the words "God" or "Buddha" or "Mohammed" or "Allah" or any of the other deities to which human beings ascribe powers greater than themselves. We don't feel that any belief conflicts with the meaning of this step.

However, we also realize that atheists and agnostics may at first view Step Two as an impossible hurdle.

What it all comes down to is a power, a force larger than ourselves. We all recognize the power of electricity and use it routinely on a daily basis. We're all aware of the power inherent in subatomic particles to create or destroy matter. And we readily acknowledge the power of social movements where numbers of individuals come together to effect change on a scale that one person acting alone might not be able to do. Therefore, it stands to reason that a group of recovering persons who have successfully completed this step might have a powerful effect on our lives because they have succeeded in doing what has not yet been possible for us to do by ourselves alone.

TODAY'S STEP: *Even if I don't know what it is, I accept that there is a power greater than myself.*

Step Two

Day 3—TAKING IT ON FAITH

"Faith is to believe what you do not see. The reward for this faith is to see what you believe."
ST. AUGUSTINE

We may not be completely filled with enthusiasm when we discover that we're expected to embrace a doctrine formulated by a group of people—none of them professionals—who don't offer us what we consider to be sufficient statistical research to justify their theories.

On the other hand, most of us do subscribe to the operating theory: "If something works, don't fix it."

AA, the grandaddy of all these self-help groups, has proven without the shadow of a doubt that "it works." And, in fact, when their *Big Book* was written, there were a number of nonalcoholic professionals who acted as co-authors and consultants, and who affirmed that when all their combined efforts and expertise had failed, this self-help group—founded by a stockbroker and a medical doctor—succeeded.

The story is told of an atheist explaining to his listeners why he didn't believe in God. "I was up in Alaska, flying my plane. Suddenly, the motor failed, and I was forced to land on a desolate expanse of snow. I got down on my knees and asked God for help. Do you think He did anything to help me? Nothing. Absolutely nothing."

"Then how come," one of his listeners asked, "you're here today?"

"Oh," said the man, "a couple of hours later an Eskimo came along on a dogsled and brought me out!"

TODAY'S STEP: *I'm beginning to believe that the power of the program really does work.*

Day 4—ACTING "AS IF"

"How much shall I be changed, before I am changed!" JOHN DONNELL

To begin this step, all you need is simply to *act as if you do believe* the message of the step, whether or not you're convinced of its workability.

Think of it in terms of building a house. You know that before the foundation can be laid, excavations must be dug. Yet, when you look at the excavation, you see nothing but an empty hole. It's very difficult to convince yourself that the completed structure will look like the architectural rendering you selected for your dream house. All you can do is trust that the architect has drawn plans that the builder can translate into a well-built, attractive home.

In the early stages of recovery, there will be unseen evidence that the process is working for you despite all your doubts and confusion. The plans have already been drawn and are based on a design that has proven to be workable. And there are people ready to reassure you that this program has demonstrated its effectiveness to them despite their skepticism.

TODAY'S STEP: *In the earliest steps toward sanity, I am willing to trust my process and act "as if."*

Step Two

Day 5—HUMOR AS A TOOL

"Humor is an affirmation of dignity, a declaration of man's superiority to all that befalls him."
ROMAIN GARY

Of the many jokes concerning the plethora of anonymous groups, one is about an imaginary fellowship called Bachelors Anonymous. When a member finds himself leaning toward matrimony, he calls his sponsor who brings over a woman who has her hair in curlers and is wearing a dirty bathrobe, no makeup, and beat-up bunny slippers. This immediately cures the bachelor's desire to get married.

Sponsorship evolved to offer new members of self-help groups the support of a friend who's been there before, someone who has a successful track record in maintaining an addiction-free lifestyle. The majority of the groups we discussed in our preface follow this same practice, simply because it has proven to be of such value.

The more we uncover our past addictions, the more we discover the absurdity of our present attitudes. As we make these discoveries, humor becomes a valuable tool in allowing us to temper self-judgment. If we assume that being clean and sober means living our lives somberly, foregoing all frivolous, enjoyable and spontaneous behavior, the price is simply not worth the effort. Although our undertaking is a serious one, it's not necessary that we approach it in a manner of "gloom and doom."

TODAY'S STEP: *I get glimpses of sanity when I can laugh at myself.*

Day 6—GROWING INTO OURSELVES

"We need to see ourselves as basic miracles and worthy of love."   VIRGINIA SATIR

Growth in recovery depends largely upon our willingness to replace many of our previous opinions and attitudes with a new set of ideas. We need new goals—ones that offer healthy ways of living, reacting and behaving; goals that enable us to interact more effectively with the significant others in our lives. We want to learn how to live our lives in ways that make a difference—not only to ourselves but also to the many others with whom we come in contact.

As little children we found it was not possible to shape our lives against the dictates of grown-ups. Very early we developed a feeling that haunted our formative years and followed us into adulthood. This feeling was one of personal powerlessness.

However, once we understand that this root feeling is an old tape we play over and over to our innermost selves, we can begin to open up to a power above and beyond us that has the potential to help us reshape our lives.

Today we see ourselves as mature human beings, capable of making decisions and changes in our lives that are based on faith and trust in a benign entity. Whether we call it cosmic consciousness, the law of cause and effect, Higher Power, karma, or whatever, this energy larger than ourselves contains the seeds of our growth.

TODAY'S STEP: *I am open to the energy of my Higher Power.*

Day 7—LOGGING ON

*"The coming to consciousness is not a discovery of
some new thing; it is a long and painful return to
that which has always been. It is when we admit
our powerlessness that the guide appears."*

HELEN M. LUKE

An article in a national magazine told of a young woman
who had abstained from drinking for a number of months,
but who was fearful that an active social life might bring her
full circle back to her old drinking patterns. Consequently,
she holed up in her apartment, refusing to go to AA
meetings because she had an aversion to joining a "cult."

She spent her evenings at her home computer, logging
on to various electronic bulletin boards late at night.
Through a modem—a phone hookup—she began access-
ing the electronic meeting places where hackers all over the
country share tips and small talk. One night she discovered
a bulletin board titled, "Alcoholics Anonymous." Night
after night she logged on to the AA menu and read the
messages from other recovering alcoholics, without typing
in any personal input. Finally, she entered some of her own
concerns, fears and problems. After six weeks, she gave in
to the invitation of one of her fellow users whose message
read: "Sobriety doesn't have to be white-knuckled. Why
not let me take you to a meeting?"

She went with him and found herself in an atmosphere
of love and support. "If I hadn't logged on," she said,
"I'm sure I never would have gotten to a meeting."

TODAY'S STEP: *My Higher Power finds me, wherever I am.*

Day 8—POINTING THE FINGER

"We cannot blame or change others. We can only change ourselves."
                     ANONYMOUS

Perhaps one of the biggest stumbling blocks we see in recovery is the human tendency toward "elitism." The person with an eating disorder looks with revulsion upon the alcoholic. The alcoholic sees the drug-dependent person as a lawbreaker, rationalizing that at least booze is legal. The drug-addicted person labels the sexual addict as immoral. The sexual addict brands the compulsive gambler as irresponsible for his or anyone else's welfare. And the compulsive gambler is contemptuous of the disgusting lack of control in bulimics, anorexics or compulsive overeaters.

The irony of such criticism is that each of us is really identifying one of our own problems. For example, people with eating disorders are revolted by their own behavior. Alcoholics who drive under the influence, know full well that they're breaking the law. People with drug dependencies defend their addiction because it's been prescribed by doctors. Addicts on the street justify their compulsion by stating that at least they're not perverts. At a deeper level, however, they are aware of their lack of morality. Sexual addicts can't avoid the evidence that their addiction does affect others. And compulsive gamblers are powerless to control the obsession that leads them—and often their loved ones—into financial disaster.

The persistence of this self-deception and the elaborate denial system with which each person defends his own behavior is one of the most difficult to break down.

TODAY'S STEP: *When I focus on my own recovery, I can take my eyes off of others who are working on theirs.*

Day 9—A HIGHER POWER IN THE USSR

"We should take care not to make the intellect our god; it has, of course, powerful muscles, but no personality." ALBERT EINSTEIN

When people balk at what they consider the religious orthodoxy of terms like a "Power greater than themselves," or "God," or "God as you understand Him," or "Higher Power," we are reminded of what happened when a group of recovering alcoholics went to the Soviet Union in 1986 to introduce AA into this supposedly atheistic country.

They had no difficulty in gaining an audience with the Soviet Ministry of Health to whom they had already sent a copy of the *Big Book*. They were greeted warmly and told that in the Soviet Union the problem of alcoholism was very serious. Anything that could help alleviate the scourge of what Mr. Gorbachev had called the "green snake" would be welcome. Further, the AA group was assured that the Soviets would have no problem with the term "Higher Power," as they felt that individuals could interpret the term any way they saw fit. In fact, although the society is officially atheistic, many Soviet citizens are devoutly spiritual, and many more are confirmed believers.

AA is now active in Moscow, Leningrad, Kiev and numerous other Soviet cities. Some groups choose to consider the group itself their Higher Power. Others admit they do need help from some higher consciousness in order to recover. Still others believe in a Judeo-Christian God who acts in human affairs.

Today I remind myself that the language of the heart is universal, and that when I reach out my hand in friendship there are many who are eager to take it.

TODAY'S STEP: *My Higher Power is not limited by religious beliefs.*

Day 10—A TOUCH OF MADNESS

"Sanity is very rare: every man almost, and every woman, has a touch of madness."

RALPH WALDO EMERSON

Let's look again at sanity versus insanity. We hate to admit that acting irrationally is one of our characteristics. We contend that we couldn't have gotten this far without having made some decent decisions, and without managing to cope with our lives, although with increasing difficulty. True.

Nonetheless, if we were continuing to make wise decisions and performing in a healthy way, we wouldn't be in the fix we find ourselves in today.

Value judgments are of no help at this stage of our recovery. "Right and wrong," "good and bad," "should and shouldn't" are worthless and prejudicial judgments. As we progress, we'll come to see that we've done many of the right things for the wrong reasons, and conversely, many of the wrong things for the right reasons.

TODAY'S STEP: *I accept that even though I have made insane decisions, I have made some sane decisions as well.*

Step Two

Day 11—RISKING THE UNKNOWN

"How does one kill fear, I wonder? How do you shoot a spectre through the heart, slash off its spectral head, take it by its spectral throat?"

JOSEPH CONRAD

Many of us have believed that by exercising our own will and intelligence we could force those around us to accept our perception of sanity as valid—despite the fact that our very world was crumbling beneath us.

The problem with this is that, because of the very nature of our problem, we were incapable of considering any alternative way of living our lives—short of disappearing off the face of the earth. We were so caught in compulsive behavior patterns that there didn't appear to be any other path than the one that was leading us toward disaster.

It's the story of the drowning man all over again. There he was, starting to go under for the third time, and still asking himself whether he should take the hand of the man in the lifeboat for fear that man might do him harm.

Fear of the unknown often keeps us frozen in an untenable position. The risk of adopting a doctrine that purports to lead to recovery, but which contradicts all our personal beliefs, raises our anxiety level to a high degree of discomfort.

But let's take another look at where we are. The first thing we need to determine, is that we're not bad people trying to be good—we're sick people trying to get well. And we're being offered a prescription that has proven itself time and time again.

TODAY'S STEP: *I can replace fear of the unknown with faith in my Higher Power.*

Step Two

Day 12—GETTING WELL

"Don't leave before the miracle happens!"

ANONYMOUS

This is not a step another person can take for you, and if you balk at thinking of yourself as "sick," remember that we see our process as getting "well." Experience tells us that no one who seeks help to solve problems with addiction, compulsion or hopelessness is entirely well. Not acting sanely doesn't exactly fit into a definition of wellness.

Turning ourselves over to "a Power greater than ourselves" in our search for wellness requires a leap of faith only we can take. Neither religion, nor the lack of it, is the issue here, because we're searching for a belief in some power that can help us move forward in our quest to live in this world with clarity, dignity and self-acceptance.

Following this program may, at times, seem an impossible and fruitless journey. Many of those who have come this way before us have felt the same way. But if we persist, as they did, we will find a new dimension to living that is well worth all our efforts. What a joy it is to learn that there are others who have successfully traveled this path before us, and to know that because they have been able to overcome their difficulties, they are willing and ready to support us as we pursue our goals. We are no longer alone.

TODAY'S STEP: *In admitting my insanity, I take a step toward trusting a power greater than myself.*

Step Two

Day 13—THE POWER OF UNDERSTANDING

"You cannot speak of the ocean to a well frog—the creature of a narrower sphere. You cannot speak of ice to a summer insect—the creature of a season."
CHUANG TZU

How often have we been accused of not living up to our potential? This seems to be the indictment leveled at us time and again since we were very small. We gave a great deal of power to these judgments, and we came to believe we'd never be able to please *them* or come up to their expectations. We told ourselves, "I'll never be enough." "If only they'd get off my back." "They'll never be satisfied." "They'll never understand."

We were right. *They* never will understand—because they can't. Those significant others in our lives who criticize or castigate us simply cannot understand why we haven't been able to exercise willpower to rid ourselves of the monkey on our backs.

For that, we need the help of those who have been through it themselves. Those persons are surely a power greater than ourselves. Only someone who has had a similar experience, who has been able to tune into our wavelength, who has the capacity to identify with us is able to understand where we are and why. And in that understanding and acceptance lies the power to restore us to sanity.

TODAY'S STEP: *I am guided through this program by the experience of others who have been restored to sanity.*

Step Two

Day 14—VINCENT'S STORY

*"I cannot imagine a God who rewards and pun-
ishes the objects of his creation [and] is but a reflection of human frailty."* ALBERT EINSTEIN

"I grew up," said the young man, "in a God-fearing
family, where church was the focal point of all our activities.
Every one of us kids could recite chapter and verse of the
scriptures when we were called upon to do so, and believe
me, we were called upon to do so a lot!

"There were strict rules governing all our behavior, and
any infraction was punished harshly. All in the interest of
becoming a good Christian, of course.

"I can't tell you how many times I heard, 'This hurts me
more than it hurts you—but it's done for God's good!'

"Then, when I came on the program and you people
told me to put my life in the hands of the God of my
understanding, I said no way! No way am I going to be
able to let a punishing God dictate to me any longer. I've
had too many years of that kind of misery!

"But then you said I didn't have to believe in that God.
I could choose what my Higher Power would be. That
power could be the group, or it could be some idealized
father image, or it could be Brahma, or Buddha, or Vishnu,
or whatever benign entity I could relate to.

" 'Benign entity' was what finally convinced me. God
knows I yearned for anything benign."

When we become "willing to be willing," we find that
new alternatives to puzzling situations make themselves
known to us almost immediately.

TODAY'S STEP: *I replace my old, fearful images of God
with the vision of a loving power I can relate to.*

Step Two

Day 15—TRUSTING OUR HEARTS

"We distrust our heart too much, and our head not enough."
JOSEPH ROUX

While waiting at a stoplight in her car, a woman was beset with worry and concern, trying to figure her way out of a dilemma that caused her a great deal of mental anguish. As the light turned from red to green, her eyes fell on the steering wheel. There she saw the words: "Master Guide—Power Steering."

When she told this story at an AA meeting, she swore she'd never noticed what was printed on the wheel before. And, yet, she knew that she had clearly received an answer to her problem. She was convinced she had been given the word to let the "Master Guide"—her Higher Power—take over and steer. Coincidence or not, she decided to let go of her concern. She released it to that power, which she did not understand, but had now begun to believe actually existed. At this point, the situation took an unexpected turn, her problem was resolved to her satisfaction by an incident she could not have foreseen.

It has been the experience of many of us that, once self-will has given way to trust in a Higher Power, many such "coincidences" occur which are too frequent and too well documented to attribute to blind luck.

It is often our heart that begins to trust first. And our heart tends to be more willing to embrace Step Two than our head. Our head is still operating on information that's been fed into it through the years, and keeps trying to direct us on familiar paths. This is why we find taking risks and changing our direction so frightening.

TODAY'S STEP: *Day by day, I entrust my problems to a power greater than myself.*

Step Two

Day 16—HUMILITY IS NOT HUMILIATION

"One must learn to love oneself with a wholesome and healthy love, so that one can bear to be with oneself and need not roam." FRIEDRICH NIETZSCHE

The more we review those desperate days that brought us to our present point of surrender, the more clearly we understand how we were skyrocketing toward disaster. Fortunately, we found within ourselves the courage and the blessed quality of humility which enabled us to admit that, by ourselves, we were helpless and hopeless.

Humility does not entail humiliation. Humility means coming to terms with the totality of our nature—the bright side and dark side. It means being willing to accept the help that will restore the inner balance that makes the dark side less oppressive.

The ability to admit our helplessness is an enormous plus. None of us likes owning up to our impotence in the face of what seem to be insurmountable odds. We prefer to think that we can always wrest victory from imminent defeat. And it is this very characteristic that will stand us in good stead as we pursue our new way of life.

Perhaps one of the most healing things we can do at this time is to give ourselves a pat on the back for the courage it took to let go of old ideas and for the open-mindedness to at least try this program on for size. Today we will not try to live up to the expectations we think others have of us. We will accept ourselves as we are, for we know that we have already become the individuals we have always wanted to be.

Today we can be comfortable enough with our own imperfections to reach out to others, for now we realize we do not need to be perfect to be loved.

TODAY'S STEP: *I am humble, but I am not humiliated. Humility is the key to restoring my sanity.*

Day 17—SPIRITUAL HEALING

"In a dark time, the eye begins to see."
                                    THEODORE ROETHKE

At the turn of the century, it would have been literally impossible to find anyone who did not subscribe to the Garden of Eden story as the true version of how man was created. But fundamentalists who believe in the Biblical story of creation have long been at odds with those who theorize that it was the "Big Bang" that brought about life as we know it.

Today, members of the Twelve Step programs are not concerned with any of these theories as a religious matter, for these programs are spiritual rather than religious. What concerns us now is finding a spiritual approach to the healing process. When we begin reaching for the Higher Power with our hearts, rather than our minds, we begin to see that power at work in our lives, even in the dark time of bottoming out. The more we get in touch with our continued efforts to make the unworkable work, the more we come to appreciate the value of our determination and persistence even when what we are trying to accomplish proves to be worthless. If we can take these qualities and apply them to our recovery program can you imagine what miracles of healing might occur?

TODAY'S STEP: *In my search for a Higher Power, I find the will to get well.*

Day 18—OBSESSION EQUALS INSANITY

"Whatever deceives seems to produce a magical enchantment."
PLATO

Many of us started down the path that led to our current dilemma in total ignorance of the dangers we were facing. Most addictive behavior starts innocently. Peer pressure, defiance of unreasonable authority, and sometimes just plain curiosity propel us on our path. It begins as a positive experience leading to instant gratification. But then we began to pursue this experience over and over. In time, what had been pleasurable began causing unhealthy and irrational behavior. Worse, we found ourselves unable to curb or control our addictions.

Some of us developed an obsessive need for food. Because we wanted to remain fashionably slim, we resorted to purging or habitual use of laxatives. We were careful to eat sparingly—or not at all—in social situations. But then we'd go home and stuff ourselves beyond belief.

Others of us, addicted to exciting and sometimes "kinky" sex, were forced to go outside of our own environment, even outside marriage, to satisfy this drive. Whatever may have started as an act of mutual enjoyment for our partners and ourselves had become a driving compulsion with no concern for the person with whom we were involved. We may even have used emotional blackmail to coerce significant others into satisfying our desires, and accused them of prudishness and lack of caring when they would not comply.

Now that we are able to see the insanity of our obsessions, we can rid ourselves of the weight we have been carrying for so long, and move through life with a new direction and a new confidence.

TODAY'S STEP: *I recognize that my addictions and obsessions were truly insanity.*

Step Two

Day 19—LETTING GO

"I could not say I believe. I know! I have had the experience of being gripped by something that is stronger than myself, something that people call God."
CARL JUNG

Many of us experience resistance to the suggestion that we forfeit control of our lives, and give that power over to some nebulous entity that is supposedly greater than ourselves.

However, if we really risk taking a look at the evidence that has piled up in our recent past, we cannot help but realize that despite our best intentions, we have been heading toward disaster.

No matter how impressive our education, our background, and our philosophy have been; no matter how hard we tried to rationalize that life had systematically been dealing us one bad break after another; no matter how often we tried to blame others for the difficulties we were experiencing, we simply had to admit that whatever the cause, our lives needed some sort of direction which would interrupt the insanity which was catapulting us on a downward spiral. Fortunately, it was our very insanity which gave us the motivation to seek help.

To avail ourselves of this help, we are going to have to be willing to release self-will and what we thought of as self-preservation, and put our trust in the hands of those who tell us that our answers begin in these steps.

TODAY'S STEP: *I know now that I need the help of a power greater than myself.*

Step Two

Day 20—CONSIDERING ALTERNATIVES

"Where there is an open mind, there will always be a frontier."
CHARLES F. KETTERING

Many of us remember that when we first decided to try our Twelve Step program, our attitudes, formed by many years of conditioning, were pretty inflexible.

Keeping an open mind was not easy for us. We had thoroughly convinced ourselves that our own path was the only possible one to follow, that we were fearful of risking what little control we still had on something that might lead us into an even deeper dilemma.

It is not surprising that we hold on to beliefs that no longer work for us, because those beliefs are *familiar*. Familiarity, despite the fact that it does not succeed in solving our problems, carries a certain degree of comfort.

Stepping off the edge, as it were, into a totally new mind-set needs every bit of courage we can muster. But once we open our minds to the possibility of exploring positive alternatives, we are well on our way to recovery.

Nothing, we can assure ourselves, is set in concrete, and flexibility allows us to see the world as a brand-new place.

TODAY'S STEP: *I embrace open-mindedness as the foundation of renewed sanity.*

Day 21—SANITY-INSANITY

"Only an open mind can be healed." ANONYMOUS

In order to accept the fact that our thinking has been less than sane, we need to look at some of our own biases. On the one hand, we make judgments and scorn those we do not view as our intellectual or social equals. Yet, on the other hand, we perceive ourselves as unworthy, unappreciated, unwanted and unloved.

We tend to measure people by their appearance, rather than by the wisdom they share with us. We need to listen for the message and not judge the messenger. We need to understand that truth can come not only from "the mouths of babes," but also from the people we would least have expected to deal in profundities.

A man once had a flat tire right outside the gates of a mental hospital. As he removed the lugs from the flat to switch them with the spare, they slipped off the curb where he'd placed them and down through the grille of a sewer drain. As he realized there was absolutely no way to retrieve them, he began to swear in frustration.

Just then, an inmate, who had been standing at the fence watching him said, "Why don't you remove one lug from each of the three other wheels and put them on the spare?"

"My gosh," said the man, "what a brilliant idea! What in hell is someone as smart as you doing in *there!*"

"I may be crazy," said the inmate, "but I'm not stupid!"

TODAY'S STEP: *My Higher Power speaks to me through others in unexpected ways.*

Step Two

Day 22—TURNING IT OVER

"What is necessary is never a risk."

CARDINAL RETZ

We possess the ability to make choices, and many of these choices have turned out to be unwise. This fact has immobilized many of us to the point where we're unwilling to make any decisions at all because we're afraid they won't turn out right. As a result, we keep trying to force other people to make decisions for us. This way we're not to blame if their choices are bad ones. We can always imply that, had we chosen for ourselves, things would have worked out better.

Without knowing it, we're really making a decision when we relinquish our power to others. We're making them responsible for our lives. This decision clearly reflects the fact that we're no longer certain of our own capabilities to get things done right. In essence, we're conceding our own powerlessness.

Once we begin to realize our true motivations, admitting our powerlessness allows us to risk turning our will and our lives over to our Higher Power—a move others assured us has worked amazingly well for them. After all, we really don't have a great deal of choice at this time: Either we continue our roller coaster ride to disaster, or we take the plunge into what may be the most exciting and fulfilling adventure of our lives.

TODAY'S STEP: *I am willing to turn my life over to a Higher Power.*

Step Two

Day 23—SLOGANS

"The ability to simplify means to eliminate the unnecessary so that the necessary may speak."

HANS HOFMANN

Many of us have found the use of catchwords and slogans helpful in focusing on each step and in strengthening our resolve as we move toward a successful recovery.

A gambler reported that he'd developed the practice of spelling words on street signs and billboards backward in his head and he'd come up with some surprising observations. " 'Evil' backwards spells 'live,' " he said. "So if I want to live I have to keep remembering that, for me, gambling is evil.

"I couldn't stop when I was winning, and I couldn't stop when I was losing. I not only lost all my money, I also bled my family and friends for every cent I could get.

"It seems ridiculous that something as simple as reversing a word can make me remember that I'm now focused on turning my will and life over to a Higher Power, that I've given up the fight. But, ridiculous or not—it works!"

Many self-help programs share a special language of their own that may seem inane and infantile when we first hear it: "Easy does it." "One day at a time." "Turn it over." "Let go and let God." "Keep coming back." "*We* can do what I can't do." These and many other slogans are offered up as if they were great profundities. But, oddly enough, just as our gambler reported, when we actually live through the experiences these very simple sayings express, we discover why they're part of the glue that keeps fellowships and support groups intact.

TODAY'S STEP: *The slogans of the program are helpful tools for regaining my sanity.*

Day 24—DEVELOPING SANE BEHAVIOR

"You know, sleep and confidence are almost the same thing; they both come together."　　UGO BETTI

Our minds, our bodies, our emotions and our spirits are all affected by illness, stress and crises. When one part of ourself is out of sync, the totality of our being is also adversely affected.

We have discovered that one of the kindest things we can do for ourselves in recovery is nourish our entire being. We find this particularly helpful in Step Two. This is because the more we do healing things for ourselves, the more clearly we come to recognize that the lifestyle we were living was less than sane.

How long has it been since you paid attention to your physical health? Took a walk along the beach, or in the country? Visited an art gallery? Enjoyed a sunset? Heard a symphony? Watched a ballet? Cheered at a sports event? Attended the theater? Had a massage? Participated in a sport? Took a trip? Or just set aside a day for yourself to read or do nothing?

Good nutrition, adequate exercise and restful sleep are important elements that help us nourish and replenish our minds and bodies.

Many of us have experienced severe sleep problems. Worry, fear and guilt are thieves that enter our consciousness and rob of us our needed rest. One interesting note about the recovery process comes from those who have been working the steps for some time. They've discovered that once they were able to confront and amend their lifestyle, night worries, anxiety and insomnia seemed to disappear.

TODAY'S STEP: *Today I allow my Higher Power to rock me to sleep.*

Day 25—MY CASE IS DIFFERENT

"Some people would not hesitate to drive up to the gates of Heaven and honk!"   ANONYMOUS

Theologians and scientists both agree that, as individuals, each of us is unique. While, on one hand, this may make us feel needed, necessary and creative, it can also be one of the greatest stumbling blocks on our road to recovery. Many of us feel that our "specialness" has not been understood or appreciated by others. As we begin working the steps our head may be telling us, "Yes, we see their point. And for most people what they're saying probably does apply." Yet, all the while, our emotions are repeating over and over, "But this doesn't apply to me. My case is different!"

Our carefully nurtured denial system, coupled with a load of honest self-deception, prevents us from identifying with others.

When we are first introduced to a new idea, we do an automatic mind-search to see whether it lies within our repertoire or seems compatible with our own convictions. Usually, if a new idea means making a change, we tend to resist it. We're accustomed to our present situation—although not happy with it. We tend to prefer living in this stalemated condition, rather than risk taking a chance.

Looking good, no matter how badly things are going, has been one of our most powerful coping tools. As a result, the fear of not looking good tends to keep us immobilized to the point where any change becomes almost impossible. Therefore, being willing to release our will and our lives to a power beyond our control takes all the strength we can muster.

TODAY'S STEP: *I trust that I can be sane again, because I can now look at myself honestly.*

Day 26—LETTING GO OF OLD IDEAS

"Rebel, n. A proponent of a new misrule who has failed to establish it." AMBROSE BIERCE
THE DEVIL'S DICTIONARY

Our Twelve Step program suggests that healing and growth are most likely to occur when we can let go of old ideas, practices and beliefs. Even though we're able to admit that we've found ourselves in a less than perfect situation, we're used to it, and we don't trust that change might work out for the better. Conformity has rarely been our strong suit. Resistance and rebellion are more our style. Indeed, these qualities in the past have helped us survive against all odds.

However, recovery is a process—not an event. A process takes time. It evolves through many phases and stages, all of which are necessary to achieve the final results. Letting go of old ideas is simply one of those phases.

The reasoning behind releasing our old attitudes and habits is well thought-out. During our formative years, and particularly as our disease began to take hold, we did things almost by rote. We fell into patterns that satisfied our self-seeking demands, and developed thought processes and defenses to justify our actions.

Not all of those old ideas were wrong. The problem is, they were so inextricably tied up with those that were, that it is only by wiping the slate clean that we can begin to develop the actions and reactions that will be in harmony with our new lifestyle.

TODAY'S STEP: *Recovery is the bedrock of sanity; I can now let go of old ideas.*

Step Two

Day 27—IMPATIENCE

"Patience is a bitter plant, but it has sweet fruit."
GERMAN PROVERB

A Japanese fable tells of a young boy who traveled many miles to the school of a great and famous swordsman. Impressed that the lad had come so far, the master gave him an audience.

"What do you wish from me?" asked the master.

"I wish to be your student and become the finest swordsman in the land," the boy replied. "How long must I study?"

"Ten years at least," replied the master.

"Ten years is a long time," said the boy, taken aback. "What if I studied twice as hard as all the other students?"

"Twenty years," replied the master.

"Twenty years! What if I were to practice unrelentingly day and night with all my effort?"

"Thirty years," answered the master.

"How is it that each time I say I will work harder you tell me that it will take longer?" the student asked, quite confused by now.

"The answer is clear," said the master. "When there is one eye fixed on your destination, there is only one eye left with which to find the Way."

Recovery is a process that requires both our eyes and all our awareness. More important, it involves letting go of our expectations of how the process will work and of its eventual outcome.

TODAY'S STEP: *When I trust in a Higher Power, I don't have to do it all myself.*

Step Two

Day 28—PATIENCE

"The reward for patience—is patience."

ST. AUGUSTINE

When we think of the steps as a philosophy rather than as a religion or doctrine, we find ourselves more willing to accept the paradoxes they present. The recovery plan tells us that we have to give up in order to win; that to keep what we get we have to give it away; that our worst transgressions may prove to be our most valuable assets.

The crux of this entire program is acceptance and action. When we combine these components with the H.O.W. process—Honesty, Open-mindedness and Willingness—they become the very foundation of recovery.

Believe it or not, we've already come a long way in our daily attendance to these pages.

We should be pleased and amazed at the progress we've made.

Our need for immediate gratification might make us impatient about the slowness of the recovery process. But, just as it took time for us to recognize the crises in our lives, it will take time for us to surmount the obstacles created by our disease. Remember, low tolerance for frustration is the norm in the early days of recovery.

The Golden Rule tells us that we should treat others the way we would hope to be treated by them. We surely would want them to be patient with us when we are slow to learn. So we must practice patience with them when they do not respond to us the way we want them to.

TODAY'S STEP: *I recognize that patience is an integral part of restoring me to sanity.*

Day 29—SNAP JUDGMENT

"If you sow kindness, you will reap a crop of friends."
ANONYMOUS

Accepting the premise that there is a power greater than ourselves requires a lot of self-searching and rethinking.

All of us, on some level, harbor prejudices and biases. We would do well to heed the Native American maxim: "Don't judge a man until you have walked many moons in his moccasins."

We find ourselves making snap judgments about others based upon how they look, how they dress or how they speak, and it becomes difficult to place principles before personalities. It's part of the process of recovery to learn to withhold judgment until we've listened carefully to what others have to offer, and determined whether it might prove to be insightful or valuable to us.

Sometimes we say things without thinking, although we had no intention of being offensive to our listeners. We wouldn't deliberately make jokes about someone else's situation if we knew that it would cause them pain. Nor would they denigrate our sacred cows if they knew how we felt. This is why it's so important for us to be open and honest about our own feelings and to respect others when they share their feelings with us.

Sensitivity is a characteristic we need to develop. But it shouldn't prevent us from voicing what we need to say. Sharing with others—even the things we find unappealing or childish about ourselves—often brings rich and surprising rewards.

TODAY'S STEP: *It's easy to overlook other people's shortcomings, when I know that my Higher Power overlooks mine.*

Day 30—TAKING STOCK—TAKING ACTION

"Faith without works is dead."　　　　JAMES 2:26

All the Twelve Steps are simple and workable. And now that we're coming to the end of Step Two, we're ready to put it into action in our lives.

Whether we believe it or not, we are prepared, for we have accepted the challenge of Step Two. We can no more erase it from our consciousness than we could comply if someone were to say, "Don't think about the Leaning Tower of Pisa." The more we would try to not think about it, the more clearly the building would be in our mind's eye.

Take a little time now to review the questions we posed to ourselves in Step One. Also, let's ask a few more questions:

Am I still resisting the concept of turning over my life to a Higher Power? Do I still balk at the phrases: "God, as you understand Him," or "Higher Power," or "a Power greater than ourselves?"

Am I willing to use those terms for the healing energy that exists outside myself and forms a vital component of my recovery?

Despite my doubts and misgivings, am I willing to commit myself to this program?

I have to admit that there is a strong feeling of relief in giving up the struggle to steer my way out of the wreckage of my past, and to believe that there truly is a power greater than myself which can and will lead me to a life of wholeness and freedom.

TODAY'S STEP: *I surrender all resistance to recognizing a Higher Power.*

Day 31—BUILDING OUR HOUSE

"Life is either a daring adventure or nothing. To keep our faces toward change and behave like free spirits in the presence of fate is strength undefeatable."
                                        HELEN KELLER

We began our exploration of the process of beginning again with the analogy of building a house. In recovery, the foundation must be laid with material that the architect has specified and that the builder can work with. Both have had previous experience in designing and building, and are therefore powers greater than we in this undertaking.

Although we might wish to choose different materials, we have no way of knowing if they will mesh with the overall plan or will be strong enough to support the stresses on the framework as the new structure emerges.

Through recovery we can begin to live in a "safe house" at last, one which is earthquake-proof, and has adequate insulation to remain cool in summer and warm in winter, and where friends and companions feel welcome and comfortable. This house may simply be a state of mind but it's sufficient to shelter us safely through the days ahead.

TODAY'S STEP: *My growing faith in a Higher Power gives me a feeling of safety.*

Step Three

STEP THREE

"Made a decision to turn our will and our lives over to the care of God as we understood Him."

Step Two was the springboard for spiritual awakening. Now, in Step Three, we are poised for that dive into the bottomless pool of trust where we begin practicing a belief we are not even sure we have.

Day by day, we will examine this step in all of its implications and ramifications. We will probably experience some doubt and skepticism about our ability to truly surrender our will and our lives to the unknown.

But we cannot have come this far without feeling that there have been some subtle changes in our attitudes and reactions. Before we're through, we'll experience even more of these behavioral and attitudinal changes.

Step Three

Day 1—CAME TO BELIEVE

"The only thing that changed was my mind."
LAURIE NEDVIN

Some folks have commented that in order to work Step Two, they found it necessary to break down the first three words:

Came . . .
Came to . . .
Came to believe . . .

Translated, this means that, first, it was necessary to show up for action. Secondly, we needed to be open-minded. And finally, we had to place our trust in a power outside of ourselves.

Now, in Step Three, we are asked to turn our will and our lives over to a power we totally fear, or with whom we're totally unfamiliar. A leap into this kind of blind faith can seem as terrifying as being told that someone has booked passage for us on a spaceship to the moon.

Even though we recognize we need all the help we can get, the thought of releasing our own self-will, despite every indication that it is partly responsible for our current dilemma, is almost too much to contemplate.

We want to declare that, armed with this new resolve, we can now pull ourselves together and get on the right track. But because we are fearful and skeptical of letting go—because we have not yet learned to trust—we tend to regret and reject this step, falling into the mode of "contempt before investigation."

TODAY'S STEP: *Each day I experience a growing faith in my Higher Power.*

Step Three

Day 2—LEARNING TO LISTEN

*"Those who can't forget are worse off than those
who can't remember."* ANONYMOUS

There is absolutely no hard-and-fast rule about what we
choose as our Higher Power. It could be a friend, a sponsor, a counselor, the group or a deity in which we have a
belief. Therefore, whatever our choice, it will work perfectly for us as long as we follow the formula that is outlined in these steps.

When we're told that we must turn our will and lives
over to a Higher Power, our first response may be: "That's
easy for you to say! But will that power get my bills paid?
Will it bring my wife back to me? Will it make my children
forgive me? Will it help me face old friends I've hurt or
misused? Will it rid me of this guilt and shame—this humiliation that overwhelms me?"

Spiritual experiences may be well and good we tell ourselves. But the practical aspects of life are what we face
daily. How in the world is some super power going to take
care of *them*? As one woman put it: "The problem with
living is that it is so daily."

We're not suggesting that practicing Step Three will
immediately solve everything that's bothering us about the
past—or what faces us in our future. But it will help us
discover that the important thing is to let go of our own
agenda, our own self-will. It will help us seek guidance, and
learn to listen to our inner voice and the counsel of our
sponsors and our recovery group.

TODAY'S STEP: *Setbacks turn into opportunities, when I
seek the guidance of a Higher Power.*

Step Three

Day 3—HOW DO I DO THAT?

"Instinctively, as do the shipwrecked, he will look round for something to which to cling; and that tragic, ruthless glance, absolutely sincere because it is a question of his salvation, will cause him to bring order into the chaos of his life."

SØREN KIERKEGAARD

Most of our troubles tend to be of our own making. Despite our best intentions to behave honestly and honorably, we got caught in a riptide of such strength that we were drawn inexorably deeper and deeper into destruction. We couldn't see any solution to our situation—until something within us proved even more powerful and helped us reach out for help.

That something, we are told, is the power greater than ourselves and that the time has come for us to let go and hand over the reins to that unknown something or someone else.

"But how," we ask, "do I do that? Do I just sit down in the middle of the room and say, 'Okay, whomever or whatever you are, take over. I give up?' "

A recovering cocaine addict shared this method with a Twelve Step group: "I put my two hands out in front of me. In the left hand I pretend to put all the dirt and crap my using had created. In the right, I put all the abilities and talents I identify as positive characteristics about myself. Then I put my left hand behind my back and say: 'I won't look at any of this right now. Instead, I'll look at what I've got going for me, and I'll work on strengthening those assets. And when the time comes to bring my left hand into view again, I'll have developed the ability—through the belief that some Greater Power is working through me—to cope with the consequences of that wreckage better than I can do now.' "

TODAY'S STEP: *Now that I can see where self-will has led me, it's easier to trust in a Higher Power.*

Step Three

Day 4—THE GROUP EXPERIENCE

"Happiness is not the absence of conflict, but the ability to cope with it." ANONYMOUS

People who have sought treatment for their addictions have uniformly reported that one of their most powerful experiences was group therapy. They found themselves identifying with others in the group and acknowledging fears and failings they had never shared with anyone before. The group became a very valuable tool in the early stages of their recovery.

Most residential treatment programs call for an aftercare plan that includes attendance at self-help groups. The undeniable power of the group experience is demonstrated by the fact that it has proven to be one of the most effective defenses against relapse.

The group dynamic is a powerful influence on our recovery—one that may offer us our first experience of unconditional love. Peer acceptance is such a healing factor in our continuing recovery. When someone tells us—"I know just how you feel; I've done that too, and I could have killed myself for doing it"—it's as if the guilt and shame we've carried for so long had somehow been lessened.

One of the primary healing qualities of groups and fellowships is the loving acceptance that evolves when people begin to trust themselves to be open with others.

TODAY'S STEP: *My group is the reflection of my Higher Power.*

Day 5—THE MIRACLE OF RECOVERY

*"The greatest undeveloped territory in the world
lies under your hat."* ANONYMOUS

Physicians have often been at a loss to explain how patients
unable to benefit from the very best medical treatment
sometimes recover completely from seemingly fatal illnesses. They admit that they're baffled about how spontaneous remission from cancer occurs. The best are
forthright enough to say that although their treatment
proved to be totally ineffectual, something very powerful
was able to effect a miraculous recovery.

Christian Science practitioners attribute to God many
phenomenal recoveries from all sorts of bodily and mental
ills. In tribal cultures, shamans successfully heal patients
through a combination of herbs and ritual chants and
dances.

In all of these cases both healer and patient acknowledge
the existence of a power greater than human beings.

These phenomena also occur in recovery from obsessions, compulsions and addictions. Where professionals
have failed to effect recovery through either medicine or
psychotherapy, a belief in some power greater than ourselves, as well as adherence to the guidelines and principles
developed in these steps, make recovery not only possible,
but highly probable.

Today we can practice gratitude for all that we are and
all that we have. We no longer dwell on the negatives for
we are in partnership with a powerful guide.

TODAY'S STEP: *My daily recovery proves that I am already
in the care of a Higher Power.*

Day 6—PLAYING GOD DOESN'T WORK

*"Courage is resistance to fear, mastery of fear—
not absence of fear."*   MARK TWAIN

The Jekyll-Hyde syndrome is both familiar and confusing
to most of us who have been victims of addictive/compul-
sive disorders. By nature we are honorable people who
would not intentionally do harm to anyone. Yet, caught up
in our compulsions, we have behaved in antisocial and
hurtful ways.

Unaided, we seemed incapable of helping ourselves.
This is why Step Three is of such importance. We simply
must release the reins of self-will. We have to stop playing
God. It hasn't worked.

Now, laid out before us are alternatives created and
practiced by people who have tried them and found them
successful. It has been proven to their satisfaction that
some sort of Higher Power does exist. We are certainly in
no position to deny their successes. As many of them have
told us, "Try it on for size. If you don't think it works,
we'll gladly refund your misery."

TODAY'S STEP: *When I let go of playing God, I begin to
experience a Higher Power.*

Step Three

Day 7—THE RULES OF THE GAME

"The only shame is to have none."   BLAISE PASCAL

We like the motto: "Bloom where you are planted." Obviously we cannot go back over our lives and make it all okay. We have to start where we are—right here, right now. We have to be willing to latch on to the faith that time will sweep away the debris we've accumulated. All we need to do now is clear the decks for our new adventure—a journey into recovery and balance.

Step Three asks us to accept where we are right now, and relinquish control of our lives and our self-will.

There will be setbacks. Most of us still seem to learn best from the mistakes we make rather than realize we've somehow stumbled on the right action. It's similar to learning to play golf. The lucky shot isn't what teaches us right form. Rather, it's when we slice or dig up divots that we become aware that we're holding the club wrong, or swinging incorrectly, or standing off center.

Today we can be thankful for all that we have. We can be amazed at the progress we are making and not dwell on those things we haven't yet accomplished.

TODAY'S STEP: *In facing where I am today, I gain the strength to turn over control of my life and my will.*

Day 8—WISHFUL THINKING

"If wishes were horses beggars would ride."
NURSERY RHYME

Not to decide is one form of decision. The habit of procrastination dies hard with many people. We hesitate, not quite ready to put a toe in the water for fear it will prove to be an uncomfortable experience. We hope that some divine providence or happy twist of fate will intervene so we won't have to take the plunge.

Most of us wish that simply by admitting defeat we could be absolved of all that has gone before. Like Scarlett O'Hara, our repeated reaction to a problem was, "Tomorrow is another day."

This kind of wishful thinking often deters us from following Step Three. We fantasize that if we win the lottery, or perform an act of heroism or are diagnosed with some rare disease that was responsible for our irrational behavior, then all will be forgiven and we can start anew. Would that it were so!

Today we will keep centering ourselves in the moment, not projecting into the future nor dwelling in the past. We can live this day to its fullest, savoring all the gifts it has in store.

TODAY'S STEP: *The future, like the present, lies in the hands of my Higher Power.*

Day 9—FORCES BEYOND OUR COMPREHENSION

"Let us weigh the gain and the loss, in wagering that God is. Consider these alternatives: If you win, you win all; if you lose, you lose nothing. Do not hesitate, then, to wager that He is."

BLAISE PASCAL

The phrase "There are no atheists in foxholes" holds true when we experience sudden and unexpected crises. If someone we love is injured or seriously ill, we automatically pray that they will be spared. Likewise we send up little prayers for a wanted job, for the home team to win, or for relief from a time of trouble. Yet we persist in denying the existence of a power greater than ourselves.

In our daily lives we still observe many superstitions. We won't walk under a ladder. We toss spilled salt over our left shoulder. We go out of our way to avoid having a black cat cross our path. And we're afraid that breaking a mirror will bring us seven years' bad luck.

These are all forms of belief in some power outside of ourselves. And although most of us deny that we really "believe in this stuff," we have an almost automatic gut reaction when such things occur.

So it would appear that, in our deepest recesses of memory and instincts, we *do* accept the existence of forces beyond our comprehension that influence our attitudes and our behavior. Perhaps we may well be able to find relief when we decide to abandon self-will—if only temporarily—and allow another power to relieve us of carrying the world on our shoulders.

TODAY'S STEP: *Faith in a Higher Power emerges from the depths of my being.*

Step Three

Day 10—LOVING WHAT IS GOOD

"Men always love what is good or what they find good; it is in judging what is good that they go wrong."
                                                    JEAN-JACQUES ROUSSEAU

When we first practiced the behavior that was to become our master, we received a positive reward. It may have been our first drink, our first pleasurable sexual experience, our first joint, our first snort, our first big win at the gambling table, our first appreciable weight loss, our sense of power in obtaining our own credit card. Each of us can fill in the category which best describes our situation.

But, in time, our desire to feel good began to rule us. We could no longer control it. Despite this, the euphoric memory of how it was at the beginning refused to dispel no matter how negatively we were affected. We were terribly confused when we saw others behaving the same way and not suffering any adverse effects. We had no way of knowing that there was something in our makeup that would hook us into addictive behavior. Then, finally, we admitted we were powerless and recognized we had to latch on to some force that could move us out of this chaos.

When we find ourselves powerless—awash in a sea of confusion and fear, we can tune into that power within ourselves that will bring us clarity and serenity. We can put ourselves under the care of that power we are coming to know.

TODAY'S STEP: *I trust my Higher Power to care for me.*

Step Three

Day 11—ACCEPTING WHO WE ARE—TODAY

"Many people today don't want honest answers insofar as honest means unpleasant or disturbing. They want a soft answer that turneth away anxiety."
LOUIS KRONENBERGER

A popular song in the Twenties had a refrain: "I love me, I love me, I'm wild about myself." Although we are not advocating quite such extravagant self-adulation, we do think it important to accept ourselves today just the way we are. Right now. It is only in acknowledging and accepting our dark side that we can realistically forge ahead with any degree of success.

When we hide from ourselves and others the part of us we perceive as shameful—afraid that if *they* really knew us, they'd throw us away—we lessen our chances of starting to set our world right. Rigorous honesty allows us to stop hiding our shameful secrets and indicates that we are willing, at last, to discard our power-play tactics and risk openness. This is when we say, "Okay, Higher Power, I can't. Maybe you can. I think I'll let you."

When that Higher Power takes over, we try to listen to its voice of guidance that speaks in our inner depths. We also try to listen to our group, our sponsor or our counselor. We constantly remind ourselves that the first thought that occurs to us in any situation might be an old conditioned-reflex response, one we had developed to defend our past habits and behavior. Therefore, we need to ask ourselves, "Is this an old idea? Is it appropriate to the situation I find myself facing at this moment?"

TODAY'S STEP: *Since I turned over my will, it's easier to be honest.*

Step Three

Day 12—BOTTOMING OUT

"The difference between perserverance and obstinacy is that one comes from a strong will and the other from a strong won't."　　　ANONYMOUS

Embarking on this journey of recovery is like setting sail with Columbus to find the New World. He's the captain, and we're supposed to trust him. But, feeling comfortable about looking for a world he guesses is there is a pretty tall order. Besides, common sense tells us that the world is flat. Suppose he's wrong? Are we just going to fall off the end?

Frequently, in recovery, we hear the term "hitting one's bottom." This implies that we've finally come to the end of all our resources—that we find ourselves helpless and well nigh hopeless. Paradoxically, this is the ideal condition we need to begin our upward climb.

Like a failing business, we have to own up to our imminent bankruptcy. And, like a failing business, we begin to feel a glimmer of hope when we're introduced to a turnaround artist who has restructured other businesses and who offers to help us set our course for future successes.

Despite the fact that his methods and suggestions differ from ours, we have to concede that he seems to be able to do what we could not. So, we agree to try it *his* way. When we let go of self-will and put our trust in a power greater than ourselves, things have a way of resolving themselves in a manner that we could not have foreseen.

TODAY'S STEP: *It's a relief to turn my life over to the care of a power greater than myself.*

Day 13—BEYOND MEDIA HYPE

"People who are wrapped up in themselves make a very small package." ANONYMOUS

Madison Avenue is a power that has dictated our lifestyle to a great extent. Provocative copy and images advertise and encourage alcohol consumption. The message is that elite, well-educated and all-American types enjoy and control their drinking. Yet, society heavily condemns alcoholics and relegates them to the lowest rung on the human ladder.

The media also advertise and applaud thinness. Yet society finds abhorrent the methods used by the eating disorder sufferer to live up to that image.

We're constantly bombarded with messages telling us that, in order to amount to anything, we have to dine at the right restaurants, drive the right kind of car, live in the right kind of a house, shop in the right kind of stores. If we don't, then we're losers. Yet, when compulsive spenders get mired in the drive for status and are unable to stop playing credit-card roulette, they're held up to scorn.

Madison Avenue advertisers should not be the power that dictates how we run our lives or how we feel. Trusting in a Higher Power opens up a whole new realm of possibilities. Once we can do that, we release the need to impress the Joneses. We begin to understand that high principles and a spiritual approach to life are far more rewarding than the drive for money, property and prestige.

TODAY'S STEP: *I let go of all false gods and turn my will over to a power greater than myself.*

Day 14—CATCH 22

"When you want to believe in something you also have to believe in everything that's necessary for believing in it."
UGO BETTI

It's understandable to want assurances that turning our will over to a Higher Power will work before we try it for ourselves. Although many people tell us it's worked for them, we don't necessarily see that as proof positive. We'd rather have firsthand, personal experience before we buy the whole package. But this is where we hit Catch 22—because the only way we can get that proof is by doing what has been suggested to us.

We may tell ourselves and others, "I really don't see my so-called problem as all that bad. All I really want is to reinstate myself with my family and my profession. I don't have any experience in releasing self-will to anyone else. I just can't buy into it. It seems pointless to put myself in the hands of some unknown force."

But when nothing changes, nothing gets better. When we realize we just spin our wheels in the sand, there is nothing to do, but to do it. We listen to those others who tell us: "I tried it. And I was amazed at the changes that began happening in my life."

Day by day, step by step, we are beginning to trust in others and in the process of recovery. A beautiful pattern is opening up before our very eyes.

TODAY'S STEP: *I am beginning to turn my will and my life over to my Higher Power unconditionally.*

Day 15—SHIFTING PERSPECTIVE

*"Going to worship doesn't make you a holy person
any more than going to a garage makes you a car."*
ANONYMOUS

Each of us has a different perspective on things. For instance,
if a man standing near us waiting for a train is reading a
magazine, we would see only the front and back covers of
that magazine. If he were to chuckle about something, we
would not have the foggiest idea what he finds so humorous.
While our perspective remains the same, he experiences
something totally different with each page he turns.

Step Three might be likened to seeing other recovering
people as represented by the covers of the magazine, and
ourselves as skeptical about what possible value they find in
the contents. We grant that the magazine has more material
in its pages than we can see from just the cover, but we are
not all that sure we are willing to purchase it in order to find
out what they think is so interesting.

How do we resolve this impasse and shift our perspective?

Well, we've got several choices. We can practice total
avoidance and not take the step. This means we're left to
work out our problems by ourselves—despite the fact that,
no matter how many previous attempts we have made, we
found ourselves "up the creek."

We might even reject the whole concept as being too
simplistic and ritualistic to be of any value, and walk away
from it. Or we can let go of our prejudices and negative
projections once and for all and commit ourselves to buy-
ing the whole package.

TODAY'S STEP: *In gaining willingness to consider another
perspective, I begin to let go of willfulness.*

Step Three

Day 16—SURVIVAL STRATEGIES

"When one door closes another opens." ANONYMOUS

Our earliest experiences of family life, peer conditioning, religious training, social restrictions and biases, economic conditions, schooling and cultural beliefs all play a large part in shaping our thinking and our behavior.

Many of us experienced a reward-punishment ethic designed to mold us into a level of conformity that others in our lives were comfortable with. We learned that if we held widely divergent opinions, it was wise to keep them to ourselves. As a result, many of us developed the habit of secrecy. Imitating our peers was the most effective way to be accepted by them and trying to follow family rules and structure seemed to lessen the likelihood of being mistreated or abandoned.

We quickly realized that if we were to win affection and approval from others, we might have to act in ways contrary to our own convictions. We learned to compromise as a way of maintaining safety.

Those of us who were rebellious saw secrecy and accommodation as the only avenue to self-preservation open to us. For others, "peace at any price" became the standard by which we ran our lives. When the pain and discomfort of our coping mechanisms became too great, we sought some means of escape. And yet, it was when we were first introduced to the chemical or type of behavior which alleviated our discomfort, that our greatest difficulties began.

Now we're being asked to walk away from our survival tools and strategies. To turn our lives over to a power greater than ourselves. What a frightening prospect! What an exciting invitation!

TODAY'S STEP: *I abandon the survival strategies that have failed me; I turn to God for help.*

Step Three

Day 17—DENNY'S STORY

"What is it that every man seeks? To be secure, to be happy, to do what he pleases without restraint and without compulsion."
EPICTETUS

"At first, my addiction was a positive and pleasant relief from pressures. It reduced my anxiety, diminished my stress, and served my purpose. In the early stages I didn't get negative feedback from people. This reinforced my behavior.

"Everything seemed positive; I had no idea I was heading for trouble. It wasn't until later that I began to hear others cry 'Can't you see what it's doing to you?'

"I didn't understand that there was something in my makeup which made me different from others, that they could indulge in some of the same behavior as I and remain relatively unscathed while I came a cropper. Consequently, I blamed the results—not on my addiction—but on the outside forces which were pressuring me.

"Beset by anxiety and tension, I found increasing comfort in turning to my 'security blanket' behavior. I became less and less able to endure uncomfortable feelings or situations for any period of time. My tolerance for frustration decreased alarmingly. My need for relief became more and more demanding.

"I clung to the euphoric memory of 'how good it was'—totally ignoring the danger signals and the mounting evidence that life wasn't working for me any longer. Although I would have told you otherwise, I was in dire need of some timely and powerful intervention to pull myself out of my pit."

TODAY'S STEP: *Now that my Higher Power is in charge, my life is becoming more manageable.*

Day 18—ANXIETY AND TENSION

"We poison our lives with fear of burglary and shipwreck and—ask anyone—the house is never burgled and the ship never goes down."

JEAN ANOUILH

When we find ourselves uneasy or apprehensive about what *may* happen, we simply need to realize we're replaying an old tape. Our subconscious is trying to take control and trigger our addictive behavior patterns. But once we identify that we're feeling anxious, we discover that we're caught up in old ideas and we have the opportunity to get some perspective on what's really going on. We can view anxiety as a clue to strengthen our resolve.

Tension offers us a similar opportunity. Tension often engenders muscular tautness, which can be relieved to some extent by relaxation techniques, deep breathing and physical exercise. Strained relationships can often be a tension-causing factor in the early stages of recovery, because many people are partially or wholly estranged from us due to the harm our disease has caused them. Now, when we feel ourselves becoming tense, we can slow down, take a deep breath, ground ourselves in the here and now, and try a new approach.

These warning signals can work to our advantage. We don't know any human being who is not beset from time to time by anxiety and tension. In the past, many of us have resorted to chemical relief. However, now that we understand the nature of our personalities, we've resolved not to depend on "better living through chemistry." We can learn to use our anxiety and tension creatively—as early warning devices.

TODAY'S STEP: *I turn my anxiety and tension over to a Higher Power and strengthen my resolve to recover.*

Step Three

Day 19—WHO AM I?

"It takes a certain level of aspiration before one can take advantage of opportunities that are clearly offered."
MICHAEL HARRINGTON

Who we think we are is often determined by the other people in our lives. We've been someone's child, sibling, friend, sweetheart, spouse and parent, and in the natural scheme of things will probably be, or already are, someone's grandparent.

But who are *we*? Now is the time when we're attempting to separate our identity from our environment. Now is the time when we are learning to be our own person.

The experience of unconditional love is probably one of the most healing factors known to humankind. The "TLC" we experience from good nurses is one example. The acceptance and approval we receive from a Twelve Step fellowship is another. When we know that we are being approved of, simply because we're making an honest attempt to recover, we begin to see and appreciate who we are. When we relinquish self-will and turn our life over to the care of a Higher Power, we receive an enormous amount of support in our struggle to discover who we really are and what we really want.

Today we remind ourselves that "God isn't finished with us yet." We are content to measure our progress in inches rather than yards.

TODAY'S STEP: *Because my Higher Power cares for me, I know I am valuable.*

Step Three

Day 20—THE WISDOM OF THE GROUP

"God is what man finds that is divine in himself. God is the best way man can behave in the ordinary occasions of life, and the farthest point to which man can stretch himself."
                                                    MAX LERNER

In turning our life and will over to a Higher Power, how do we eliminate feelings of guilt and shame? In recovery, the law of cause and effect runs its course. While the consequences may seem negative, they simply represent the playing out of the scenario that our addiction created. It helps to know that as we change our old behaviors, we need never again be victims of our compulsive/addictive disorders.

Support groups can be of tremendous value to us in recovery. While we may not find kindred souls among all those working toward the same goal, when we listen to the messages they share—rather than judging the nature of the compulsion and addictions of the speakers—we will find many points of reference and a surprising depth of wisdom that can be extremely helpful.

When we all come together—each with his or her separate fears, prejudices, social and philosophical biases—somewhere, somehow we find the strength in numbers that we could not muster alone. God, as we understand Him, assumes the many shapes and identities as conceived by individuals in the group. This is how the group consciousness operates on the level of a Higher Power—and where the healing wisdom emerges from and finds its center.

TODAY'S STEP: *Through my group, God's will for me is made known.*

Day 21—HOW WE SEE OURSELVES

"If you scatter thorns, don't go barefoot."

ANONYMOUS

A well-known psychotherapist tells this story of working in the closed ward of a mental hospital where the more disturbed patients were quartered. He handed a simple test to all the patients, and when they'd completed it, he handed out the same test again. "Now," he said, "take this test as if you were a sane and normal person." In each instance the second test, taken by the same patients, was strikingly better than the first. Because they followed the promptings of a power greater than themselves (in this case the doctor), and because they were encouraged to act "as if," they all improved.

When we seek the guidance of a Higher Power who can help us to overcome our problems, we're well on our way to just such an accomplishment. But if we think of ourselves as shallow; as lacking in finer feelings; as second-class citizens, we're diminishing that power.

Too many children have been branded troublemakers by parents or teachers who never took the time to find out what caused the disruptive behavior. Some of these children accepted that judgment as valid, and continued to behave in defiant and rebellious ways. Branded as renegades, they decided to live up to their label. So it was with some of us.

We're not bad people trying to be good. On the contrary, we're survivors. We're wounded, striving to recover from a disorder that has caused us to think and behave in ways contrary to our true natures.

TODAY'S STEP: *I will count all my blessings, acknowledge all my talents, and treat myself as if I were my very best friend.*

Day 22—SKEPTICISM

"Glory is not in never failing, but in rising every time we fall."   ANONYMOUS

One of the reasons so many of us have had difficulty releasing our lives and will is that we've prided ourselves on our own self-sufficiency, and we can cite evidence to prove it. Because of past experience, we've had a hard time learning to trust others and to share our emotions with them. We've become so used to keeping our feelings to ourselves and to solving our own problems, that it's extremely difficult for us to admit we've reached a stage of personal helplessness.

Paranoia sets in when we suspect that we've stumbled upon a cult whose only mission is to brainwash us into marching in lockstep with their band. The concept that some spirit is going to pick us up and carry us safely into a better and more comfortable existence is not only too abstract for us to grasp, but also seems totally lacking in logic or common sense.

But no one expects us to buy the whole package when it's first presented to us. Still, where we find ourselves today is of our own making. Obviously, our way isn't cutting it. We've tried other alternatives, and they haven't worked either. We don't seem to have anything to lose—and possibly a great deal to gain—by tabling our skepticism and accepting the program on faith.

TODAY'S STEP: *I allow myself to rely on a Higher Power.*

Step Three

Day 23—TURNING THE TABLES

"It is one of the most beautiful compensations of life that no one can sincerely try to help another without helping himself." CHARLES DUDLEY WARNER

A large part of recovery is based on faith. And faith comes hard to those of us who are the "walking wounded." We can't help but feel that we've been dealt an unfair hand, that if *they* really knew the pain and hurt and disappointments we've suffered, they would be more understanding and compassionate.

But the reality is that they've watched in sorrow and helplessness as our addictions progressed and caused changes in us both physically and emotionally. Frequently, and unknowingly, those close to us may have encouraged our dysfunctional behavior by taking on the roles of placater, critic, parent or dependent in order to cope with our baffling attitudes and actions. It has pained them to see someone they love change from a warm and caring individual into a tormented, driven antagonist.

The problem here is that, instead of helping us to overcome our problem, their pain often acts as a catalyst to plunge us ever deeper into our compulsive behavior. This explains, in part, why many of them may not be very supportive when we accept help from strangers in our recovery program. They feel that they've stuck by us through thick and thin, and are angry that we turn to others for support. In recovery, the tables are turned. It's now time for us to be more understanding and compassionate with them.

TODAY'S STEP: *My relationships are also in the care of a Higher Power.*

Day 24—TRYING A DIFFERENT ROUTE

"Never mistake motion for action."

ERNEST HEMINGWAY

Acceptance is one of the biggest stumbling blocks on our path to recovery. It's hard to let go of the ideas we feel have been in our best interest, even though they've led us into disaster. We think that if we just keep trying harder we'll get the desired results. This, despite the evidence that time after time our situation got worse—not better.

Step One clearly demonstrated to us that admitting our powerlessness and the unmanageability of our lives were prerequisites to recovery. However, as we progress, we need to remember that we'll continue to be plagued by our past beliefs and attitudes. It's as if the familiar music starts to play, and our feet move—with accustomed routine—in the remembered dance steps.

Many of us have resisted marching in lockstep and conforming to rigid guidelines. This sense of our individuality will serve us well down the road. Right now, though, we're embarking on a new journey whose rules for survival require our willingness to try a different route. Even though this path might seem to be roundabout, it has proven to be the safest and surest way to achieve our objective.

The more we let go of old ideas, biases and prejudices, the more we find ourselves moving at ease among our fellow men and women.

TODAY'S STEP: *I replace willfulness with willingness.*

Day 25—LEARNING THROUGH FAITH

*"The formula for perpetual ignorance is to be satis-
fied with your biases and current knowledge."*

ANONYMOUS

Psychologist-philosopher William James once said that
many religious or spiritual experiences were educational in
nature. Rather than stemming from a commitment to any
orthodoxy, creed, or dogma, they came from some profound phenomenon wherein people realized—after the
fact—that they had experienced a deep belief and awareness for which there seemed to be no logical explanation.

Those of us who are not comfortable with the terms
"Higher Power" or "God" might feel more at ease accepting James' theory. And, in time, as we progress, we'll begin
to notice changes in both our attitude and actions that
indicate we're seeing ourselves and the world in a different
light. The more frequently and more completely we are
able to let go of self-will, the more events will begin to
occur that we could never have foreseen.

On the surface it seems foolhardy to assume that simply
by declaring our willingness to let go, and let whoever or
whatever take charge, that all will be resolved. And yet, this
is an essential part of recovery.

TODAY'S STEP: *Just for today, I am willing to let go and
let God.*

Step Three

Day 26—FREE-FALL

"To get everything, you must let go of everything."
TAOIST PROVERB

An Alpine climber, exploring alone, suddenly felt a crevasse open beneath his feet. As he started to fall into the abyss, he grabbed onto an edelweiss plant that was so deeply rooted it arrested his descent.

In fear and trepidation he called out, "If there *is* a God, please help me now!" The heavens parted and a blinding white light shone down. A thunderous voice boomed out, "Do you trust me, my son?"

"Yes. Oh, yes, yes, yes, yes!" screamed the climber.

"Very good, my son. Now let go of the edelweiss."

The man thought for a moment, and then called out, "Is there anyone else up there I can talk to?"

So it is with many of us when we face the prospect of letting go of one of our life problems. While we may concede that a Higher Power does exist, we question whether He, She, It or They is really interested enough in us to solve our dilemmas.

Haven't we been told since childhood that, if we wanted a thing done well, we should do it ourselves? How can we trust in the unseen and unknown to do for us what we're afraid is an impossible task?

The only way we'll ever know is to let go of the edelweiss.

TODAY'S STEP: *I trust that my life is in the hands of a loving power.*

Day 27—THAWING OUT

"To understand is to forgive, even oneself."
ALEXANDER CHASE

Our lives are a lot like icebergs. We see only the third that rises above the surface. But most of the weight lies submerged, and we have no idea of its width and breadth. Only through exploration with highly technical know-how can we determine how much territory is really being covered.

At this point in recovery we're only just beginning to understand that we've barely skimmed the surface of our own makeup, despite the fact that we're certain we know ourselves well. But as we work the steps, again and again we'll discover long-forgotten circumstances that have deeply shaped the width and breadth of our lives.

Like the iceberg, whose cap melts with persistent sunshine, releasing more and more of what lies below, it is in the illumination and release that come with understanding that we begin to have a clearer perception of ourselves, our needs, patterns. It is only by releasing the "old melt" that we find the capacity to uncover our hidden structures.

TODAY'S STEP: *The true direction of my life is being revealed to me, day by day.*

Day 28—AUTOMATIC PILOT

*"Habit is habit, and not to be flung out the window
by any man, but to be coaxed downstairs a step at
a time."*
                                                      MARK TWAIN

We've been programmed into our present form from the
very beginning of our lives. This framework of beliefs and
behaviors was constructed long before we could understand what was happening to us.

Who we are today has roots in where we were born;
what our parents were like; whether we had siblings; where
we went to school and for how long; who our friends were;
whether we had any illnesses or disabilities; what religion—
or lack of it—was instilled in us; whether we were
upper class, middle class, or lower class; whether we lived
in the city, the suburbs, or the country; whether we grew
up in one place or moved around a lot; what language we
spoke; what cultural ethic we were born into.

A large part of our behavior today is conditioned by our
early programming that occurred before we were able to
think or act independently. This conditioned behavior is
similar to the task-oriented learning of tying one's shoelaces. Once mastered, the task requires no more conscious
thought; it becomes an automatic act. Much of what we
think of as our will is actually habit and programming
disguised as conscious choice. When we see "will" as nothing more than mindless programming, it is easier to turn it
over.

TODAY'S STEP: *I willingly relinquish habits which do not
serve me.*

Day 29—OPENING TO THE NEW

"Either I've been missing something or nothing is going on."
KAREN ELIZABETH GORDON

In Step One we talked about the young bride who sliced off the end of the ham before she baked it, never stopping to think why she did it. Her mother had done it, so it was obviously the correct thing to do. Her mother, in this case, was her Higher Power when it came to baking a ham.

Perhaps this seems a farfetched analogy. However, if we consider that we've been doing, saying and thinking many things in our lives that we learned through similar conditioning and we continue to do those things without any conscious thought, we've been performing more or less like an automaton. Our guiding power has been habit rather than judgment.

As we begin to uncover this truth, it becomes even more evident that we need the guidance of some power greater than ourselves to help guide us through the morass of our past experiences and actions. The search for our identity and for the meaning in our life today is helped immeasurably when we become willing to step out of that old conditioning and open ourselves to new ideas and new ways of seeing and being.

TODAY'S STEP: *The daily decision to turn my life over makes more and more sense.*

Day 30—OLD BIASES

"One doesn't discover new lands without consenting to lose sight of the shore for a very long time."
ANDRÉ GIDE

A song from the Rogers and Hammerstein musical "South Pacific" aptly describes the conditioning we experience in our formative years. It tells of the dilemma of a young naval officer who has fallen deeply in love with an island girl. He recognizes the impossibility of marrying her and bringing her into his world because of the prejudices that exist toward minorities. He laments:

"You have to be taught to be afraid
    of people whose skin is a different shade."

As we gradually start uncovering all the biases and bits of misinformation we have gathered in our lifetime, we begin to discover that the very act of releasing our hold on them indicates that we're beginning to trust in something that will work for our ultimate good. We no longer cling to timeworn practices. In fact, we've become willing to free ourselves of the misconceptions of our past.

TODAY'S STEP: *Recognition of my willfulness leads to freedom.*

Day 31—NOT GUILTY

*"Success is relative: It is what we can make of the
mess we have made of things."*   T.S. ELIOT

How often have we been told we're crazy; that we lack
willpower; that we play the victim; that we're selfish, weak
and insensitive? And how often have we accepted these
labels as valid?

While, on the one hand, we may have to plead guilty to
some of these value judgments, on the other hand, we're
gradually discovering that we're not guilty of the disease
itself. We contracted this disease because we were unaware
that our particular biophysical makeup made us susceptible
to it. Not guilty, however, does not mean that we're not
responsible for our behavior. In time, we'll learn that this
too was more the result of our disorder than any fault of
our basic nature.

In order to recover, we must keep in mind that, just as
our difficulties did not come about overnight, neither will
our recovery.

Recovery is a process—not an event. In due process,
the road to recovery will open up for us in ways that will
amaze us.

TODAY'S STEP: *I willingly surrender to recovery.*

Step Four

STEP FOUR

"Made a searching and fearless moral inventory of ourselves."

The real work begins in Step Four. In the first three steps we admitted our powerlessness; agreed that of ourselves and by ourselves we were not able to effect recovery; and made the decision to trust a power greater than ourselves to be our guide.

Now we are about to embark on a process of self-evaluation, an inventory in which we will assess the qualities we possess—both negative and positive—to determine our future course of action.

We've found it advisable to do a *written* inventory. This is because our minds have a tendency to ricochet off the subject at hand and to dwell on emotions rather than on hard facts. We also suggest that you keep what you have written for future reference.

Our goal in Step Four is to experience a lightening **of** the load we've been carrying, and to begin to believe that we can create a comfortable and rewarding lifestyle.

Step Four

Day 1—LOOKING FOR THE GOOD

*"Every morning I get up and look at the Forbes list
of the richest people in America. If I'm not there I
go to work."*
                                        ROBERT ORBEN

Beginning the Fourth Step tends to create a feeling of
impending doom in many of us. We devise various inge-
nious methods of delaying, detouring, or deferring our
personal housecleaning. The fear that many shameful skeletons will emerge from our closet leaves us procrastinating
indefinitely lest we forfeit what self-esteem we have left.

During a group therapy session, a counselor who had
gained the respect of the people there, asked this question,
"If I were alone with you—just you and I talking—would
you be willing to tell me something about yourself you've
never told anyone else?"

The reactions were mixed. Some said "Yes." Some said
they weren't sure they would. Some said their lives were an
open book and they had nothing to hide.

"Tell me then," said the counselor, "who among you
has thought of something good about yourself?" No one
had.

Our inventory needs to include both assets and liabilities. It is a fact-finding mission similar to those done in the
business world to assess exactly where a company stands in
order to create greater success and productivity.

TODAY'S STEP: *I have the courage to look at both my
strengths and my weaknesses.*

Step Four

Day 2—ACTING AS OUR OWN CONSULTANT

*"Blessed are those who can laugh at themselves,
for they shall never cease to be amused."*

ANONYMOUS

Although we've admitted that our lives have become un-manageable, and have acknowledged that we're no longer in the driver's seat, we hesitate to tackle this phase of recovery. We're filled with free-floating anxiety about what will be revealed. The Scottish prayer: "From ghoulies and ghosties and long leggety beasties, and things that go bump in the night, Good Lord, deliver us," is an apt description of our uneasiness.

At this point it's good to step back and look at ourselves objectively. We're like a consultant hired to confer with a business firm that isn't performing up to its optimum potential. As our own consultant, we can see that our inventory is not an indictment—actually it's a blueprint for success.

Making the inventory allows us to see where our compulsive behavior has created havoc in our personal lives. It allows us to see the pattern that has led to imbalances in our body, mind and spirit. Taking a good hard look at our assets and liabilities helps us decide how we can create a more satisfying future.

TODAY'S STEP: *My inventory gives me the opportunity to improve upon my past.*

Step Four

Day 3—BEGINNING THE ASSESSMENT

"A day of worry is more exhausting than a week of work."   ANONYMOUS

Our inventory is really an assessment of where we are today. But in order to understand where we want to go, it's necessary to look at where we've been. We need to know which of our actions created negative results, not only for ourselves, but also for others. Then we need to uncover the cause of those actions.

When we continue to experience "bad luck" in situation after situation, when we feel people are treating us unfairly through no fault of our own, isn't it interesting that the single common denominator in each case is that *we* were there? Chances are, if we were the only member of the cast on stage in each scenario, it was probable that our performance was the one out of sync.

When we remember that people are not doing things *to* us, but are doing things *for* themselves, we can release those old familiar feelings of being a victim.

When we begin to question whether our current thinking and actions are bringing us growth and satisfaction, we can direct our attention away from blaming others and focus it where it needs to be—on ourselves.

Switching our focus in no way diminishes us as people. Rather than condemning ourselves, what we're doing is freeing ourselves from the bondage of self.

TODAY'S STEP: *I release blame as I examine my own part in each situation.*

Day 4—DANCING WITH THE SEVEN DEADLY SINS—PRIDE

"It's a fine thing to rise above pride, but you must have pride in order to do so."

GEORGES BERNANOS
THE DIARY OF A COUNTRY PRIEST

One way to begin our inventory is to use as a framework the seven deadly sins: pride, lust, greed, anger, gluttony, envy and sloth.

Let's start with pride. It has many facets to consider. The dictionary defines pride as a sense of one's own dignity, or value, or self-respect, as well as pleasure or satisfaction taken in ones' work, achievements, or possessions. Only at the end of the entry is pride defined as an excessively high opinion of oneself, that is, conceit.

If we're doing a true inventory, the positive aspects of pride need to take their place in our survey. Denying our positive attributes is an inverse form of snobbery: If we can't be the best, then we'll take pride in being the worst.

Grandiosity and perfectionism are symptoms of pride. When we strut, preen, condescend, and display a superior attitude, what we're really doing is wearing a mask to cover our deep-seated feelings of inadequacy. We're like the blowfish, which when threatened by its enemies, blows up to an enormous size to prevent them from attacking.

We take pride in our ability to outwit and outsmart people; in our superiority in the cars we drive, the houses we live in, the clothes we wear, and our artistic or business successes. In proper balance, these things are all positive attributes. But when we flaunt them to make others unhappy, they take on a negative aspect.

TODAY'S STEP: *I take pride in my willingness to let go of false pride.*

Day 5—PRIDE AND CRITICISM

"Pride is the lack of one's own faults."
HEBREW PROVERB

There are two kinds of pride: One in which we approve of ourselves, and the other in which we cannot accept ourselves. However, once pride is purged of its false properties, it becomes a useful tool, a positive factor in growth and self-esteem.

The tenacity with which we hold on to certain characteristics is easy to understand once we realize that these characteristics provide protective armor shielding us from contempt or criticism by others.

None of us welcomes criticism. It's simply human nature to view most criticism as destructive—and this makes it difficult to accept when it's meant to be constructive. We try to defend ourselves from it with the same type of energy that we use to defend ourselves from danger, hunger or disease.

Coming to terms with the destructive side of pride is probably one of the most difficult, yet positive things we can do to break through our exquisite denial system. It's been said that self-pride, which is much like vanity, is like a magnet pointing to only one object—self. As a result, it repels everyone else.

In "The Nun's Story," the Novice who had tried so hard to please her Mother Superior confessed in chapel, "Dear Lord, when I find myself fulfilling all my responsibilities, then I am guilty of the sin of pride."

TODAY'S STEP: *I can accept true pride as a useful tool.*

Step Four

Day 6—DEALING WITH GUILT, SHAME, AND ANGER

"In order to change we must be sick and tired of being sick and tired." ANONYMOUS

Compulsive and/or addictive diseases are not predictable. Why some people become hooked into a progressive debilitation and others do not remains something of a mystery.

The onset of such diseases is obscure in time, cause and progression. While the symptoms may not necessarily follow a classic course, the results are typically negative. This makes it hard for us to wade through the maze of characteristics that compromise our dilemma and to admit sole responsibility.

Guilt, shame and anger often make us retreat from such candor. We feel guilt as self-reproach; shame because we sense that others will, or have, lost respect for us because of improper behavior, and anger manifests itself as the desire to place blame or fight back.

If we were able to go back in our memory and pinpoint the exact details of when and how we began to lose control, we still might not be able to understand how we ended up on this roller coaster ride to disaster.

TODAY'S STEP: *I release my shame, guilt, and anger over my disease.*

Day 7—SEX

"The sex instinct is one of the three or four prime movers in all that we do and are and dream, both individually and collectively."
PHILIP WYLIE

In times gone by, lust was considered one of the most deadly of the seven sins. Today we have a far more liberal view. Explicit sex scenes in movies and TV depict lust as a normal "boy meets girl" activity. Unfortunately, this allows us to feel that our own sexual excesses have been legitimized.

Many of us have been guilty of using sex as a means to justify our ends. We have been unfaithful to our spouses, or if we were single, have knowingly had affairs with others who were married at the time. We have seduced just for the thrill of seduction, with no concern or respect for the person with whom we've had intercourse. We've demanded that our partners submit to our own carnal desires and erotic fantasies without any concern for their feelings. We've withheld sex as a means of punishment, or to demonstrate our own power and superiority.

TODAY'S STEP: *I now have the courage to look at my sexual conduct honestly.*

Step Four

Day 8—COVETOUSNESS

"If envy were a fever, all the world would be ill."
DANISH PROVERB

Covetousness is the excessive desire for another's possessions. When addictive behavior and a disintegrating personality have brought about a loss of money, property and prestige, it's easy to see why we experience ourselves as victims. Our excessive longing for other people's possessions is really about our own sense of loss. This is what makes it important at this stage of recovery to be very honest about how the losses in our life really came about.

Admitting our own shortcomings means that we accept the fact that we're responsible for our lack. Realistically, we must also acknowledge that, even if we weren't in this sorry state, there will always be those who, by virtue of birth, good fortune, ability, or talent, will accomplish and possess more than us.

Despite all the self-help books on how to achieve fame and fortune, many of us will never attain the success enjoyed by the jet set or the financial wizards who are paraded across our consciousness by the media. When we're dealing with covetousness, we need to acknowledge that we have all experienced the very human reaction of wishing that we, too, had all these possessions. But what we must strive to do is rid ourselves of any active animosity toward those who are more fortunate than us.

TODAY'S STEP: *I acknowledge my envy of others' successes.*

Day 9—ANGER

"In taking revenge, a man is but even with his enemy; but in passing it over, he is superior."
FRANCIS BACON

Anger is a perfectly normal feeling. But society judges it as if it were an evil demon, warping our intelligence and judgment. In reality, anger is a feeling of displeasure resulting from injury, mistreatment or opposition. Our reaction to feelings of displeasure is to fight back at the supposed cause of these feelings. This is quite understandable.

And yet, anger has many faces. It may take on the aspects of indignation, rage, fury, wrath or hostility.

Indignation is a typical response to things that seem unjust, mean or insulting. At times we respond to this feeling impulsively, or with negative behavior that we then defend as righteous. Wrath and hostility imply deep indignation. These are feelings of enmity or ill will that push us toward revenge or punishment.

All too often, anger manifests itself in violent outbursts bordering on madness. In these irrational moments, we may have done harm to other persons or their possessions. "Crimes of passion" frequently result from such outbursts.

If we have used anger to act out in the past, the time has now come for us to reassess the price we've paid for that behavior. It's not a sin to feel angry—but we need not act on the feeling.

TODAY'S STEP: *I can feel and recognize my anger without venting it on others.*

Day 10—GLUTTONY, ENVY AND SLOTH

"Sin is an acronym for 'self-inflicted nonsense,'
Fear an acronym for 'false evidence appearing
real.' " ANONYMOUS

Gluttony, envy and sloth round out our review of the seven
deadly sins. It's not hard to see how they influence actions
and emotions that work against our feelings of well-being
and self-acceptance. A wise sage once said, "All we want is
all there is—and then some."

Gluttony can certainly be equated with greed as well as
with stuffing ourselves with large amounts of food. Gluttony is often fueled by the fear that we won't "get ours":
that somehow we will be shortchanged in life.

We never seem to have enough money, enough recognition, enough property, enough sex, enough entertain-
ment, enough toys. We continually compare our insides to
other people's outsides, and without realizing it, we shift
from "keeping up with the Joneses" to "keeping ahead of
the Joneses," never quite realizing how unreasonable these
demands on ourselves may be. Then, when we fail to
achieve our unreasonable goals, we brand those who have
succeeded as opportunists and charlatans, assuming that
those who have climbed the ladder of success have done so
by squashing every "have not" who stood in their way.

Many of us have experienced the frustration that envy
creates. As a result, we give up on life and descend into the
pits of inactivity and procrastination. And these add up to
sloth. We become drop-outs in the game of life, blaming
our failures on everything and everybody but ourselves.

TODAY'S STEP: *I have enough.*

Day 11—DEFECTS

"Sadness flies on the wings of the morning and out of the darkness comes the light." JEAN GIRAUDOUX

When we recap those seven deadly sins and see our own culpability in each of them, we use this information, not as an indictment of our lack of character, but as guidelines to direct us on our path of recovery.

Wearing sackcloth and ashes has never been productive for the human spirit, and it is only when we are able to see a way out of our misery that we become willing to make the effort to change.

In the past, although we frequently apologized to others for hurting them, and wept crocodile tears about our misdeeds, we neither felt any true regret, nor could we guarantee that we wouldn't turn right around and do those same things all over again.

This superficiality was our defense system. It protected us from experiencing the pain caused by our actions. Often we found ourselves going full-speed ahead on a disaster course without having any idea how to put on the brakes.

Now, with a growing awareness of what prompted so much of that old behavior, we can set our sights on more productive actions with a clear expectation that the results will be positive. We now have the knowledge, help and support to change those negative feelings to positive ones.

TODAY'S STEP: *In examining old patterns honestly, I find the roots of today's difficulties.*

Day 12—RESENTMENT

"Learn to forgive. With bitterness in your soul you can never be happy."   ANONYMOUS

The *Big Book of Alcoholics Anonymous* has some excellent guidelines on how to do an inventory. Their experience of taking stock identifies resentment as the primary defect that can unlock the mystery of our unmanageable lives.

The word "resentment" has its root in the Latin word "sentire"—to feel. Resentment actually means re-feeling in its most negative sense.

A useful way of dealing with resentment is to make a list of those persons toward whom we hold resentments and then take a look at "why" we feel that way. Have these people affected our self-esteem, our security, our personal relationships, our sexual relations or our ambitions? In what manner have these people behaved to cause this reaction from us? Are they patronizing? Do they threaten our professional standing or careers? Have they bested us in competition, either socially or through their superior business tactics? Have they turned others away from us? Are they unresponsive to our seductiveness?

More often than not, we find that the underlying cause of these resentments is fear: Fear of being discounted; fear of losing our stature in the community; fear of financial failure; fear of being deserted by our friends, fear of losing our ability to attract the opposite sex. There are also many other fears underlying resentment that we could add to our list.

TODAY'S STEP: *I examine my resentments rather than indulging in them.*

Day 13—DIGGING DEEPER INTO RESENTMENT

"Regret is an appalling waste of energy; you can't build on it; it is only good for wallowing in."

ANONYMOUS

Yesterday we considered the causes of resentment and looked at the underlying emotions it provokes. But this subject deserves more than just a cursory appraisal. Resentment seems to be the prime cause of backsliding because it's the feeling that deters our progress toward freedom and self-worth.

This step shows us the value of the "uncover, discover, and recover" concept—and it works best when we follow that sequence. Knowing that we've used many justifications to validate our resentments against others, we first review the "why" of the feelings against those persons on our list. Then we dig deeper into the circumstances and conditions that precipitated our reaction. While we don't deny that people have inflicted injustices upon us, and that we've been unfairly treated by many, nevertheless, for a full recovery, it serves us better to look at our part in those instances, and to acknowledge where we've been at fault.

Remember, the inventory is meant to be a fact-finding process, not an indictment of ourselves or any other person. It's a road map pointing us in the right direction—the one that will bring us safely to our destination.

TODAY'S STEP: *In taking stock of resentments, I discover my own contribution to each one.*

Step Four

Day 14—FUELING RESENTMENT

"It is better to know some of the questions than all of the answers."   JAMES THURBER

A man who came from a small town in Middle America entered a national competition. Although he was a neophyte in this field, he felt he had the qualifications to win.

The competition was held in a large city, and the contestants were headquartered in a very elegant hotel where a reception was held prior to the coming event.

At the reception another contestant identified himself as coming from "the city of champions," and asked our friend where he was from. "Middle Podunk" replied our man, adding that it was in the same state as his questioner.

"Never heard of it," said the stranger, and walked away.

Seething, our friend left the reception, went to his room and made the decision that, no matter what, he'd beat that s.o.b. in the competition.

He didn't make it the first time around. But, spurred by his resentment against his adversary, he worked hard the following year to perfect his skills. Anger and revenge were the motivating factors that energized him. And the next year he won the competition.

"Now," he said, confronting his enemy, "you know where Middle Podunk is!"

"Oh!" said the man. "When we first met I'd just moved into the state. I didn't know where anything was."

Our friend who had spent all those months engulfed in anger and resentment while his nemesis was happily pursuing his own life without any negative bugaboos tormenting him, will always wonder whether his natural ability, rather his resentment, would have won him the trophy or not.

TODAY'S STEP: *I release the habit of holding on to resentments.*

Step Four

Day 15—GETTING ON WITH OUR LIVES

"The world is quickly bored by the recital of misfortune, and willingly avoids the sight of distress."
W. SOMERSET MAUGHAM

Yesterday's story of the man tormented by resentment for a year over a casual remark made by a stranger illustrates how often our perception can be off base: Someone makes a statement that, to them, has no hidden message whatsoever, yet we think, "What did he really mean by that?"

So often the object of our resentment goes along in a totally carefree way while we develop headaches, stomach problems and bad backs. It has been said that some physical reactions are nature's way of alerting us to what feeling is causing these conditions. For example, ulcers may be another way of expressing, "I've had a gutfull." Hemorrhoids can mean, "He gives me a pain in the butt." Back pain could be telling us, "I want her off my back."

We are a synthesis of body, mind and spirit. When one part of this trio is out of sync, the other two feel the effects. Imbalance and anxiety, even disease, can result. This is when we begin to perceive that resentments are totally without value for us. They are past history with no validity in our lives today. They only sap our psychic energy and prevent us from getting on with our lives.

When we let go of old hurts, resentments, beliefs and biases, we can experience ourselves as empty vessels, waiting to be filled with a new sense of freedom and resolve.

TODAY'S STEP: *I free myself of resentment, one day at a time.*

Step Four

Day 16—WRITING THE INVENTORY

"The measure of your real character is what you would do if you knew you would never be found out."
ANONYMOUS

Sometimes our confused and muddled thinking makes us feel as though we have a committee in our heads. One young man said it well when he compared his brain to a popcorn machine spewing thoughts in all directions without any concern for cohesiveness. To quiet all these voices, experience has taught us to put this step on paper.

Some of us have found it easiest to write our own life history, and to list and describe all the people who were responsible for our upbringing or instrumental in our growth. Next, we need to examine those relationships to see what dynamics occurred. Where were we at fault? Where were others at fault? What kinds of emotions are surfacing because of these memories?

It is helpful to list all the special relationships we experienced in the past, and the opportunities lost when something we hoped to accomplish didn't work out because we weren't able to live up to our promises. At this point, we need to look at our emotional insecurities, and examine our need for power, acceptance, control and approval. This allows us to begin to sort out the factors implicated in our compulsive behavior.

In our life histories we'll very likely discover that the people we've listed have both positive and negative influences on us. With any luck, we'll also begin to see clearly the positive and negative aspects of our behavior.

TODAY'S STEP: *I am surprised at how easy it is becoming for me to write my inventory.*

Step Four

Day 17—OVERCOMING HONEST SELF-DECEPTION

*"One of my problems is that I internalize every-
thing. I can't express anger; I grow a tumor instead."*
                                              WOODY ALLEN

"Honest self-deception" is one of the most difficult hurdles for us to overcome. We've so sincerely convinced
ourselves of the authenticity of our own perception that it
becomes nearly impossible for us to consider any other
point of view.

We're much like the fundamentalist who was taught in
his formative years that the words of the Bible—such as,
"An eye for an eye . . . a tooth for a tooth"—are meant
to be taken literally. Obviously, if we were to act on that
dictum we'd be living in a chaotic society with continual
outbreaks of violence.

There isn't a person living who hasn't experienced some
wrong, and who has not wronged others. Many of these
wrongs have left imprints that follow us through our own
lives and—consciously or unconsciously—govern a great
many of our actions and reactions.

As we write out our inventory we need to keep in mind
that its object is to focus us on our own characteristics—
not those of others. We especially need to pinpoint the
ones that have created discomfort and bad relationships in
the past. Most often we find these feelings have engen-
dered guilt, anger, resentment, fear and shame. What we're
seeking is the behavioral pattern that appears in our own
actions that will show us the *nature* of our wrongs.

TODAY'S STEP: *I fearlessly confront the ways I have been
deceiving myself.*

Step Four

Day 18—WRITING IT DOWN

"I do not know what I may appear to the world; but to myself I seem to have been only like a boy playing on the seashore, diverting myself in now and then finding a smoother pebble or a prettier shell than ordinary, whilst the great ocean of truth lay all undiscovered before me." SIR ISAAC NEWTON

Because we believe that the nature of truth depends upon the individual or group that holds it, we often tend to see events from a skewed perspective. We play judge, jury, prosecuting attorney and defense attorney, convinced that our judgment is correct. No wonder it's so hard to make the shift from self-justification to admitting that our thinking has taken a wrong turn and has created havoc and bitterness.

This is why making an inventory is such an important part of the process of clearing the way for recovery. But it's a difficult step, and many people think that it's too much work to put this inventory in writing. They believe it's much easier to simply search their memories and identify the nature of their wrongs.

However, time and again, experience has shown that the opposite is true. Our popcorn-machine minds shoot out so many random and extraneous thoughts that the central theme gets lost. Writing it all down, on the other hand, creates more order and focus, and enables us to discover the recurring patterns in our actions.

Those who have found great benefit in writing a life history say this exercise has uncovered more for them than any other method. Although we should each follow the procedure that best suits our needs, we must question why we're hesitant to write out our inventory.

TODAY'S STEP: *As I write my inventory, I gain the self I lost.*

Step Four

Day 19—HALF TRUTHS

*"Pure truth, like pure gold, has been found unfit
for circulation, because men have discovered that it
is far more convenient to adulterate the truth than
to refine themselves."*
                                          CHARLES CALEB COLTON

There once was a thief who stole a watch belonging to a
priest. Later that day he entered the confessional and
stated, "Forgive me Father, for I have sinned. I stole a
man's watch."

"My son," said the priest, "you must return the
watch."

"Please Father," said the man, "you take the watch."

"No my son" replied the priest, "I do not want the
watch."

"But Father, the man from whom I stole the watch
does not want it back."

"Then," said the priest, "say five Our Fathers and ten
Hail Marys, and go forth and sin no more."

The thief did indeed tell the truth—but not the whole
truth. He rationalized that since he had confessed his sins
and was absolved by the priest, he could keep the watch.

Have we, like that thief, indulged in half-truths? Have
we used denial to intimidate others and create a smoke
screen to hide our behavior? Have we had repeated job
difficulties? Experienced deep loneliness? Suffered broken
relationships, financial and health problems?

If so, we would do well to take a good hard look at how
those instances have contributed to our addictive behavior.

TODAY'S STEP: *By admitting my half-truths, I become
whole again.*

Step Four

Day 20—CRUCIAL QUESTIONS

"We acknowledge our faults in order to repair by our sincerity the damage they have done us in the eyes of others."
LA ROCHEFOUCAULD

Has your pride ever prevented you from being honest with others? Where and when?

What was the result?

Have you made others responsible for your actions? How and when?

Do you believe that outside forces control all that goes on in your life: that you are helpless and not responsible for what happens to you?

Have you cheated anyone out of money that rightfully belongs to them?

Have you betrayed confidences entrusted to you by others?

Have you been untrue to the significant other person in your life?

Have you shirked your responsibilities to your spouse, children, or parents?

No doubt other questions have occurred to you. The more probing and candid you can be, the more relief you will feel when you have finally discarded the burden of a lifetime of secrets.

TODAY'S STEP: *When I ask myself all the right questions, the answers are clear to me.*

Day 21—SEARCHING AND FEARLESS

*"You have to do your own growing up no matter
how tall your grandpa was."*   ANONYMOUS

The terms "fearless" and "thorough" are not in Step Four
by mistake. Nor is the term "moral." Those who have
gone before us in the Twelve Step process discovered that
only by making a deep and soul-searching examination
could they begin to effect the kind of recovery that could
withstand the stimuli that sparked their dysfunctional behavior.

What we are searching out in our inventory is not only
the behavior that we see as unproductive, but also the very
nature of that behavior.

Does that behavior stem from fear, or from resentment,
ignorance, defiance, or from a need to retaliate because
others have treated us unfairly?

Those who have successfully completed Step Four report that the human tendency to generalize, skip or under-
value specifics results in an inventory that is, at best, a
mediocre attempt. To truly rid ourselves of unproductive
thinking and actions, we need to be detailed enough to
detect the patterns that must be changed in order to create
a more satisfying life.

TODAY'S STEP: *I have the courage and patience to be
searching and thorough in my inventory.*

Day 22—READY & WILLING

"Nothing is impossible to a willing heart."

JOHN HEYWOOD

Let's take another look at health, finances, interpersonal relationships, jobs, creativity and self-esteem—especially the negative aspects that have resulted from our attitudes and behavior in each case.

Many of us discover that our best intelligence, our best philosophy, our best intentions have not been sufficient to prevent us from arriving at our present dilemma. But before we point the finger at ourselves and cry "Shame!" let's first try deferring our judgment. Let's listen to the advice of others who have won through their own personal challenges.

All those who have written their life histories say they found that this exercise uncovers more for them than anything else they've tried. They attest to the fact that a successfully completed Step Four brings one a great sense of relief and freedom. They acknowledge that our problems are often the result of good intentions gone awry, and that we're responsible for the negative results that have occurred as a consequence of our actions. But the happy outcome of this inventory is that once we've discovered the formula, we have the opportunity to correct the behavior that has caused us so much difficulty in the past.

Our willingness to tackle the Fourth Step is probably one of the most positive indications that we're on the road to recovery. We admit it's not an easy task. Many people have told us that they had to be "willing to be willing" before they could become willing!

TODAY'S STEP: *Because I am willing, my resistance to self-discovery is fading.*

Day 23—ACCENTUATE THE POSITIVES

*"Man will only become better when you make him
see what he is like."*
ANTON CHEKHOV

By now we've surely discovered some very negative things
about ourselves. For some reason, it seems to be human
nature to see our faults more easily than our virtues.

However, the time has now come to start writing down
the good things about ourselves. It's time to list all the
assets that are part of our makeup. Ironically, we often find
this to be the most difficult assignment we've faced so far.
So many of us are filled with guilt and fear, with regret and
remorse, that we find ourselves hard-pressed to list more
that a few grudging things we find positive about ourselves.

When someone asks us, "Tell me something good
about yourself," we frequently answer them very superfi-
cially. But this avoids the issue of truly assessing our important talents, skills, aptitudes and abilities. These are our best
tools for shaping new healthy patterns of behavior. Hard
though it is for us to parade our positives, parade them we
must.

TODAY'S STEP: *I acknowledge and cherish my virtues.*

Day 24—A FOR ARTISTIC

"The same man cannot be well skilled in every-thing; each has his special excellence." EURIPIDES

We're now going to bombard ourselves with our strengths, and this gives us a chance for fun and games. While the exercise may appear to be childish, it has worked successfully for many people.

First, we get ourselves a legal-sized pad of writing paper. In the left-hand margin, going down the page, we list the letters of the alphabet—A through Z. Next to each letter we write down one of our positive attributes, skills, abilities, or talents that begin with that letter: for example, A—artistic, B—brave, C—considerate, and so on.

We don't have to drum up multiple entries—just enough to get on our side.

Those who have played this game say they resorted to the dictionary for their "q's," "x's," and "z's." Many came up with imaginative definitions. It isn't written in stone that we must use these problem letters. But it might be fun to see what we come up with. For example, we might use "questioning" for "Q." Questioning, which we're doing right now, is an essential attribute in assessing our positive and negative characteristics. Just to be sporting, we'll throw in "ex" as a substitute for "X," and "zippy" for "Z" to indicate we're lively and full of energy.

TODAY'S STEP: *I search for my assets as thoroughly as I search for my liabilities.*

Day 25—BALANCING THE BOOKS

"The essence of being human is that one does not seek perfection."   GEORGE ORWELL

The qualities we look for in playing the Alphabet Game are those we were born with and those we developed. This is not the time to editorialize on the fact that we may once have had some of these positive characteristics but have lost them as a result of our behavior and subsequent lack of self-esteem.

We're using scrutiny and honesty to look for the assets we can build on in our search for recovery. Were we to list only liabilities, we would feel hopelessly stalemated.

It's a truism that once we learn to ride a bike, we never unlearn it. Although we may find the latest models a little hard to get used to, it doesn't take long before we master the ability again.

Now we can take our list of positives, and compare it to the list of defects we wrote down in our inventory. Which of these defects can be overcome by using the positive alternatives we've uncovered about ourselves? For instance, say we find "fear" on the negative side. We can cancel it out with "courage." We might also substitute "compassion" for "indifference."

TODAY'S STEP: *My good qualities can help me overcome my defects.*

Day 26—A LETTER FROM FRIENDS

"Freedom is the will to be responsible to ourselves."

ANONYMOUS

The next thing we might do in our campaign to bombard ourselves with our strengths is to ask three people close to us to write us a letter listing only the admirable things they see in us. We need to impress upon them up front that this is being done as an exercise that we've been asked to do, and that even though they see some of our faults clearly, these aren't part of this particular exercise.

This is where the power of a support group begins to be a big help in our journey toward enlightenment. One or two members in the group might be the appropriate people to ask for help in this exercise. Some folks have asked their siblings, spouses, friends, clergy or counselors to do this—always emphasizing the need to keep the focus on the positive aspects.

Once we've read those letters, we add their appraisal to the attributes we've already put on our alphabetical list. Now we can begin to compare the way others see us with the way we see ourselves. In this way we can begin to get a clearer picture of what we're really like.

TODAY'S STEP: *With the support of others, I gain a better, clearer self-image.*

Day 27—TAKING OFF THE ARMOR

"Let's talk sense to the American people. Let's tell them the truth, that 'there are no gains without pains.'"
ADLAI STEVENSON

Our past decisions were the direct result of our addictions—plus the need to please others. We often let other people make our decisions for us. This lets us off the hook because now we can disclaim all responsibility for the outcome. It's been far easier to identify other forces and people as the causes of our behavior.

The enormous value of Step Four is that we now take charge of ourselves, accepting both our assets and liabilities as our responsibility. We learn that it's by our own efforts—and our Higher Power's—that we are capable of ridding ourselves of defects.

Up to now we've been interested in the impression only that we were making on others. We swagger in, wearing a shining suit of armor but are terrified that someone will lift up the visor and see the little shriveled person within. In the past, this armor has been a necessary protection. We felt so vulnerable that we couldn't operate without putting on an "act."

Fear of abandonment and rejection has prompted us to do and say many things that were actually contrary to the way we felt. But we can never develop self-respect as long as we depend on others to set our standards for us. As one young man expressed it: "The best description I'm able to give you of myself is that I was like a chameleon. I changed behavior and opinions to adapt to whichever person or group I happened to be with. I was literally a nonperson—a reflection in other people's eyes."

TODAY'S STEP: *I let go of blaming others or trying to impress them; I can see myself clearly.*

Step Four

Day 28—PEELING THE ONION

*"My opinion is a view I hold until . . . well, until
I find something that changes it."*

LUIGI PIRANDELLO

Peeling back the layers of our past to uncover those facets
of behavior that have led to our present straits is much like
peeling an onion. Just when we seem to be making progress, we find a very thin film between us and what we
thought was the next layer. And we're confounded by the
realization that we've discovered something important
about ourselves that we'd totally blocked.

This holds true for the positive and negative alike. Now
and then we're amazed to uncover some splendid thing
we've done in the past and totally forgotten. This positive
attribute should immediately be added to our list of
strengths. We're going to keep using our treasure house—
our inventory, our alphabetical list of strengths and our
three letters as we move through the steps to come.

As we progress through the steps, our outsides gradually begin to match our insides. This process, though, takes
time. Our goal is to discover, uncover and recover. At this
point we're well on our way to doing just that.

TODAY'S STEP: *In searching through my past, I uncover
buried treasure.*

Step Four

Day 29—HEALING OUR SHAME

"The real fault is to have faults and not to amend them."
CONFUCIUS

Day by day we're getting in closer touch with our own truth. We're facing reality with less and less trepidation. How many times have we been told "The truth shall make you free," and *not* heard it. Until we ourselves have had the experience that proves the adage, we cannot internalize and digest the true meaning of that statement.

We are also beginning to understand the fact that physical reactions can be triggered by subconscious thoughts. For example, our emotions can create headaches, backaches, stomach problems—even chronic diseases such as asthma. We still carry around and play these same tapes from early childhood. One of the most powerful of these negative imprints is the shame we felt when we simply weren't making it in the eyes of our parents. We were certain there was no way on earth we could ever win their unqualified approval.

As we grew older, we simply transferred those feelings to other significant people in our lives. Sometimes we would withhold love and support from them to make up for what we felt had been withheld from us. We behaved toward them with coldness and indifference, for we were fearful that if we invested ourselves in trusting, we'd be risking further rejection.

The process of writing our inventory—uncovering and validating our positive attributes—will, in time, reassure us that we have no further need for such defensive behavior.

TODAY'S STEP: *I am discovering the truth, and it is setting me free.*

Day 30—OLD IDEAS

"Understanding is the beginning of approving."
ANDRÉ GIDE

On our pilgrimage to recovery we've begun to work through the phases of "uncovering" and "discovering." If we've been thorough about Step Four, we should have a clearer understanding of ourselves. We've recognized that the many things we did for the wrong reasons and the many things we did for the right reasons are all part of our past, part of our frame of reference. We've also seen that we're on a whole new course—one that will enable us to experience a much more satisfying existence.

Fear of discovering what we're *really like* prevented many of us from examining our vulnerable spots. Now we can experience the relief that comes when we begin to lower our inner shields and to see ourselves as productive, worthwhile human beings.

When the *Big Book of Alcoholics Anonymous* tells us, "We let go of all our old ideas," it means *all* our old ideas, not just those we found to be counterproductive. The reasoning behind this is that as our disease progressed, all our thoughts became conditioned by the false information our addiction fed into our brains. Our thinking processes became slanted to conform to our skewed perspective.

Recovery is an ongoing process, not a singular event. It requires commitment and the willingness to defer judgment—trusting those who have successfully trod the road before us.

TODAY'S STEP: *I am willing to let go of all my old ideas in order to recover.*

Step Four

Day 31—WE'VE DONE IT!

"The pure and simple truth is rarely pure and never simple."
                                            OSCAR WILDE

As we complete this step we find ourselves enmeshed in a variety of feelings—guilt and shame all tangled up with hope and optimism.

But what an enormous feeling of relief floods through us now that we've finally been willing to look at our dark side, and to recognize that we have sufficient assets to counteract many of our defects of character. We're like a corporation we thought was headed for bankruptcy. Making an assessment and getting rid of old practices allows us to introduce new ways of doing things that will make us a successful business once more.

The following quote from Mahatma Gandhi beautifully describes the value of Step Four.

> It is not the critic who counts, nor the man who points out how the strong man stumbles, or where the doer of deeds could have done better. The credit belongs to the man who is actually in the arena; whose face is marred by dust and sweat; who strives valiantly; who errs and may fail again, because there is no effort without error or shortcoming; who does actually strive to do the deeds; who does know the great enthusiasm, the great devotion; who spends himself in a worthy cause; who at the best, knows in the end the triumph of high achievement, and who at the worst, if he fails, at least fails while daring greatly, so that his place shall never be with those cold and timid souls who know neither victory nor defeat.

TODAY'S STEP: *I complete my inventory and reap its rewards.*

Step Five

"Admitted to God, to ourselves and to another human being the exact nature of our wrongs."

This is a good place to borrow another line from the *Big Book of Alcoholics Anonymous* because it aptly describes how many of us may be feeling right now: "What an order! I can't go through with it!"

This is the step where humility smacks us right between the eyes.

It was one thing to write out our inventory for ourselves. As for sharing it with God—if there *is* a God, He'd know all about us anyway. But we're also being asked to share our inventory with *another person*! This is asking too much! Why can't we simply assess ourselves and get on with the business of cleaning up our lives?

Why not? Because there's something very good waiting for us on the other end. As we follow the process of Step Five to its conclusion, we'll come to understand more fully all the reasons for—and advantages of—taking this step exactly as it is written.

Step Five

Day 1—ADDICTIVE HISTORY

"If you tell the truth you don't have to remember anything."
MARK TWAIN

When we were very little, we dreamed about what we wanted to be when we grew up. We did this in part because adults used to ask us all the time, "What do *you* want to be when you grow up?" We also did it because it is normal for little children to fantasize an ideal existence for themselves.

As we grew older, our dreams began to fade under the influence of the giants in our life who dictated the path we were to follow. Some of us were traumatized by being told we'd never amount to anything. Others were ordered to live up to our potential (whatever *that* was supposed to be). Still others of us were expected to follow in our parents' footsteps.

Some of these expectations didn't become harmful until they started clashing with our own personal yearnings and ambitions. While many of us followed those parental dictates with good results, others of us assumed—but hated—the roles assigned to us. Playing those roles created negative thinking, negative attitudes and behavior. It's exactly these characteristics that we need to examine now to come to a clearer understanding of our addictive history. An addict with no sense of addictive history can never admit to anyone the exact nature of his wrongs.

TODAY'S STEP: *I share my addictive history fearlessly.*

"All human beings have gray little souls—and they all want to rouge them up." MAXIM GORKY

The root of the word "personality" is "persona." This is defined as "a character in a dramatic or literary work"—literally a mask for actors. In psychology, the definition of "persona" is, "The role we assume to display our conscious intentions to ourselves and to others."

As we grew up we simply accepted the evaluations other people made of our character, and built a mental image of ourselves that wasn't necessarily accurate.

Over time we became adept at wearing masks to project what others wanted to see. Because concealment, defense, deception and our need to adapt to our environment were necessary for our survival, these masks became our primary means of defense. As a result they're very difficult to give up. We're afraid if we take them off we'll become a cipher—a zero—in the eyes of others. We have hidden, protected, disguised our true selves. The very thought of mentally undressing under the scrutiny of anyone else is terrifying.

When we trust that those who are close to us wish for us the same ultimate good that we wish for them, we become less afraid and more self-disclosing. For the first time in a very long time, we're beginning to trust enough to risk dropping our masks.

TODAY'S STEP: *I can take off my mask with perfect confidence.*

Day 3—CLEARING THE DECKS

"There is something about a closet that makes a skeleton restless." ANONYMOUS

Difficult as change is, it does lead to new good. We tend to cling to the familiar even if that familiar is causing pain and discord. We feel uncertain about taking steps to move from what we know into the unknown. Besides, we're not convinced that change is going to work for us, anyway.

We can point to the fact that we've tried all manner of changes—change of jobs, of spouses, geographic changes—and none of them have proved to be the answer. We see no logic in the supposition that, after we've bared our soul, and admitted our past defects, there will be clear sailing ahead. Taking into account the problems we have faced, we're not even sure that some of our past behavior wasn't necessary.

What we don't yet realize is that there was a payoff to our dysfunctional behavior. Despite its negative effect it gave us a certain amount of satisfaction in the doing. It was "self-will run riot"—the behavior of a two-year-old whose demands for self-gratification are insatiable.

We cannot clear the decks for change, we cannot clear away past wreckage, without first identifying it, as we did in Step Four. The next move is to be willing to verbalize what we've found so it can be dealt with in a healthy manner.

TODAY'S STEP: *Coming out of the closet willingly and admitting the exact nature of my wrongs is a change for the better.*

Day 4—VICTIMS

*"If you are pointing the finger at someone, three are
pointing back at you!"* ANONYMOUS

We may be having difficulties with the Fourth and Fifth
Steps because we do not view ourselves as transgressors,
but rather as victims.

For example, take divorce. Many of us who've gone
through the experience feel we did everything in our power
to save the marriage. It was our mate who refused to
change.

We point to the fact that we were self-sacrificing, patient
and understanding of our partner's failings, that we practiced forgiveness again and again despite continued epi-
sodes that were very hurtful to us.

In taking our inventory, we admitted to the seven
deadly sins only as they related to our envy of others who
had a stable marriage. Our pride was simply the act of
trying to put on a good public face, despite the pain we
were experiencing; our greed was our desire for a more
abundant and fulfilling lifestyle; our anger we considered a
perfectly normal response to the treatment we were suffering.

As we work Step Five, we can begin to admit to our
contributions to our life's difficulties. We can stop being
victims.

TODAY'S STEP: *I release the need to blame others for my
own shortcomings.*

Day 5—SELF-PITY

"When your dreams turn to dust, vacuum."

ANONYMOUS

Our identity as a victim doesn't hold water once we begin to admit to ourselves the exact nature of our wrongs and how they have affected our relationships. Gradually, we begin to see that, as one of our friends so aptly put it, "Every pot goes out to find a lid to fit it."

When we can release this victim fixation, we can begin to examine our own role in the chaos of our lives. Finally, we begin to understand what led us to the admission that we were powerless over our circumstances, and that our lives had truly become unmanageable. We discover that we played a very active part in making a relationship unworkable, even though we truly thought we were doing all the right things. But we also find that much of what we *did* do stemmed from early conditioning and beliefs that came from our families, our cultures and our religions.

If we are to pull ourselves out of this morass of misconceptions, it's vital that we stop pointing fingers at others and look straight at ourselves. We'll see clearly that we possess some characteristics that work against us in a very powerful way. Paramount among them is self-pity. Equally nonproductive is the illusion that we're doomed to a life of pain, frustration and lost chances. Through self-examination and self-determination we can reverse this downward spiral and open up new opportunities and admit to ourselves, God and another human being our own part in various victim scenarios. We can trade in self-pity for self-acceptance and in the process gain positive associations with others.

TODAY'S STEP: *I can examine painful relationships and understand the rewards of honesty.*

Step Five

Day 6—CAROL'S STORY

*"The bitter and the sweet come from the outside,
the hard from within, from one's own efforts."*
ALBERT EINSTEIN

Carol told this story about getting ready for the Fifth Step. She decided she'd type out her inventory from Step Four so it would be legible enough for her sponsor to read— despite the fact that she'd never learned to type. However, her sponsor was a professional writer, so Carol felt it was very important that her inventory be letter-perfect.

Almost instantly she struck a wrong key. Now, Carol was in a quandary. If she erased it, her paper wouldn't look perfect. So she searched her mind for a word that would fit the letter she'd mistyped. Needless to say, this did not end up as a searching and fearless inventory. It was, though, the best she could do at the time. Carol was so afraid of looking inadequate that she couldn't bear to present a less than perfect paper.

Luckily, Carol's sponsor, who had overcome her own serious eating disorder, was able to assure her that no one grades our inventory and succeeded in helping her complete a satisfactory Fifth Step.

Nevertheless, the importance of what Carol accomplished must not be diminished. Despite the fact that the job was a superficial one, she *did it*. She demonstrated the willingness to follow directions—a primary ingredient in any recovery program.

TODAY'S STEP: *I release the need to do a perfect inventory, and I get on with it.*

Day 7—THE TRIPLE WHAMMY

"It is not the criminal things that are hardest to confess, but the ridiculous and shameful."
JEAN-JACQUES ROUSSEAU

The value of our inventory is never more clearly demonstrated than when we admit the nature of our wrongs to ourselves and others. Without that written evidence, our minds search for every excuse, rationalization and justification in the book.

We could remain masked and inscrutable to ourselves and others were we not faced with the triple whammy that Step Five delivers.

"To God, to ourselves" are the two preliminary phases that prepare us for the moment when we face another human being with our disclosures. But there is absolutely no way we can be candid with that other person until we ourselves have made full and complete disclosure *to* ourselves.

This unmasking, this tearing away of our self-deceptions, is very painful. We have to drop the "act" that was our coping mechanism. We have to release the image that we and others have painted of ourselves. We have to let go of the fiction that we've been hapless victims of cruel fate. At this point, there's nothing left to do but honestly confront the truth that no one but ourselves is responsible for the spot we have found ourselves in today.

This, at long last, is when we're able to embrace our dark side—our "shadow."

And this is where we start.

TODAY'S STEP: *I am no longer afraid to admit the exact nature of my wrongs.*

Day 8—BAD NEWS AND GOOD NEWS

"One loyal friend is worth ten thousand relatives."
EURIPIDES

Once we work the Fifth Step and share the results of our Fourth Step inventory with others, we begin to realize that we're gaining more and more insight into the *why* of our addiction. With increasing clarity, we see that our own behavior has been the major cause of our unhappiness.

As we uncover the characteristics that led us down the path to our disease, we slowly realize that it wasn't our life situation that was at fault. It wasn't our parents' fault. It wasn't "bad luck." It wasn't any person, place or thing that pushed us over the edge. The reality is that we had begun to develop some dysfunctional habit patterns. At first they seemed innocuous enough. But in the end, it was these patterns that led to the chronic progression of our disorder.

The good news here is that the more we uncover and discover, and the more candid we become about sharing this with another person, the closer we are to our recovery. Along the way we'll learn that what looks like a catastrophe at first glance becomes a golden opportunity.

There are people today in the Twelve Step process who are able to accept things that we're still making ourselves miserable about. And they stand ready to help us work through every step of our recovery. All we have to do is ask.

TODAY'S STEP: *It becomes easier and easier to admit the truth to myself and others.*

Step Five

Day 9—A SPIRITUAL PROGRAM

"If God did not exist, it would be necessary to invent him." VOLTAIRE

"God" is a word, a term that has been used universally to depict a presence variously envisioned as powerful, benign, punitive, clever, omnipotent, cruel, loving, vindictive, wrathful or omniscient, depending upon the views, needs or beliefs of a given group of people.

Those who subscribe to the ethic of formal religion follow the prescribed procedures advocated by their system of belief, whether it be Buddhism, Islamism, Judaism, Taoism, Hinduism, Christianity, or others. Some Christian churches see God as an anthropomorphic being who keeps a tally on their sins, and who—when they die—assigns them to heaven, hell or purgatory, depending on their record sheet.

Mormons believe in families reunited on one of the three levels of heaven. Catholics and Episcopalians believe in life everlasting. Jews believe that heaven and hell are part of our daily lives right here on earth. Other faiths subscribe to reincarnation.

Whatever we believe will not conflict with the working of these steps, for the program is *not* religious. However, it *is* spiritual. For years, not only those who were affiliated with formal religions but also agnostics and atheists chose to accept the word "God" as the term for their Higher Power.

TODAY'S STEP: *As I work my program, I develop my own personal concept of God.*

Step Five

Day 10—"ADMITTED TO GOD"

"When down in the mouth, remember Jonah. He came out all right."   THOMAS EDISON

Before we approach the person with whom we are to share Step Five, we must first privately confess to ourselves and to God.

Granted, this presupposes that we're using "God" as a term that defines either a power greater than ourselves or a Higher Power. Some folks use "H.P.," others use "universal mind or spirit," still others "God" or "Goddess within." Many people in their early stages of sobriety choose to allow the group conscience to guide them. There is no quarrel among any of us as to which term you choose.

It is in the doing that results begin to show themselves. Without the willingness to at least act as if we were putting some sort of trust and belief in a Higher Power, we remain mired in the belief that of ourselves, and by ourselves we can master our own recovery, despite the fact that our past performance totally disproves this illusion.

Deeply rooted habits of self-justification are hard to break. They constantly tempt us to find rationalizations for our past wrongs. And although we may argue that there's no sense in admitting them to God because—if He *is* God—He already knows them, we're hopelessly stuck until we let go of any resistance to doing the step exactly as it is outlined.

TODAY'S STEP: *In a leap of faith, I admit to the God of my understanding the exact nature of my wrongs.*

Step Five

Day 11—ACCEPTANCE

"When one door closes another opens. But we often look so long and so regretfully upon the closed door that we fail to see the one that has opened for us."
ALEXANDER GRAHAM BELL

When we did our inventory we were aware that the time would come when we were to admit our faults to someone else. Now that the moment has arrived we find ourselves uncomfortable about sharing all our guilty secrets with another person. It was hard enough to face up to the nature of our wrongs when we were alone with pad and pencil. But now we're face-to-face with another person, and we're afraid we'll be harshly judged.

What usually happens as we own up to our failings, is that the individuals with whom we're sharing our confession begin to identify with some of our disclosures because they've had similar experiences. This helps us to open up even more, for we recognize we're not the only one who has suffered guilt and remorse. We're flooded with relief when we sense their nonjudgmental acceptance. This is when we discover the universal truth that each of us feels that our failings signify the bottom of the barrel of human behavior.

The Twelve Step process recognizes that we must become as little children: trusting and following the lead of those who have gone before us. When we do this, we begin to gain access to our inner wisdom. We become free from affectation. We become teachable. We become open to positive change.

TODAY'S STEP: *In sharing my inventory with others, I find myself accepted.*

Day 12—AS SICK AS OUR SECRETS

"Resolve to perform what you ought. Perform without fail what you resolve."   BENJAMIN FRANKLIN

We choose with great care the person with whom we wish to discuss our inventory. We resolve to be totally honest, holding back nothing that we feel may be met with disapproval.

We also want to be sure we can trust that person to keep what we disclose in the strictest confidence. It is important that we make a clean breast of those defects we have discovered in our Fourth Step, and we need to know that what we disclose will not go any further than the two of us.

If we're still intent on making a good impression, we're totally negating the purpose of this step. This means we'll probably keep repeating many nonproductive practices until we are willing to make a clean breast of all our defects. Only then will the time come that we no longer need to hold onto the painful memories of our past.

Those of us in the program believe that people are as sick as their secrets. The more we suppress, the longer it takes us to recover. The value of Steps Four and Five is that, first, they succeed in bringing those secrets into the light of day so they can be discarded. Secondly, they also unearth many hidden assets that will serve us in good stead as we begin to create a more balanced and healthy lifestyle.

TODAY'S STEP: *I unerringly select the right people to share my secrets with.*

Day 13—FACE-TO-FACE

*"Whenever the going seems too easy, make sure you
are not going downhill."*   ANONYMOUS

There is great value in sharing this step with another human
being because, as we face that person, we find ourselves less
apt to deceive them or ourselves. The eyes have been called
the mirrors of the soul, and there seems to be a powerful
contact made when our eyes meet those of someone who
is there to help and support us, someone who will act
neither as critic nor judge.

The very act of speaking aloud has enormous value.
Instead of just looking at what we've written, and having
it float around in our head, we're actually hearing ourselves
freely and honestly admitting to all our guilty secrets. And
once they're verbalized, we're free to rid ourselves of their
burden.

Steps Four and Five are, without doubt, two of the
most powerful ones in our program. They solidify the
commitment we've made to truly follow the directions laid
out before us. And they signify another giant step toward
surrender.

Our confidant is now free to guide us into an understanding of the deeper nature of our wrongs and not just
the specific details of each negative behavior. But without
having disclosed the specifics first, we'd have had no clues
pointing us toward the patterns that have kept us bound to
our addiction.

TODAY'S STEP: *In sharing my inventory more of the truth
is revealed to me.*

Step Five

Day 14—A SYMPATHETIC EAR

"It takes two to speak the truth—one to speak and another to hear." HENRY DAVID THOREAU

Often the people with whom we share our Fifth Step have worked through this same procedure with someone else. As a result, they're sensitive to our fears and to our difficulty in articulating our feelings. Having benefited from the advice, counseling and experience of those who have gone before them, they're able to bring these capabilities into play as they share some of their own history with us.

Professionals—doctors, lawyers, clergy, therapists, and religious science practitioners—are skilled in dealing with the disclosures many others have made to them. Sometimes they are the wisest choice for confidant when we verbalize our inventory, particularly if what we have to admit might be of a legal or confidential nature.

Despite this caveat, many of us choose to share with our sponsor or another group member, trusting that we have nothing to fear from their reaction. There is a certain amount of relief in knowing that this person has had similar experiences and thus is not likely to moralize or therapize, but simply wants to help us get on with the business of cleaning house and learning to live more comfortably with ourselves.

TODAY'S STEP: *I am led to a wise, compassionate person to hear my inventory.*

Day 15—OUR TRUE SELF

"I have been everything unholy. If the Spirit can work through me, it can work through anyone."
ST. FRANCIS OF ASSISI

The admission of powerlessness that we acknowledged in Step One had a humbling quality to it. Now we're asked to humble ourselves again by telling another human being all our missteps and frailties.

Yet, this is not a step in which we wallow in remorse or self-recrimination. We do not dwell on phony self-condemnation or whining self-pity. Nor do we expect to be judged or punished. Rather, we anticipate the sense of relief that we'd experience if we were operated on for a life-threatening tumor that turned out benign.

Certainly we've made mistakes. We've blundered. We've deceived ourselves and others. We've hurt people, behaved outrageously, caused tears and disappointments. We've inflicted heartaches, humiliations and innumerable other things.

But, in time we'll learn that this behavior runs contrary to our true self. For our basic nature is of that self that was born without sin. We simply do not subscribe to "original sin." Rather, we think in terms of "original blessing." We believe that at the moment of birth we are whole and perfect human beings, as yet unadulterated and unhampered by a confusing and sometimes hostile world.

TODAY'S STEP: *As I admit my faults, the barriers to wholeness come down.*

Day 16—HONEST SELF-DECEPTION

"You can fool too many people too much of the time."
                                                                JAMES THURBER

Let's take a look at past mistakes, at blunders, at deception. Things we did both to ourselves and to others. Let's examine misunderstandings, misjudgments and all the other negative aspects of our thinking that we can bring to light.

The closer we look, the clearer it becomes that faulty judgment had become a common occurrence in our repertoire of behaviors. Given a choice of alternatives, we inevitably chose the one that worked against our best interests. Then, to top it all off, we'd rail at the persistent amount of bad luck that beset us, seeing ourselves as victims of a cruel fate.

As for deception, we learned that the greatest difficulty lay, not so much in deceiving others, but in the deception we practiced on ourselves. The kicker is that for many of us it was *honest* self-deception—and therefore extremely difficult to penetrate.

We played judge, jury, prosecuting and defense attorneys in our own heads, and decided that, by sheer deductive reasoning, we'd won our case. Of all the forms of deception, this is by far the most difficult for any of us to see through. We're so sure of our own evaluation that we find it well-nigh impossible to entertain a different point of view.

The process of admitting these mistakes to ourselves requires letting go of self-deception and self-justification. Until we admit to ourselves the exact nature of our wrongs, we cannot succeed in admitting them to God and to another human being.

TODAY'S STEP: *I no longer need to deceive myself about past mistakes.*

Step Five

Day 17—LETTING THE CHIPS FALL

"People who think they know everything are very irritating to those of us who do."   ANONYMOUS

Before we share our inventory, we need to let go of our anxieties. To do this, we pause and invite the Higher Power we can believe in to help direct us as we divulge our wrongs to another human being.

We need strength and energy for this task. What better time to rely on the spirit we're developing within. Rather than wandering away from our disclosures, we're able to release fear and worry. We're ready to take the plunge into the sea of honesty and candor. We tell ourselves we're willing to let the chips fall where they may, and although we're not really sure we feel that way, we proceed as if it were true. After all, what have we got to lose?

Many of these steps are a far cry from the way we've acted in the past, so we should not be too concerned when we feel awkward and a bit insincere in doing them. The doing is the key. Not the thinking. *You can live yourself into good thinking—but you cannot think yourself into good living.*

We take the action. We take it with a faith that may be as tiny as the proverbial mustard seed. But it's sufficient enough to carry us through this and the following steps.

TODAY'S STEP: *Today I take positive action toward completing Step Five.*

Step Five

Day 18—BEYOND THE NO-WIN

"We don't need more strength or more ability or greater opportunity. What we need is to use what we have."
BASIL S. WALSH

It's not necessary for anyone else to read what you've written in your inventory. But some people have found it helpful to bring it with them when they do their Fifth Step. It can be a useful reminder of the specific items you wish to discuss. Some people choose to outline the nature of their wrongs. Others list their assets and liabilities in order to detail more fully their past behavior patterns.

Those with Catholic backgrounds have had long experience in the confessional and they tend to be relatively comfortable with this dynamic. In fact, many of them choose to take the step with their priest. Others who have been in counseling may choose their therapist to be their confidant. Still others elect to share with their sponsor. Whomever we choose—whether a lay person or professional—we want to be sure that we've selected someone with whom we can be perfectly honest.

The "why" of our past behavior will be revealed to us as we begin to realize that we were caught up in a no-win dilemma—one that was impossible to escape from without qualified help and support. In time we'll learn to recycle this past experience as guidelines for our recovery.

TODAY'S STEP: *I am beginning to understand that my negatives can become positives.*

Step Five

Day 19—UNCOVERING THE DEPTHS

*"Your past is always going to be the way it was.
Step trying to change it."* ANONYMOUS

Step Five made a powerful impact on Georgia, who described it as "an unbelievable experience."

"I really couldn't believe that I'd have such a feeling of release and relief in following this formula.

"As a matter of fact, I was very skeptical about the benefits of telling someone else all my failings—my resentments, my fears, my cowardly behavior, my lies, my unfaithfulness. But it worked!

"My sponsor (because that's who I chose to take this step with) identified with some of the experiences I shared, and also reminded me that we also needed to look at my positive characteristics. We went over the seven deadly sins, my grudge list, and all the other data that I'd compiled, and then we talked about how to change liabilities into assets.

"If you'd told me this step would have such a profound effect on me, I'd have thought that was just the party line. You know, where everyone sings the same song, marches in lockstep, and feels that if they don't testify to an incredible sense of relief, other people will feel that they are too shallow to have really worked the step. But when I finally did it, I discovered there was a profound truth underlying the whole process."

TODAY'S STEP: *Hearing how Step Five has benefited others, I have come to trust the process.*

Day 20—TAKING ENOUGH TIME

"No mistake is fatal unless you make it so."

ANONYMOUS

We've defined "admission" as "letting in." What this means is that we do not share our inventory in an abbreviated manner. We drop all subterfuge and evasion. We hold up, one by one, in complete detail, every defect we have unearthed in our inventory list. We keep nothing back, nor do we attempt to justify or rationalize our past performances.

We simply get on with it, and do not consider the step done until we've covered every aspect of our Fourth Step work. We dispense with false pride and reaffirm our decision to practice the H.O.W.—Honesty, Open-mindedness and Willingness—as we pursue our path to recovery.

Some people accomplish this step in one sitting. Others may need repeated visits with the person they're sharing with. We've had people report they spent the entire day going through their inventory list, while others have completed the step in a few hours. Each of us is different. Each of us must honor our own process.

We heartily recommend not trying to rush through this procedure. The person with whom we share has valuable feedback to offer. Also, he or she can help us clarify aspects that confuse us, and give us the kind of reassurance, acceptance and approval that allows us, at last, to throw off our yoke of subterfuge and pretense.

TODAY'S STEP: *I do my inventory work thoroughly and at the proper pace.*

Step Five

Day 21—THE BAG OF TRICKS

"If I were two-faced, would I be wearing this one?"
ABRAHAM LINCOLN

"I'd paid back every debt I owed," said Harry. "So why do I have to admit to cheating people out of anything? I did this before I agreed to try this program, so I see no reason to label this as one of my defects of character."

Harry's sponsor patiently and carefully led him back along the path to the beginning phases of his addiction. He helped Harry identify the underlying factors that had led to the time when Harry first began to lie, cheat and steal. Finally, Harry's sponsor was able to get him to admit that the reason he'd paid all his debts was that, if he hadn't, he'd have been faced with a lawsuit. Harry's sponsor did this with gentleness and compassion, and this allowed Harry to identify even more defects that needed attention.

Through the process of "uncover," "discover," "recover," we progress into deeper self-knowledge and acceptance. This process allows us to uncover long-forgotten incidents. In them, we discover the origins of earlier, carefully disguised characteristics that had become recurring themes in our bag of coping tricks. The object of this search is not to make us feel more guilty or ashamed of ourselves, but to clearly point out how the mosaic of our life has been made up of tiny missteps.

TODAY'S STEP: *I allow myself to uncover, discover and recover.*

Step Five

Day 22—NOTHING TO HIDE

"As long as you live you'll win some and you'll lose some."   KEN KEYES, JR.

The world does not change to accommodate a person who has been crippled by an accident or disabled by a disease, and the world will not change for us because we've been traumatized by our disorder.

We change, however. And in doing so, our world takes on a less frightening aspect.

We've suffered depression, anxiety, remorse, irritability, frustration and despair. These are all perfectly normal emotions, considering our past history. Many of those feelings will stay with us for some time, and we need to accept this as a logical condition of recovery. Our addiction didn't appear full-blown in our lives. It took time to develop. Recovery will take time as well.

When we dare to take off our masks of pretense and self-deception, we're able to gain a more accurate description of who and what we really are. With nothing to hide, we can go about our lives with a degree of dignity that we've not experienced for a long time. We can begin to accept life on life's terms. We know there will be problems and difficulties. But we also know that our newfound strength and commitment give us the courage and fortitude to face them. Insight will take the place of fear.

In the process of admitting our wrongs to ourselves, we learn more than we could have imagined. How much more can we learn, then, by completing this step and admitting our wrongs to God and others.

TODAY'S STEP: *I confidently remove the mask of self-deception.*

Day 23—LIVING THE PARADOX

"The art of living is more like wrestling than dancing."
MARCUS AURELIUS

There is a definite catharsis that occurs when we rid ourselves of our secrets. And yet, some of us may experience a sensation of emptiness or loss. In time, this will change as we pursue our resolve. We'll discover that our old identity needs to be re-formed to fit into a positive recovery mode.

When we question how we can turn negatives into positives, we need to remind ourselves that *Failure is not final*. It simply means we've missed the mark. As we move on in recovery, we begin to understand that what caused us to feel guilt and shame was due more to the chronic progression of our disease than our character. And once we're free of our compulsive addiction, we'll have no need to repeat those negative patterns of the past.

It's a paradox that the very qualities that were defeating us can now become our greatest assets. Both our elaborate denial system and our persistent self-deception can be made to serve us by alerting us to the necessity of letting go of past attitudes, reactions and behavior. As we unearth and admit to these defects, we begin to understand how to monitor the trigger mechanisms that caused us to act in an unproductive manner.

TODAY'S STEP: *In uncovering my defects, I discover how they can become assets.*

Day 24—DIGGING DEEPER

"If I had known I was going to live this long, I'd have taken better care of myself." ANONYMOUS

There are a few more stumbling blocks to our continued progress that we need to add to our inventory. These are: rebellion, self-deception, sentimentality, defiance, blame-placing and phony remorse.

How do we turn these negatives into positives? Steps Six, Seven, Eight and Nine will give us guidelines in clearing them away. For now these blocks simply act as clues to help us do a thorough job of Step Five. Let's define them clearly:

• Rebellion: Are we resisting making a totally clean breast of our failings?

• Self-deception: Are we still seeing ourselves as victims?

• Sentimentality: Do we persist in dwelling on the memory of how good it once was?

• Defiance: Are we belligerently defensive about past actions?

• Blame-placing: Do we believe that it's what other people have done to us that caused our problems?

• Phony remorse: Are we working this step in a self-deprecating way, saying that we were totally to blame when we really believe we were not?

The deeper we dig, the more we'll find things we want to acknowledge and discard.

TODAY'S STEP: *I examine all hidden blocks that get in the way of completing Step Five.*

Step Five

Day 25—GETTING THE MOST

"Success means getting your 'but' out of the way."
ANONYMOUS

Ken Keyes, Jr. has written a number of books that he's chosen not to have copyrighted because he wishes to share them as a gift with us.

The following excerpt is from one of these books, *Prescriptions for Happiness*, which is published by Living Love Publications, Coos Bay, Oregon. From time to time we'll quote him again.

> Most of your life problems can no longer be effectively handled by primitive "fight or flight" responses. You usually deprive yourself of getting the most from people and situations around you when you come on with power or let your fears make you run away. To develop the most satisfying outcomes, most of your problems require more insight and a practical back-and-forth working with the situation over a period of time. Try to remember that it's always your emotion-backed demands that are really the practical cause of your own unhappiness. The art of happiness means learning to be with and to work and play with the cast of characters you've brought into your life. Retreating won't do it. Coming on like a ten-ton truck won't do it either. Emotionally accepting and patiently working with life situations will get you the most that's gettable!

TODAY'S STEP: *I am learning how to be patient and to trust others.*

Step Five

Day 26—PRETENSES

"We can do what I can't do."　　　ANONYMOUS

There are many support systems available to us in our quest for recovery. In the preface, we listed some of the self-help groups that have proliferated in our society since AA became nationally known. It has been our experience that belonging to self-help groups greatly enhances our progress in recovery. Their support helps us begin to establish our own sense of identity and to build trust.

When we pay attention to what other group members tell us about themselves, we become aware that we can relate to some aspects of their behavior, their feelings and attitudes. As we do this, our inventory broadens. We begin to identify even more of the causes of our own discomfort and unreasonable actions.

Over time we've developed tactics that have enabled us to cope with the deepening progression of our compulsions. Because of our faulty perspective, we've judged these tactics to be reasonable and logical. Our ability to surrender them now and to see them as a form of denial is a true test of our desire to recover. With the help of those who have gone before us, we find the courage not only to dispense with our defense mechanisms but also to allow others to see us stripped of all pretense.

TODAY'S STEP: *As I listen to others tell the truth I find the courage to stop defending and pretending.*

Day 27—NEGATIVES BECOME POSITIVES

"The important thing is this: to be able at any moment to sacrifice what we are for what we could become."
CHARLES DU BOS

A positive approach is of inestimable help when we work Step Five. We're realistic enough to know that this step requires a great deal of effort and enormous optimism, for we're putting our trust in a procedure with which we've had no previous experience. But, we're not under any delusion that the minute we complete Step Five we'll experience total freedom from all guilt and responsibility for our past. Guilt and shame are natural by-products of what we feel about our compulsive behavior.

That we feel guilt and shame is, in itself, a positive thing. It indicates that we're learning to accept personal responsibility rather than laying the blame on others.

Also, once the clouds of self-deception start to dissipate, we begin to understand that much of the guilt we feel can actually be attributed to the nature of the chronic progression of our addiction. Once freed from the yoke of that addiction, we need never repeat those actions that have caused us to harm ourselves and others.

By taking each negative in turn, and examining its effects and admitting its exact nature to ourselves and another human being, we develop personal responsibility.

TODAY'S STEP: *In working Step Five, I can free myself of guilt and shame.*

Step Five

Day 28—OLD LABELS

"Happiness is good health and a bad memory."
INGRID BERGMAN

When a friend asked Thomas Edison how many times he'd tried to perfect one of his inventions, he answered, "Oh, perhaps ninety-nine or a hundred."

"You mean," said the friend in amazement, "that you've failed that many times?"

"No," answered Edison, "I've simply found that many ways not to do it."

We've done so many things for what we believed—or were told—were the right reasons, that it's now hard for us to judge what's right and what's wrong for ourselves. Are right things done for the wrong reasons more acceptable than wrong things done for the right reasons?

There really is no contest here. We simply have to reexamine long-held value judgments and reassess whether those judgments are appropriate in our lives today. More often than not, we'll discover that we operated more out of conditioning than reasoning. By discarding the labels "good" and "bad," and looking instead at what has created positive or negative results, we can begin to chart our course in the direction that will be of the most value to us.

When we see our failures as only temporary setbacks, we realize that we are finally learning how to be kind to ourselves.

TODAY'S STEP: *As I learn from past mistakes, I release any sense of failure.*

Day 29—PURGING THE PAIN

"Hope is the feeling you have that the feeling you have isn't permanent."
JEAN KERR

Being able to accept ourselves exactly the way we are at this point is a vital factor in recovery. This is because when we begin to tell another person of our wrongs, there's a great temptation to editorialize, rationalize and apologize.

This is not the intent of Step Five. We have to resist putting on a good face to gain the other person's approval. This is so hard to do, for approval is almost as vital to our survival as are food, shelter and love. Our ability to risk rejection when we do this step is a true measure of our humility. It confirms our resolve to go about the business of recovery with no holds barred—with complete willingness to let the past be exposed in all its embarrassing detail.

The dammed-up emotions of years spill out when we speak of our past. And we are filled with an enormous sense of relief when we're finally able to purge ourselves of all our guilty secrets. Much of our pain dissipates when we share the load we've carried for so long. We now know we never have to fabricate lie upon lie to explain our actions to anyone again. We're finally free of subterfuge and pretense.

TODAY'S STEP: *In my inventory, I courageously reveal my real self, releasing the need for approval.*

Step Five

Day 30—TURNING THE CORNER

"Nobody can make you feel inferior without your consent."
ELEANOR ROOSEVELT

We have worked through one of the most difficult and powerful steps in our program. Now is the time for us to congratulate ourselves for having come so far. At this point we're ready to tackle Steps Six and Seven. These help us review all that we have unearthed about ourselves so that we can let go.

We have entrusted our secrets to another, and we feel secure that whatever confidences we have shared will go no further than between the two of us.

Sometimes this step leaves us feeling uncertain. We've spent a long time with one set of values and opinions, struggling mightily to defend and justify ourselves. Now we're not really sure how we're going to manage our lives without them.

It may take a little time before we truly feel we no longer have to live a life of pretense and subterfuge. We know, from personal stories we've heard, that there comes a moment when we experience a sense of freedom that has been outside the realm of our comprehension for a long while. It's as if we've shed a scabrous carapace that armored us against what we used to see as a hostile world.

Today we can see that simple truths and right actions are becoming the stabilizing factors in our lives.

TODAY'S STEP: *I reap the rewards of sharing my inventory.*

Step Five

Day 31—PURPOSE

"The truth shall make you free." JOHN 8:32

As Ken Keyes, Jr., has written, "There's only one person in the world who can really make you happy. There's only one person in the world who can make you unhappy. How about getting to know this person more deeply?"

And that is exactly what we have been trying to do in Step Five.

True, the inventory in Step Four uncovered a great many truths we had hidden from ourselves. But with Step Five and the added insight and input of the person we chose to share it with, we have discovered a wealth of information about both our assets and our liabilities.

We have come to understand that we carried with us many old ideas, gleaned from our families, our environment and sometimes our religion, which did not hold up under the scrutiny of honest self-appraisal.

We also discovered that some of the traits we thought were of no value whatsoever turned out to be very positive assets in our search for dignity and well-being.

And, most of all, we have discovered that within ourselves we have the capability of pursuing a way of life that is both rewarding and meaningful.

TODAY'S STEP: *I accept myself as a valuable human being, worthy of respect.*

Step Six

> *"Were entirely ready to have God remove all these defects of character."*

Here we go again—into the "letting go" mode. We first did it in Step Three, but now we're supposed to believe that the only way our defects can be removed is to trust a power, whom we're still uncertain of, to do the job for us.

Well, not exactly. The principle that faith without works is dead, holds true for Step Six. The Twelve Steps in their entirety are part of the process of recovery. None of them, however, suggests that we passively relinquish all personal responsibility.

Sometimes we have to *act* as if a defect has been removed, even though we don't *feel* it has been. We experience reluctance to let go of those defects we feel are part of our personalities, arguing that without them we'd appear very dull and uninteresting.

As we begin to learn that we can live our way into good thinking, but cannot think ourselves into good living, Step Six becomes more valuable and understandable.

Step Six

Day 1—DROPPING THE ARMOR

"Self-respect: The secure feeling that no one, as yet, is suspicious."
H.L. MENCKEN

Now we're really ready to clean house. We've identified the nature of our wrongs. We've shared that inventory with God, ourselves and another human being. And the decks are cleared for us to take the action that proves even to ourselves our willingness to proceed. Now that we've uncovered and discovered, we're ready to discard.

But, this is where we run into a whole new issue—the startling realization that we treasure some of our defects of character! They've been a part of us for so long, and they've served our purposes in so many ways that dropping the familiar armor that has protected us from the onslaught of other people's criticism feels much like standing naked in school. In the past, some of us have operated on the theory that a strong offense is the best defense. It's hard to let go of that posture when we're feeling inadequate and defenseless.

Remember that the word "God" can be translated into whatever guiding energy you've chosen to embrace as your Higher Power. But be aware also, that Step Six presupposes that you accept this power as a senior partner in your recovery process.

TODAY'S STEP: *I let go of defensiveness about my defects of character.*

Day 2—PACKING OUR BAGS

"He who would travel happily must travel light."
ANTOINE DE SAINT-EXUPERY

When we get ready for a trip we have to decide what we're going to pack in our suitcase to meet our needs away from home. Some of us are very methodical about this procedure. Others of us just stuff things willy-nilly into our bags, hoping we've chosen appropriately.

Using the suitcase analogy to work this step, it's clear that the first thing we have to do is dump the entire contents. As we begin to repack, we only want to take those items that work for us—those that are valuable and usable right now. Many familiar and well-worn articles will have to go.

We need to take note of those familiar things that have worked to our disadvantage, and ask for the courage we need to let them go. We have to check our closets and bureaus for appropriate items that have been stored away unused for some time. Now's the time to look them over and to remind ourselves of how valuable they are, and start putting them to good use.

TODAY'S STEP: *On the path of recovery, I travel light—and lightheartedly.*

Step Six

Day 3—THE HISTORY OF THE PICKLE

"As long as we feel victimized, we have lost the power to change." ANONYMOUS

The pickle was once a nice, fat cucumber. When it was left in the brine for a prescribed length of time, it emerged as a pickle. But once it had become a pickle, there was absolutely no way in the world it could ever become a cucumber again.

"What's that got to do with the subject at hand?" you may ask.

Everything. Once we've been caught up in, or addicted to our drug of choice, or compulsive behavior or an aberrant lifestyle, we can never go back to the way we were before it began. No matter how recovered we are, we will never be able to do in moderation what began by serving us, but in time became our master.

The bad news is that it's extremely hard to watch others doing with impunity the things that are forbidden to us.

But the good news is that we've become something new—a pickle instead of a cucumber. And this new form allows us to be better, more productive and happier than we've ever been in our entire lifetime. Extravagant as this promise seems, it has been proven true, time after time, by those who have gone before us.

As we celebrate the new form, it becomes easier to let go of the old. And in that celebration, we become willing to let God remove these defects of character.

TODAY'S STEP: *I rejoice in the new form my life is taking.*

Step Six

Day 4—ONE IS TOO MANY

"Patience is the best remedy for every trouble."
PLAUTUS

Once we've made the decision to let go of our defects, it's foolish to expect immediate results. If they don't materialize quickly we start to waffle. Like making a New Year's resolution to cut sugar out of our diet. Pretty soon we find ourselves rationalizing that after all we don't need to be fanatics about it. We could probably have just one or two after-dinner mints or perhaps a few mouthfuls of sherbert.

Talk to anyone who has successfully stopped smoking for a number of years, following failed attempt after failed attempt, and they'll tell you that the surest way to fall back into addiction is to smoke "just one." Recovered alcoholics report that: "One is too many. And a thousand aren't enough." Overeaters Anonymous members say that the moment they introduce one mint or one taste of sherbert into their systems, they're off and running.

It's the same way with our other defects of character. We need to resist the temptation to slip back into them in the same way—and with the same tools—that we resist slipping back into the addiction or compulsion that brought us into the program in the first place.

Recovery is a much more complex process than we might have thought at the beginning. This is why it takes time and patience to really focus on our own responsibilities rather than complaining about the bad hand life has dealt us. At the onset, it's awkward and hard to conform to this step, but the payoff is enormous.

TODAY'S STEP: *I avoid the temptation to fall back into my old ways.*

Day 5—SHOWING UP

"If you can't hide it, paint it red!"   ANONYMOUS

We begin this step simply by suiting up and showing up. We should not expect the process of recovery to be accomplished in one fell swoop. Most of our defects have taken time to develop, and they will take time to resolve. None of them are one single thing—simply physical, mental, emotional or spiritual. They are a complex combination of all these aspects.

In addition, while we may identify with similar problems presented in the stories of others, our defects and shortcomings remain uniquely our own, because they've developed within the framework of our own lifestyles and relationships.

As we work Step Six, we need to concentrate on our own defects, not those of others. It's so easy to point the finger and rationalize that it's because of what *they* did that we behaved the way *we* did. On the other hand, it's also true that our behavior hasn't been the cause of all the pain and discomfort that has befallen us and those close to us. But, for now, our focus in recovery must be solely on ourselves.

TODAY'S STEP: *I have patience to keep the focus on myself.*

Day 6—GETTING THINGS DONE

"Procrastination is the art of keeping up with yes-
terday."
                                                    DON MARQUIS

Time now to look over the inventory we compiled in the
Fourth Step and decide which of our defects we're willing
to have removed.

Our goal is freedom from addiction, and we cannot
accomplish this without thoroughly clearing away what
we've come to see as the wreckage of our past. The first
step, of course, is to stop doing what we were doing,
because until we succeed in changing our behavior, we
have no chance to recover. Our rationalization may have
been, "I'll stop when I finish this job," or, "I'll stop if
he/she comes back to me," or, "I'll stop right after the
holidays."

All of these delays add up to procrastination. So, if we
see procrastination as one of our defects, we have to ask
ourself how we'd act if we did not procrastinate. What
would our behavior be like? One way is to give serious
thought to how those who succeed in doing things when
they should be done manage their time, and then try to
imitate their behavior. We call this "acting as if."

But if our reply is, "I've always been a procrastinator. I
just don't think I can change at this late stage," what we're
really saying is, "I'm unwilling to follow your path because
my case is different."

TODAY'S STEP: *My procrastination is history! Today I am*
ready to have this defect removed.

Step Six

Day 7—PUTTING OUR MONEY WHERE OUR MOUTHS ARE

"Life is like playing a violin in public and learning the instrument as one goes on." SAMUEL BUTLER

From here on in we'll assume that most of us are satisfied with our concept of a Higher Power.

We've already established that those who do not subscribe to the Judeo-Christian ethic may just as efficaciously put their belief in a "cosmic consciousness," or the law of cause and effect, or whatever they choose. The important thing here is to accept the fact that all by ourselves we cannot accomplish this challenge.

This is when we leave our fantasy world and enter the world of reality. We stop dwelling on the harm that others have done us, and start looking at the ways we've responded. In the process, we let go of the notion of ourselves as helpless victims, and we also let go of the resentments we thought justified our anger. Then we look again at our inventory and rank our defects in order of priority. And we tackle number one first.

Time after time, we've tried making bargains with ourselves and with our Higher Power to get out of any scrapes. We've promised that once we're free of our predicament, we'll never repeat the actions that brought us to this state. Yet, time and again, we've fallen into the same old behavior. Now, however, we're ready to step out the door into a new existence.

"Entirely ready," this Sixth Step says. What a heavy order! This means we embrace this step with no reservations. We're now ready to put our money where our mouth is.

TODAY'S STEP: *I embrace a Higher Power as the key to removing my defects.*

Day 8—CROSSING THE THRESHOLD

"The toughest thing about success is that you've got to keep on being a success." IRVING BERLIN

When some speech therapists treat stammerers or stutterers, they have their clients go to a supermarket, choose a long line, and when they come abreast of the checker, ask where they can find an item that is particularly difficult to pronounce. This is done, not to humiliate them, but to build up enough self-esteem to realize that they are deserving and worthwhile people, and that their speech difficulty in no way diminishes them as dignified human beings.

When we set about the business of clearing up these negative characteristics and behavior patterns that have plagued us in our recent past, it's helpful to know that although we *have* a problem, we are *not* the problem. We are afflicted with a treatable condition that responds admirably to the program we've begun to follow. And, like the stutterers, our difficulties in no way diminish our worth as human beings. We are worthy of recovery, and of having our defects removed. Knowing that makes it easier to gain the willingness to have God remove them.

TODAY'S STEP: *I recognize that I am worthwhile, in spite of my flaws.*

Day 9—LAYING THE GROUNDWORK

"O Lord, help me to be pure, but not yet."

ST. AUGUSTINE

We have to close one door in order to open another. But it's amazing how reluctant we are to let that first door close. We persist in trying to keep it slightly ajar in case we find it necessary to return to our old familiar path. Painful, admittedly, but familiar. It almost feels better to stay in our pain than to risk embracing the unknown.

We experience nostalgia for the good old days when we didn't know that our characteristics were defects. We try to bargain, telling ourselves, "I'll give up all *those* if I can just keep *this* one." We reevaluate our judgment on our inventory work and say to ourselves: "Maybe I've been too hard on myself. Maybe that one isn't really a defect. I probably went overboard in trying to be so scrupulous!"

Although this step may appear to be a passive one, that's far from the truth. We don't simply sit still and say, "Well, here they are. All my defects. O.K. Higher Power—take 'em away." We review our inventory list. We spread it all out before us and use it to choose our first project.

TODAY'S STEP: *My inventory is the foundation for my further recovery.*

Day 10—FEAR HAS MANY FACES

"The more things a man is ashamed of, the more respectable he is."   GEORGE BERNARD SHAW

While the stereotypical image of meekness is a fearful, cringing figure, we view meekness in an entirely different light.

When we suggest developing the quality of meekness to facilitate working this step, we think of patience and humility, both of which are potent factors in our formula for success.

Granted, we do experience a certain amount of fear and uncertainty in letting go of some of those characteristics which have kept others at a distance, but because we've identified them as defects of character, getting rid of them is a "must."

Fear, itself, has many faces. More often than not, it masquerades as other emotions such as anger, resentment and self-deception.

This is one of the reasons that we've had such difficulty defining the true source of our discomfort, and why it becomes necessary for us to work through these symptoms before we can eliminate fear itself.

Despite the fact that resentment is often the most difficult defect to eliminate, experience has proven it to be an excellent candidate with which to begin Step Six.

TODAY'S STEP: *I am finding the courage to let go of my character defects.*

Step Six

Day 11—GETTING UNSTUCK

*"It is only possible to live happily ever after on a
day-to-day basis."*
MARGARET BONNANO

Problems can translate into healthy challenges if we approach them with optimism. We've already acknowledged that we're the ones who created the situation we find ourselves in. But we've also discovered that we have the courage and—hand in hand with our Higher Power—the ability to change negatives into positives.

The gap between how our lives are, and how we want them to be, creates tension. But tension is a two-way street. It can act as a catapult to thrust us into a more productive life pattern, or it can drag us back into the pit we're struggling to escape.

We have to recognize that until we cease trying to place the blame on people, places, or things; until we stop denying our responsibility; until we stop defending our reasons for past behavior, we're hopelessly stuck.

If, on the other hand, we look at what our denial and defensiveness are covering up—and what they are trying to tell us—we begin to see opportunities to turn those self-same liabilities into assets.

TODAY'S STEP: *I accept my Higher Power's ability to change my negatives into positives.*

Step Six

Day 12—REPLACING DEFECTS

"It's a rare person who wants to hear what he doesn't want to hear."   DICK CAVETT

The surest way to erase a defect of character is to replace it with a positive attribute. If we're lazy, for example, we can begin by carefully scheduling our activities during the day, and alloting them specific time-frames for their completion. A word of advice. It's often necessary to guard against going overboard on an exercise like this because most of us tend to operate on the premise that anything worth doing is worth doing to excess.

As we start letting go of some of our defects, we begin to experience a certain amount of anxiety. Despite the fact that they were not benefiting us, they had become valuable to our equilibrium. Removing them puts us out of kilter. It's the same dynamic as having a tooth removed, or an appendix taken out. We know that their removal is in our best interests, but they've been of value to us in the past, and we feel somehow diminished when they are taken away.

A recent divorcee, who had experienced physical abuse from her husband put it this way: "Somehow it would be a relief when he finally hit me. I knew it was coming sooner or later, and after the episode I always felt better because on some level, I felt I deserved the pain."

TODAY'S STEP: *I am gentle with myself; I allow time to adjust to change.*

Day 13—RESENTMENTS

"The trouble with the rat race is that, even if you win, you're still a rat."
LILY TOMLIN

Resentment is often a stumbling block to recovery because it crops up when we least expect it. So, it helps to give resentment a long, hard look to assess whether it's preventing us from working effectively toward our goal.

In our search for self-knowledge and self-acceptance, we've uncovered many negative characteristics that caused us to behave in an unacceptable manner that was hurtful to others.

When we assessed the harm we'd done to others, we were also quick to report that they had hurt us too, and we felt a strong desire to make them pay for their behavior.

Here's where we truly separate the grown-ups from the children.

Our task is to focus on the changes we need to make to live more comfortably with ourselves. The minute we dwell on what *they* have done, resentment begins to cloud our vision and prevent us from doing an adequate appraisal of our own culpability. It's resentment that allows us to justify the unacceptable as our only recourse. And it's resentment that keeps us reliving those past experiences. In fact, resentments can blow them up to such importance that we feel vindicated in planning retribution.

Until we've put ourselves right with our world, we can't afford to waste an ounce of energy pursuing this kind of satisfaction.

TODAY'S STEP: *I am entirely ready to turn my resentments over.*

Day 14—POINTING THE FINGER

*"Responsibility's like a string we can only see the
middle of. Both ends are out of sight."*

WILLIAM McFEE

Step Six, like Step Four, is designed so that we focus only
on ourselves—on those defects of character which have
been hurtful to us and to others. Unquestionably, there
have been many painful events in our lives when we were
the victim rather than the perpetrator—when the actions of
others have caused us pain and distress.

But our business today is not what has been done *to* us,
no matter how painful it might have been. In time we will
be able to reassess, and work through, the grief and disappointment we've experienced at the hands of others. For
the present, we need to keep the focus on ourselves. We
can't afford the dubious luxury of pointing the finger at any
other person, place, or thing, lest we lose sight of our
primary purpose—to put our *own* house in order.

The temptation to blame others for causing our behavior can be a serious stumbling block to recovery. There will
be a time, when we are right with ourselves, that we can
heal some of those old scars. Until then, our job is to
complete this journey within the framework of these
Twelve Steps.

TODAY'S STEP: *I firmly put the focus back on myself and
my need to recover.*

Step Six

Day 15—NURSING OUR HURTS

"There's no need to hang about waiting for the Last Judgment—it takes place every day."

ALBERT CAMUS

Eddie Nolan, a small-town boy, had made a big name for himself in New York. He gave generously to charity; endowed colleges, universities and hospitals; and was always ready to lend a helping hand.

A schoolmate who hadn't seen Eddie for fifteen years arrived in town one day and called him at his office. His intent was to invite Eddie to be Master of Ceremonies at their 25th high school reunion. He was told that Eddie was tied up, but that the message would be relayed to him.

When he didn't hear from Eddie by the next day, he called again. This time the boss's secretary was out, and her assistant answered the phone. She saw the note from the day before, but didn't know that Eddie hadn't seen it. Assuming Eddie didn't wish to deal with the caller, she told him that the boss could not take any calls. This so angered the man that he told her to cancel his previous message, which she did.

Hurt and resentful, he told all the home folks what a big head Eddie had developed, wrote him a sarcastic letter, and chose someone else to keynote the event. This supposed snub caused him to react with anger, to hurt someone else's reputation, and to spoil what would have been a wonderful celebration for himself and others.

Maybe the stories behind our hurts and resentments aren't as dramatic as this one, but there are consequences, anyway, of our readiness to take affront so easily. Can we learn to give others the benefit of the doubt and to communicate before assuming they mean to hurt us?

TODAY'S STEP: *Today I give other people the benefit of the doubt.*

Day 16—EATING WORMS

"Don't be discouraged. It's often the last key in the bunch that opens the lock." ANONYMOUS

The child within us has a tendency to make unreasonable demands on others. Then he or she feels petulant and discounted when *they* fail to rise to our expectations. We feel hurt, and we want to hurt back. We get touchy when we feel those close to us are not sympathetic to our needs, and we begin to look for more and more evidence that we're being treated badly.

How often have we found ourselves in situations where we've become aggressive rather than assertive in asking for our just due? This usually leads to frustration and impotence when our behavior is met with disapproval and the total withdrawal of support.

At this point, we plot and plan how to retaliate for these supposed snubs. We fantasize all sorts of situations that will make *them* regret the way they treated us. We'll win the lottery, we think. We'll demonstrate an act of heroism, and receive national acclaim. An obscure relative will die and leave us a fortune. We'll contract an exotic and incurable illness. Then *they'll* be sorry. Then *they'll* wish they'd treated us better. It's that old nursery rhyme: "Nobody loves me, everybody hates me. I'm gonna go out and eat worms."

TODAY'S STEP: *As I become aware of my unreasonable demands on others, I can no longer take my drama so seriously.*

Day 17—IMBALANCES

"The door of opportunity won't open unless you do some pushing."   ANONYMOUS

There are shorthand terms that help us boil down wordy and complicated descriptions of certain behavioral and emotional problems. They're useful because they're both accurate and pithy.

The term, "biopsychosocial" is one of these. It clearly outlines the set of conditions that have led many of us to addiction. Body (biological or physiological), mind (psychological), and culture (social) interact to set the stage for our addiction, compulsion or problem. All parts of us are thrown out of kilter when just one of these factors is off center. This is because all three work in concert to produce a healthy and comfortable existence.

We lack the ability to function well when we're physically ill, emotionally disturbed or are experiencing an unhealthy life situation, whether its root is in work, finances, relationships or a catastrophic event. Anything that makes us feel better becomes desirable. In the past the desire to "feel better" often meant a chemical or behavioral cure. This, in turn, is what led us to our compulsive/addictive practice.

As we become aware of how our character defects create inner imbalances, we become increasingly uncomfortable with them and finally are willing to have them removed.

TODAY'S STEP: *I accept the need for balance in all areas of my life.*

Day 18—ONE DAY AT A TIME

"Genius is one percent inspiration and ninety-nine percent perspiration."   THOMAS ALVA EDISON

One of the keys to recovery is to take things "one day at a time." It's unreasonable to even think of trying to eliminate all our defects immediately. Remember how long it took us to arrive at the point in our lives when we were willing to ask for help.

But now that we're here, learning to turn our failures into successes, it's vital to look at where we failed in order to understand what we must do to succeed.

A few days ago we talked of resentment being a prime target for our housecleaning efforts. We examined the futility of laying the blame on others, and we accepted that we'd failed miserably in trying to extricate ourselves from our downward course.

Now's the time to start shifting our perspective. Thomas Edison's statement that he hadn't really failed, but he'd simply found countless ways not to do a thing, is good counsel. So let's divest ourselves of our negative attitudes and proceed with the expectation that—with the help of our Higher Power—our defects can be removed.

TODAY'S STEP: *I am ready for my Higher Power to restore balance to my life.*

Day 19—THE FATAL FLAW

"The optimist proclaims that we live in the best of all possible worlds; and the pessimist fears this is true."   JAMES BRANCH CABELL

All of us, at one time or another, have felt that we had a dark side—a fatal flaw, and if others knew of it we'd be blackballed from the human race. This fatal flaw concept seems to be pervasive in recovering people. Step Six is the place to deal with it.

As a breed, we tend to think in terms of black and white, in extremes. We're hooked on perfection. If we can't be the best, then we'll be the worst. We play "Can you top this?" games with others on the recovery path, never quite realizing that the feeling that we're either the best or the worst is a form of grandiosity.

We sometimes mask our need for approval with arrogance. Many of us are so insecure in our innermost selves that we feel the need to inflate our egos with posturing and pretense in the hope that others will see us as worthwhile or important. Or, we take the opposite tack and become so timid and self-effacing that we make others uncomfortable with our wimpiness.

Step Six offers us a chance to accept ourselves as we really are—a chance to own and acknowledge our defects and assets. And this puts us in a splendid position to divest ourselves of our negative characteristics.

TODAY'S STEP: *By accepting both my defects and my assets I can change for the better.*

Step Six

Day 20—"LET GO AND LET GOD"

"I can't. He can. I think I'll let Him."

ANONYMOUS

As children bring their broken toys
With tears for us to mend,
I brought my broken dreams to God
Because He is my friend.
But then, instead of leaving Him in peace to work
   alone,
I hung around and tried to help with ways that
   were my own.
At last, I snatched them back and cried,
How could you be so slow?
My child, He said, what could I do?
You never did let go.

TODAY'S STEP: *Today, I let go and let God.*

Day 21—RUTS

"A man will do more for his stubborness than for his religion or his country."   EDGAR WATSON HOWE

When we find ourselves cornered, our instinct is either to run or to stand up and fight to defend ourselves. We propose all sorts of rationalizations about why we're in this fix, and we stubbornly cling to our alibis. Even when we accept the responsibility, we still attempt to justify our actions. And we come up with some really inventive reasons for why we behaved the way we did.

We just as stubbornly cling to old ideas and old habit patterns. We've got that old-time religion: "It was good enough for Father and good enough for Mother—and it's good enough for me."

We all agree on how difficult it is to change habit patterns, and that it takes a lot of effort. Yet, like that jaywalker who, although repeatedly injured, persisted in jaywalking time and time again, we persist in trying our old ways "one more time" because "this time it will be different!" It is almost as if there's some kind of magnetic attraction to the same character defects.

TODAY'S STEP: *With God's help, I am ready to acknowledge my character defects.*

Day 22—FOOTWORK

*"What you have become is the price you paid to get
what you used to want."*   MIGNON McLAUGHLIN

Sometimes, when we hear people telling us to "Turn it
over," "Let go and let God," "Give it to your Higher
Power," it sounds as if they've found a symbolic depository
for all their problems, and take no further responsibility for
their solution. Right? Wrong.

This is where we start doing some "footwork." Without some action on our part, all we've proven is that "Faith
without works is dead."

It would be wonderfully convenient to rid ourselves of
the debris of our past by the simple act of putting it in other
hands—like the Good Fairy zapping us with her magic
wand. But that isn't the true meaning of Step Six.

What we're really expected to do when we work this
step is to begin changing old patterns of behavior simply by
not doing things the way we did them in the past.

We start by looking at the gap between where we are
and where we want to be, acknowledging that it was our
past actions that created the divide. Our next bit of footwork is to begin to turn these habit patterns and daily
rituals over to God.

Today, we can tap into that inner strength that has lain
dormant in the past. We know now that we have the power
and the ability to use it well.

TODAY'S STEP: *With God's help I am able to do my
footwork; I can acknowledge my defects with love.*

Day 23—CHANGING THE OLD ROUTINE

"If you could really accept you weren't O.K., you could stop trying to prove you're O.K."

ANONYMOUS

Because we need to keep our goal as our number one priority, it becomes more and more necessary to change our actions and attitudes. This sometimes involves activities that might seem juvenile or ineffectual. This is where we practice open-mindedness and suspend judgment, and we give "acting as if" a try.

One technique many of us have used to jump start these changes is altering our morning routine. Most of us have a ritual we perform in going to the bathroom, brushing our teeth, starting the coffee, picking up the paper, turning on the TV or radio. So try changing the order of the activities. If the first thing you do is brush your teeth, try picking up the paper instead. Soap up your body before you shampoo instead of after.

The value of this shift in the old routine is that it triggers our thinking mechanisms to remember the goal we've set for ourselves. Each time we change a behavior, we're alerted to *why* we're doing it, and it helps us to key into our resolve one more time.

One man who dates his recovery back some twenty years said that his trigger mechanism was to shave on the left side of his face rather than his customary practice of starting on the right. He said, that to this day, each morning, he thinks of the man who first suggested that he try this exercise, and he's given this same advice to many of his other friends.

TODAY'S STEP: *In the smallest changes, I plant the seeds of greater ones.*

Day 24—INTOLERANCE TO ACCEPTANCE

"I don't care how you think things should be, it's the way they are that counts." ANONYMOUS

If intolerance is one of our defects, how do we change it?

First, we take a clear-eyed look at where it all began. Was it a trait we learned from our parents because they were prejudiced about races or religions? Was it something we developed because of peer pressure—of wanting to belong? Did we suffer a bad experience at the hands of a certain individual or an organization? Were we frightened or angered by a misdiagnosis by someone in the medical field? What was it that has caused us to react in such a judgmental fashion ever since?

Once we know the source of our intolerance, we're in a much better position to deal with it. However, there are times when we can't quite put our finger on the imprint that created our prejudices. Should this happen, we only need to acknowledge that we are intolerant and for our continuing peace of mind we need to let go of this attitude.

So what do we do?

We start by "acting as if" we were not intolerant—even though our feelings have not yet caught up with our actions. Underlying this leap of faith is the belief that if we had no prejudice of any kind there would be no desire to bad-mouth any person or institution. We'd be able to accept people and things just the way they are without feeling the need to display our dissatisfaction with them.

TODAY'S STEP: *I become willing to develop tolerance and acceptance of others.*

Day 25—VIRTUE FOR VIRTUE'S SAKE

"Life is so generous a giver but we, judging its gifts by their covering, cast them away as ugly or heavy or hard. Remove the covering and you will find beneath it a living splendor, woven of love, by wisdom, with power."   FRA GIOVANNI

Bitterness and righteous indignation are heavy loads to carry with us every day. Without realizing it, we fuel these fires by dwelling on the real—or imaginary—slights inflicted on us by others. For example, we point to snobbery and elitism as characteristic of certain social and financial groups, and we play this scenario over and over in our minds until it takes on enormous importance.

We fantasize a situation in which we pay them back in their own coin. We dwell on all sorts of "appropriate" punishment for the harm they've done us—an eye for an eye.

If these kinds of daydreams were productive, we'd probably advocate using fantasies of this sort as a recovery tool. However, they've proven to be just the opposite. They damage our growth and impair our feelings of self-worth.

If we add a corollary to the Golden Rule: "Do unto others as you would have others do unto you—but don't expect others to do unto you as you would do unto them," we begin to get the picture.

The way out of this negative loop is to try on a new behavior, experiment with virtue for virtue's sake, and behave in a principled manner, no matter how others may treat us. As we have said before, it isn't easy, but it's worth a try! After all, we've already made it to Step Six—something must be working.

TODAY'S STEP: *I am willing to be freed from bitterness, resentment, envy and the desire for revenge.*

Day 26—FROM SELF-PITY TO GRATITUDE

*"It's not a bad idea to get in the habit of writing
down one's thoughts. It saves one from having to
bother anyone else with them."*   ISABEL COLEGATE

We play out the "Poor Pitiful Pearl" and "Poor Pitiful
Paul" syndrome over and over again when we wallow in
the self-pity brought on by the sorry state of affairs in which
we find ourselves.

Self-pity is high on the list of nonproductive behaviors.
It depletes our energy and plunges us into such an apa-
thetic state that we're practically immobilized. We can
point, with accuracy, to the fact that we're in a pretty
negative place. No one would argue that our current op-
tions seem severely limited. So it seems that feeling sorry
for ourselves is a pretty reasonable reaction.

Here comes another bit of advice that may seem simplistic, or inconsequental. And once again, all I can say is: Give
it a try. We've found that it really works.

Simply start compiling a gratitude list for those things
we *do* have, rather than dwelling on what we lack. Making
a list doesn't mean just mentally trying to count what, if
any, blessings we might have. It means writing it out, just
as we did in our Fourth Step. The value of putting words
to paper has far greater impact than we expect, for it
underlines our resolve to release our self-will and judgment
and to allow ourselves to take the advice of others.

TODAY'S STEP: *I cultivate the habit of gratitude.*

Day 27—ONE HOUR AT A TIME

"We are here and it is now. Further than that all human knowledge is moonshine." **H.L. MENCKEN**

It's the doing, not the thinking, that brings results. Our faith in the process begins to solidify when our lives start taking a definite turn for the better. All of a sudden, the gap between where we are and where we want to be doesn't seem so vast. Finally, we have tangible proof that complete recovery is possible.

A very successful attorney told us this story about a day in which all sorts of stresses and adverse circumstances began to pile up.

"I set my alarm to go off every hour. When it rang, I immediately stopped what I was doing and made a phone call to either someone in my group, or a friend who was aware of what I was hoping to accomplish in my recovery process. If I couldn't reach someone, I went off by myself and did one of the guided imagery exercises I'd learned. I'd give myself five to ten minutes to really concentrate on the things I had going for me, or I'd meditate on serenity. Then I'd get back to whatever was at hand.

"Although my need for relief was running high, I found that by reducing the day to one hour compartments, I got done what I had to do, and made it through another day. What's more—and I think this was the most important part of the whole thing—I felt *good* about myself."

Today, we can take time to go off by ourselves and meditate on all the wonderful gifts we possess. We will not discount ourselves and we will think only positive thoughts.

TODAY'S STEP: *I can take care of myself in times of stress*

Step Six

Day 28—JUSTIFIABLE ANGER

*"I have learned silence from the talkative, toler-
ance from the intolerant, and kindness from the
unkind. I should not be ungrateful to those teachers."*
KAHLIL GIBRAN

In his book, *How to Stop Worrying and Start Living* Dale
Carnegie says: "When we hate our enemies, we give them
power over us—power over our sleep, our appetites and
our happiness. They would dance for joy if they knew how
much they were upsetting us. Our hate doesn't harm them
at all, but turns our days and nights into a hellish turmoil."

No matter how much harm we feel has been done to us,
and how much we feel our anger is justified, our job now
is to take our eyes off the microscope and pick up the
mirror. We are responsible for our own actions and reactions, we have no power over anyone else's actions or
emotions, nor do we want them living rent-free in our
heads. Lord knows, we have enough work to do on ourselves without muddying the water with other people's
behavior.

A woman told her sponsor a truly sad tale of disappointment and despair. She ended by saying: "You know, I feel
I've really been betrayed." "That's because you have been
betrayed," said her sponsor. "Now that your perception
has been validated, and your very understandable pain has
been acknowledged, it's up to you to accept that unpalat-
able truth, and get on with your business of making a new
life."

TODAY'S STEP: *I relinquish the gratification of justifiable
anger.*

Day 29—INAPPROPRIATE REACTIONS

*"Our consciences are littered like an old attic with
the junk of sheer conviction."*   WILFRED O. CROSS

Are there really certain personality traits that those of us
with compulsive/addictive natures share?

This subject has been open to debate for some time.
We feel that everyone has exactly the same menu of emotions. However, the more deeply we progress in our addiction, the more exaggerated some of these characteristics become.

For example, no one is particularly fond of having to
wait long periods of time for anything. Impatience and
frustration are natural reactions to having to stand too long
in a supermarket line; to being put on "hold" when making a business call; to sitting in a plane for more than an
hour because the flight hasn't been cleared for take-off.

However, the inability to endure any uncomfortable
feelings over even a short period of time is directly related
to the disorder we are now battling. Some of us become
angry, agitated and vocal. We create much more of a stir
than is appropriate to the situation. Others recede into
stony silence, which breeds indigestion and ulcers. Whatever the feelings, we push them to excess.

TODAY'S STEP: *Recognizing the defect of inappropriate
reactions, I can ask God to help remove them.*

Step Six

Day 30—TIME AS HEALER

"Time is a dressmaker specializing in alterations."
FAITH BALDWIN

Other personality characteristics that have been ascribed to compulsive/addictive personalities are: isolation, wishful thinking, sensitivity, perfectionism, impulsiveness and anxiety. Rather than indictments, we consider these qualities as guides to aid us in our pursuit of recovery.

If we did not use grandiosity as a shield to protect us from the criticism of others, would they see how really vulnerable we are?

Would self-pity really disappear if we didn't begin by thinking of ourselves as victims?

Like grandiosity, defiance has been our shield. Can we lower it? What if we dared come out of our shell and involve ourselves with others? Can we risk being rejected?

If we stopped dreaming that by some miraculous twist of fate we would become rich and famous, would life be worth living?

When we've worn our sensitivity as a badge of honor, wouldn't shedding it make us look too callous?

Could we release our need to be perfect without disappointing those who admire us?

If we curtailed our rash actions and impulsivity, would that make us look less "macho" or self-assured?

And how, in heaven's name, can anyone be free from anxiety?

The answer to all of these questions is: "Time."

TODAY'S STEP: *I accept that recovery takes time.*

Step Six

Day 31—WINDUP

"When you reach for the stars, you may not quite get one, but you won't come up with a handful of mud either."
LEO BURNETT

We've come a long way in our recovery process. We've discovered and uncovered the nature of our wrongs, shared them with another human being and are beginning to see our defects melting away.

We're aware that Steps Six and Seven require a great deal of effort and an enormous amount of trust. It's not easy to relinquish the habit patterns we've viewed as survival kits to a God we're not at all sure we understand.

But we are beginning to see results. And these results have become the beacon lights that will help guide us through the second half of our Twelve Steps.

In his book, *Prescriptions for Happiness*, Ken Keyes says: "Did all your uptightness, fear, anger, jealousy, worry, resentment, grief, irritation, and heartbreak solve your problems?"

The answer for all of us is a resounding "No." So let's continue to follow new patterns established in Step Six and uncover and discover more of those negatives we're turning into positives. Now we truly understand that the world hasn't been "doing it" to us—we've been "doing it" to ourselves. As we move ever more deeply into a new way of being, we know that turning over our character defects is the key to creating an increasingly productive life.

TODAY'S STEP: *I take pride in the amazing progress I have made with Step Six.*

Step Seven

STEP SEVEN

"Humbly asked Him to remove our shortcomings."

Steps Six and Seven work in concert. First, we become ready to have our defects and shortcomings removed, and then we put our money where our mouth is, by asking our Higher Power to take the lead in doing the job.

Humility, which essentially gives us the ability to learn, plays a major role in Step Seven. All the preceding steps have led to the uncovering and discovering of our defects. Now we're ready to discard them as part of our quest for recovery.

Our shortcomings are never more clearly defined than when we begin looking at them without guilt. When we accept responsibility for past actions, we need never feel these humiliations again. As we come to understand this, we become even more willing to examine the wreckage of our past, because we know we'll soon be done with it.

Day 1—KEEPING THE FAITH

"It's been my experience that folks who have no vices have very few virtues." ABRAHAM LINCOLN

In the Second Step we talked of being restored to sanity by a power greater than ourselves. In the Third, we made a decision to turn our will and our lives over to that power. In the Fifth, we admitted the nature of our wrongs to God. And in the Sixth, we announced our readiness for His intervention.

With the Seventh Step comes our true expression of faith. Now we must eliminate any remaining fantasy that we can really handle our own recovery. Without arrogance, we must ask His assistance in removing our shortcomings.

We've all been brainwashed by the good old American rallying cry that all we need to do is pull ourselves up by our bootstraps, dust ourselves off and make a brand-new start.

And this is true—to a certain extent. Certainly, our own efforts are a major factor in our recovery. And yet, without the help of a greater power, we'll find ourselves floundering in that same old rut we've worked so hard to escape. Our personal courage and drive are important assets, to be sure. But the moment we have doubts about the strength of the program and begin to believe, once more, in our own omnipotence, the downward spiral threatens once again.

TODAY'S STEP: *I will replace fear with faith.*

Day 2—HUMILITY IS NOT HUMILIATION

"Humility has its origin in an awareness of unworthiness, and sometimes too in a dazzled awareness of saintliness."
COLETTE

The word, "humbly," which appears in this step, makes some of us more than a little concerned that we're expected to abase ourselves in order to successfully accomplish its intent. Such is not the case, for what we're talking about here is humility—not humiliation.

Humility is the ability to perceive things as they really are, and to acknowledge truthfully where we stand in relation to them. Humility is neither groveling nor meekly bowing to the will of others, nor is it displaying false modesty about our attributes and abilities. It's rather like examining a grain of sand on the beach, contemplating how big we are in comparison, and then looking at the ocean and realizing how small we are from that perspective.

The qualities we tend to admire most in people are those of simplicity and naturalness. We're most comfortable with people who are up front about their likes and dislikes without being disagreeable; people who neither diminish nor overstate their abilities.

We seek this same kind of balance ourselves. And it is through working both Steps Six and Seven that we're able to achieve the kind of self-acceptance that translates into acceptance by others.

TODAY'S STEP: *I understand the true nature of humility and I can comfortably embrace it.*

Step Seven

Day 3—FALSE HUMILITY

"If you are reluctant to ask the way, you will be lost."
MALAY PROVERB

In the past, many of us developed techniques to escape the wrath of others. One convenient method was to take full blame for everything that happened in our past relationships, no matter how much blame may not have been ours.

We found this to be an excellent defense because, to a degree, it deflected the other person's anger, disappointment or criticism. By presenting ourselves as defenseless and vulnerable, it made it almost impossible for others to persist in their accusations. Most people find it difficult to hit someone who's already down.

But Step Seven clearly instructs us to let go of all these phony postures and artifices. We do this by learning to operate on a level where we not only acknowledge all our weaknesses and liabilities, but also no longer plead false modesty in denying those strengths, talents and assets with which we are endowed. We neither demean nor diminish our strengths, nor parade them in a boastful fashion. We do not deny our shortcomings or constantly draw attention to them. Our starting point is a realistic assessment of our current status.

TODAY'S STEP: *A genuine and balanced humility is my strength.*

Day 4—UNWILLINGNESS

"If you want a place in the sun, prepare to put up with a few blisters."
ABIGAIL VAN BUREN

By the time we arrive at Step Seven, we've undergone a great deal of self-evaluation and self-appraisal. Sometimes it feels as though more is being demanded of us than we're willing to give. We've accomplished so much by this point, why can't we just kick back and rest for a while? Besides, isn't this pretty redundant? Didn't we cover all this in Step Six?

Indeed, there are similarities. But Step Six emphasizes readiness, while Step Seven indicates willingness. And then there's that subtle difference between shortcomings and defects. But if we think of shortcomings as falling short of our capabilities, and realize that the removal of defects can be inhibited by lack of willingness, then the effectiveness of the partnership between these two steps becomes clearer.

This understanding is helpful right about now, when another defect tends to rise up and plague us—procrastination. This is a tremendously powerful habit that gets in the way of our letting go of old patterns and ideas. Procrastination tends to create inertia, which we then defend by saying we've surely worked hard enough already. In reality, though, what it does indicate is an unwillingness to persist in uncovering and discovering any more negative things about ourselves.

TODAY'S STEP: *I stop procrastinating and become willing.*

Step Seven

Day 5—THE VICTIM

"People who feel good about themselves produce good results." ANONYMOUS

Today's the day we need to remind ourselves that our inventory didn't simply uncover defects of character. It also revealed our positive side—the strengths that helped sustain us in those times when we felt we were victims of unfair treatment or unfortunate circumstances.

How often have we felt like the man beset with incredibly bad luck. Although he was a spiritual, ethical, moral man, he was cuckolded by his wife, cheated by his partner and humiliated by his children. As if that weren't enough, his house burned down, his business failed, his wife left him and his children stole his savings.

Despite all this misfortune, he went out in his field to pray, trying to keep his faith intact. He flung his arms in supplication and looked up at the sky. At that precise moment, a bird flew by and its droppings hit him squarely in the eye.

In utter defeat, the man wiped his eye, looked heavenward again, and cried, "Why God? Why me? For other people they sing!"

Unquestionably, we have suffered many bitter blows to our self-image. This is one of the reasons our compulsion held us so long in its grip. Whether this obsession was with people, places, things or substances, it created a definite erosion of our self-respect.

At this point in our program we need to decide whether we will continue to feel the victim, or whether we will use our new tools and new perspective, and walk away from those old hurts and attitudes once and for all.

TODAY'S STEP: *I let go of old hurts and misfortunes in order to build a new life.*

Day 6—HITCHING OUR WAGON TO OUR HIGHER POWER

"No man can think clearly when his fists are clenched."   GEORGE JEAN NATHAN

Our Higher Power has no interest in manipulating us like puppets on a string. True, the path has been laid out, and the guidelines defined, but each of us is unique, and each of us must find our own star to hitch our wagon to.

If we can believe that for all our differences, each of us represents one of the many faces of God, then we can accept the fact that we're not isolated creatures, apart and distinct from one another. Rather, we're human beings— each individualizing into the many. Knowing that we're related through our minds and souls, it becomes easier to shuck the elitism of "I" and start thinking in terms of "we." It also becomes easier to put our hands in God's hand, and trust that we will be led into healthy thinking and behavior.

Those of us who may be agnostics or atheists have been going along, up to this point, in reluctant agreement that a Higher Power does exist. However, hitting Step Seven may prove to be a stumbling block to some.

Once again, postponing judgment and "acting as if" prove to be effective recovery tools. These techniques can be invaluable as we put that Higher Power to the test by our willingness to seek guidance and direction through prayer, meditation and listening carefully to our intuition.

TODAY'S STEP: *However I define my Higher Power, I am ready to call on Him now.*

Step Seven

Day 7—HIGH HOPES

"Propaganda is the art of persuading others what you don't believe yourself."
ABBA EBAN

How do we go about asking our Higher Power for help? Meditation is one way. Holding a conversation—in our heads or in writing—is another. Then there's prayer. It need not be formal, although the getting-down-on-your-knees practice is favored by many, for it teaches us about the surprising power of humility. However we choose to pray, it is an expression of faith, and haven't we always heard that "faith can move mountains?"

As children we were told that if we wished upon the first star that shone in the evening sky, our wish would come true. If we didn't get our wish, we became doubting Thomases—but if our wish did come true, we became true believers. Later in life we began to recognize our power to turn our dreams into reality—if we held our hopes high and were willing to do the necessary footwork.

High hopes are what we need when we begin to work Step Seven. They're an indication of probable success in whatever goal we set for ourselves. The person who starts out with an optimistic approach tends to have an edge on those who harbor doubts and skepticism. This doesn't mean that those of us who approach this step with grave misgivings are doomed to failure. It simply means that the path becomes much easier when we're willing to put our beliefs and disbeliefs to the test.

The same ethic we explored in Step One—"surrendering to win"—begins to manifest when we do Step Seven in this spirit.

TODAY'S STEP: *I approach the healing of my shortcomings with high hopes.*

Step Seven

Day 8—GOOD THINKING

"Oh yet we trust that somehow good will be the final goal of ill."
                                    ALFRED LORD TENNYSON

In Step Seven we concentrate on ridding ourselves of old tapes, old ideas and old patterns. Our objective is to open our minds and emotions to new possibilities; to think of ourselves as competent human beings whose capabilities and talents are continually developing and emerging.

In order to make room for positive action and reaction, we first need to rid ourselves of the old behaviors and characteristics that stand between us and our growth and well-being. These stumbling blocks have been in place for some time and removing them can be a tough task. We fall into old habits and old ideas so automatically, that it takes constant reappraisal to see where we are: either stuck in the same old patterns or living ourselves into good thinking.

Projections of gloom and doom are the bogeymen in our recovery path, mostly because we've had little firsthand experience with the kind of life our program advocates. All of us fear the unknown. This is where a little faith and trust in those who have gone before us can be very handy. They've seen both sides and continue to assure us of the enormous benefits that lie just around the bend.

When we can remind ourselves that many of our past fears never materialized, then we can stop projecting negative thoughts and get on with the business of living today with a positive attitude.

TODAY'S STEP: *Today my attitude is positive and hopeful.*

Step Seven

Day 9—ENLIGHTENED RESTRAINT

"I am a kind of paranoiac in reverse. I suspect people of plotting to make me happy."

J.D. SALINGER

Most everyone agrees that good character is an asset, and that it is admirable to play by the rules. Yet most of us fall prey to that perversity of human nature that makes us occasionally bend the rules to suit our current needs and desires. Then we rationalize our own lapses by saying, "Everyone else does it. Why shouldn't I?"

It's when "occasionally" becomes "constantly" that we know we're in trouble. When all we can see is our desire for immediate satisfaction and gratification, it means we've opted to get what we want when we want it without giving any thought to the results of our actions. Impulsiveness— the proverbial trap of not looking before we leap—is hard to curb once we've let it become a habit with us.

But if we're to make any progress at all, we need to recognize each of these demanding impulses, and run it through our inner computer. This is partly to check on whether they're appropriate for our current resolve. It's also partly to tap into our Higher Power for guidance.

In the past we've been motivated by self-centered fear. The fear that we'd either lose something important to us, or fail to get or achieve something we wanted very badly.

Now, in Step Seven, we're able to release those fears and ask our Higher Power to help us to practice enlightened restraint.

TODAY'S STEP: *With the help of a Higher Power, I am able to control my destructive impulses.*

Step Seven

Day 10—ANALYZING FAILURE

"Failure is the condiment that gives success its flavor."
                                        TRUMAN CAPOTE

Why do we so often see ourselves as being the very personification of failure? What are the ingredients of failure? How do we analyze it?

F: Fear. Frustration. Futility. Falling short. Fallacies. Fallibility. Forgetfulness. False pride. Foul-ups. Frailty.

A: Anger. Animosity. Adversity. Arrogance. Arbitrariness. Antipathy. Anxiety. Alienation.

I: Indifference. Impulsiveness. Isolation. Ill will, Incapacity. Impatience. Impropriety.

L: Lethargy. Lying. Lechery. Laziness. Lust. Lugubriousness.

U: Unworthiness. Unctuousness. Undutifulness. Unfaithfulness. Unsociability. Uselessness.

R: Resentment. Regret. Remorse. Rationalization, Revenge. Rage. Rebellion. Recklessness. Regression.

E: Envy. Extremism. Egotism. Elitism. Emotionalism.

Some of these characteristics are probably very familiar to us. The goal of Step Seven is that having already identified them, we now petition our Higher Power for help in removing them.

TODAY'S STEP: *Because I call on my Higher Power for help daily, I turn failure into success.*

Step Seven

Day 11—TRIUMPH

"Not in the shouts and plaudits of the throng, But in ourselves, are triumph and defeat."

HENRY WADSWORTH LONGFELLOW

Now that we've looked at the components of failure, let's analyze some of the factors that make up triumph.

T: Teachability. Truthfulness. Tolerance. Temperance. Tact. Trustworthiness. Tenacity. Thankfulness. Thoughtfulness.

R: Rationality. Reasonableness. Responsibility. Reverence. Resourcefulness. Realism. Respect.

I: Integrity. Intelligence. Intuition. Introspection. Idealism. Illumination. Insight. Imagination. Initiative.

U: Understanding. Usefulness. Uncriticalness. Upstandingness. Undauntability. Unity.

M: Mastery. Motivation. Morality. Mental health. Maturity. Meditation. Modesty.

P: Patience. Persistence. Playfulness. Pleasantness. Passion. Perception.

H: Hopefulness. Heart. Humility. Happiness. Hard work. Humor. Harmony. Healthy habits. Help.

Just knowing the qualities that are needed for success is not sufficient. We have tried to emulate these qualities in the past, under our own power, and have fallen short time and again. It is only through the process of identifying defects that create failure, being willing to eliminate them, and calling on our Higher Power to help us, that we remove the barriers to success. That same Higher Power can help us strengthen the positive qualities we have just listed.

TODAY'S STEP: *With the help of my Higher Power, I can see that success is possible for me.*

Day 12—A LITTLE HELP FROM MY FRIENDS

"The Good Lord never gives you more than you can handle. Unless you die or something."

ANONYMOUS

In recovery, we need to discard old habits and replace them with new behavior. This process reminds us that we cannot think our way into good living, but we can live our way into good thinking.

It is strange that, despite repeated attempts to do a thing the way we believe it should be done, and our failure to reach our goal each time, we persist in performing the same actions over and over again. Repeated failure does smack of a certain degree of powerlessness. And this should be a clue. When this keeps happening, it shouldn't be too hard to admit that our lives are unmanageable.

Changing our behavior seems to be the most logical method to start changing our lives. Friends can be of great help to us at this point, particularly when they're willing to share their own experiences with us. It's very reassuring to know that we're not alone in our foibles, and that others who have gone before us have had an equally difficult and confusing time of it.

One of the values of a self-help group is that it allows us to talk openly with one another without fear of destructive criticism or banishment from the fellowship. The experience of receiving feedback that is neither judgmental nor punitive encourages us to open up about ourselves. It helps us identify the bypaths we traveled during the chronic progression of our addiction with greater insight and honesty.

TODAY'S STEP: *I know that my needs will be met; my group gives me loving support in removing my defects.*

Day 13—THE FORMULA

"If there is another way to skin a cat, I don't want to know about it."
                                                          STEVE KRAVITZ

As we're walking on a path through the woods, the light becomes dimmer and dimmer. Finally, we come to a place where there's absolutely no light at all. We hesitate. If we take one more step into the unknown will we fall into an abyss? Suddenly, from somewhere comes a voice: "Take the next step," it says. "Either God will put solid ground under your feet, or He will teach you to fly."

Fairy tale, fable, or parable, it's a lovely story about taking things on faith.

Despite the trial runs we may be giving our belief in a Higher Power, Step Seven may well push our limits. But be reassured there's no "hook" here, no hidden agenda—just the useful techniques of "acting as if." Each of us is free to believe or not to believe. But since the trial run seems to be paying off—for the moment—why not keep giving the formula a try.

TODAY'S STEP: *My Higher Power guides me as I enter into unfamiliar territory.*

Step Seven

Day 14—STRENGTH BOMBARDMENT

"Underneath this flabby exterior is an enormous lack of character."
OSCAR LEVANT

Do you remember doing the "strength bombardment" of our assets in Step Four? We used each letter of the alphabet to list all our strengths, capabilities and talents. Then we asked three persons close to us to write a list of the positive attributes they felt we possessed.

Just about now it might be very helpful to resurrect those lists and reappraise them.

We've spent the past six weeks or so trying to release some of our character defects and shortcomings. Although we've been reminded again and again not to overlook our assets, most of us tend to focus on our failings.

But how are we going to develop greater flexibility and creativity, and open up new possibilities in our lives if we aren't continually aware of our strong points? We need to have some balance. As important as it is to realistically assess our negatives, it's equally necessary to know we have enough positive attributes to make the struggle worth our while. We need to know we've got to break those old habits and self-defeating beliefs and behaviors, and to supplant them with a more positive plan for our future relationships and lifestyles.

Today we can affirm possession of everything we need to achieve our goals. We release any thoughts that may prevent us from succeeding, and express ourselves with confidence and determination.

TODAY'S STEP: *I can call on my strengths to help me transform my weaknesses.*

Day 15—THE DOCTOR'S STORY: PART I

"The only prison we need to escape from is the prison of our own minds."　　　ANONYMOUS

Steps Six and Seven create a high degree of anxiety in many of us who have been educated in parochial schools because we run into a conflict between what we've been taught about God, and how that fits with what the program seems to be telling us.

For the next few days we'd like to share what a recovering physician told us about his experience.

"In parochial school and throughout my Catholic education I'd always been taught that God Himself spent His time watching to see if I'd shaped up yet. That He'd given me everything I needed to be a better boy, young man, adult—and all I needed to do was try harder and I could be the person God intended me to be.

"Meanwhile, He was terribly disappointed in me—and in the world in general. In fact, He'd even sent a flood to wipe out the whole thing so we could start over and do it right. Not only that, God had originally put us up in an extremely fancy garden. But he'd gotten so mad when one of our personality defects showed up, that He kicked everybody out, slammed the door on the place, and nobody's heard of it since.

" 'If you'll just try harder, you can do better' was the message I got all the time I was going to Confession every Saturday, and during the time I was going to pharmacy school."

TODAY'S STEP: *I release any religious teachings that stand in the way of my Higher Power's help.*

Day 16—THE DOCTOR'S STORY: PART II

"Few things are harder to put up with than the annoyance of a good example."   MARK TWAIN

"For years I asked God to help me," our friend continued. " 'Help me! Help me! For God's sake, God, help me,' I cried. And I wondered why He refused to help me. Today, I realize He is not willing to help me do *my* will, but is entirely willing to have me help Him do His will. He's entirely willing to have me work for Him, but is not willing to work for me. He insists on being in charge—even when it comes to my defects, all of me, the good and the bad.

"He knows that if He helped me accomplish what I want accomplished—my will—I'd be grateful at the moment. But very soon, I'd be taking all the credit and thinking, 'Look what I've done!' My ego would take over. (Apparently His is bigger than mine.)

"The result is that, while I do have an initial choice, He is in charge of the outcome. He makes the final decision as to who I am. He created me, not only initially, but also currently—one day at a time, and on a moment-to-moment basis. My job is to not hate me for still having certain defects, but to love and tolerate me in spite of them. In fact, it's important that I get friendly with the defects that God has decided I should continue to have. He'll never take them all away—even if I ask."

TODAY'S STEP: *I willingly surrender my will and work to do God's will for me.*

Day 17—THE DOCTOR'S STORY: PART III

"Trust in God, but tie your camel."

PERSIAN PROVERB

There's a prayer in the *Big Book of Alcoholics Anonymous* that says, "My Creator, I am now willing that You should have all of me, good and bad. I pray that You now remove from me every single defect of character that stands in the way of my usefulness to You and to my fellows. Grant me strength, as I go out from here to do Your bidding. Amen."

Our physician friend says this prayer has great meaning for him. "I've also used several other prayers that have helped me through tough spots," he says. "First, there's the Serenity Prayer: 'God grant me the serenity to accept the things I cannot change, the courage to change the things I can, and the wisdom to know the difference.' And then there's the Third Step Prayer: 'God, I offer myself to Thee to build with me, and do with me as Thou will. Relieve me of the bondage of self, that I may better do Thy will. Take away my difficulties that victory over them may bear witness to those I would help of Thy power, Thy love, Thy way of life. May I do Thy will always.' I repeat these prayers every day, at least once. Some days more often."

TODAY'S STEP: *Prayer strengthens my communication with my Higher Power and shows me His will.*

Day 18—THE DOCTOR'S STORY: PART IV

"Some folks think they are thinking when they are only rearranging their prejudices." ANONYMOUS

"It's like everything else in life," says the doctor. "I can do anything I want, but God is in charge of the results. I can decide not to have a certain defect anymore, but God makes the final decision as to whether or not to remove it—and whether or not the removal is permanent or temporary.

"My program tells me that it's not up to me to root out my defects. Indeed, I'm powerless over them. It means I've been trying to exercise control over something over which I have no control. I can't control my personality the way I can change the program on my TV set. But I can make some choices. I can become willing to have God remove certain defects if I care to—but I, personally, can't root them out and throw them away willy-nilly.

"Even after doing all the steps, doing everything I could to rid myself of guilt, I still had my sense of guilt. It interfered with my self-esteem, with my growth, with my emotional recovery. Finally I decided that my sense of guilt was out of proportion to my actual guilt: that my sense of guilt was actually a defect of character. And I decided to use Steps Six and Seven on it."

The doctor said that he felt strange asking a God, whom he'd been taught wanted His subjects to feel guilt more than anything else, to remove his excessive sense of guilt. But it worked. And for the first time he began to enjoy life and the program.

TODAY'S STEP: *I take action to remove my shortcomings, but turn the result over to God.*

Step Seven

Day 19—WHAT WILL PEOPLE THINK?

"Anyone can do any amount of work, provided it isn't the work he's supposed to be doing at that moment."
ROBERT BENCHLEY

The story of the woman who commits suicide because her feelings of guilt and shame prevented her from reaching out for help is repeated far too often in compulsive/obsessive disorders. The fear of being ridiculed by other people is one of the most pervasive stumbling blocks to recovery.

Spouses who have stayed in sick or dysfunctional relationships are fearful they'll be perceived as spineless or weak if people knew what a sorry existence they'd been enduring. Many of them see separation or divorce as proof positive that they didn't have the chutzpah to straighten out their marital mess. On top of that, it looks as though they had very poor judgment to have chosen that particular spouse in the first place. Their rationale is: "There must be something wrong with *me* to have chosen that partner!"

Looking back, we have to admit that our dependence on the power of self-will and self-analysis has not worked. In fact, it's brought us nothing but pain and disillusionment. The only thing we can do at this point is to surrender our will and our lives to a power greater than ourselves to achieve a more balanced and satisfactory existence.

TODAY'S STEP: *Releasing all shame and guilt, I humbly ask for help.*

Day 20—BELIEF IN GOD

"How is it Lord, that we are cowards in everything save in opposing Thee?" ST. TERESA OF AVILA

"I cannot in all honesty say that I've been able to develop a belief in God," said the man. "I hear you folks talking about Him all the time as if you have a personal pipeline, and as if you're all in total agreement as to what He's like. I just don't buy it.

"Look, I'm not unintelligent. I know that there's a payoff to tapping into spiritual values. I know I'm missing something. But I refuse to be a phony and say I believe in something or someone when I don't. It seems to me that that kind of conformity doesn't jibe with the honesty which you tell me is one of the prerequisites for recovery."

It's not unusual to hear one of us saying something like this. But there's no need to try to convert anyone into accepting our individual understanding of God. As a matter of fact, we have no consensus about what God is or isn't.

Some people say "Take the O out of 'good' and you have God." Others say, "H.I.M. stands for 'Higher Intelligent Motives.'" It truly doesn't matter whether our belief is a profound or superficial one. "Acting as if" is sufficient—provided we do the footwork and follow the formula instead of altering the program to suit our individual specifications.

TODAY'S STEP: *When I lack faith, I simply act as if.*

Step Seven

Day 21—THE INNER CHILD

"Inch by inch, it's a cinch. But by the yard, it's very hard."
ANONYMOUS

The courage to accept that which we cannot change—to accept things as they are—is a vital ingredient of humility. The world we live in is not by any stretch of the imagination a sane one. Maintaining an inner calm when faced with the uncertainty and turbulence that surrounds us means we must develop a sense of self-acceptance. One that tells us that, despite outward conditions, things will work out as long as we continue on our chosen path.

We must be aware that it's not very likely that all our character defects will be removed. We're not aspiring to sainthood. We simply wish to exist in our world with reasonable comfort and contentment.

Learning to be gentle and patient with our inner child is one way of understanding our human frailties. There will always be frustrations, heartaches and disappointments. We'll act inappropriately at times. We will fall back into negative habit patterns. But through it all, rather than becoming impatient with what seems to be a disturbingly slow process of recovery, we'll begin to be amazed at the progress we've made.

We're not striving to present an image of perfection. We're simply and humbly asking that our shortcomings be removed.

TODAY'S STEP: *I am patient and loving with myself as my shortcomings are removed.*

Day 22—GUILT

"Better keep yourself clean and bright; you are the window through which you must see the world."
GEORGE BERNARD SHAW

When old habit patterns start to reassert themselves, we shouldn't panic. We need to be tolerant and gentle with ourselves. The patterns of a lifetime cannot be erased at once despite all our determination and resolve. It is essential that we accept these lapses, and treat ourselves as our own best friend. We certainly allow others leeway in their shortcomings and failings. We minimize their feelings of guilt and concern. But, when we commit the same offenses, we come down on ourselves like a ton of bricks.

We had no idea, at the onset of our problems, that we were embarking on a roller coaster ride to disaster. Certainly, we feel guilty for the havoc we have created, but it is essential that we realize that we were *not* guilty of intent to do harm to ourselves or others.

In the recovery process, responsibility, not guilt, is placed squarely on our shoulders, making us accountable for our actions and reactions. Now that we're free from the addictive process, we must resist any temptation to blame people or circumstances for our difficulties.

We repeat: *failure is not final.* It's simply missing the mark. And today we have the opportunity of adjusting our sights toward a more satisfactory goal.

TODAY'S STEP: *I accept full responsibility for my mistakes, and cease blaming others.*

Step Seven

Day 23—IF THERE'S ANYONE OUT THERE

"In Burbank there's a drive-in church called Jack-in-the-Pulpit. You shout your sins into the face of a plastic priest."   JOHNNY CARSON

"You know," said the speaker, "I've been around this program for over five years, and I'm just beginning to understand its incredible power. But I'm still not able to pray. I just don't feel comfortable in doing it. I'm fine when it comes to meditating. I hear what some of you say when you tell me that prayer is talking to God, and meditation is listening. But I don't seem to be able to tap into the same pipeline as you. That's not to say I don't have mental conversations with some power or being or presence. I just can't define what it is.

"When I first started the program I had no problem with using the group as my Higher Power. And I've always said the Lord's Prayer along with the group—but I say it more from rote and conformity than from belief. It's weird, I *do* have the feeling that I'm never alone. It's not a spooky feeling, but it's not a spiritual feeling either. It's just a comfortable sort of thing that makes me know I'm on the right track.

"So as far as the Seventh Step is concerned, I just threw it open to the universe. I said, 'If there *is* anyone out there, please help me get rid of this garbage—I can't seem to do it myself.' And it worked. I don't know how or why. I just know that it did."

TODAY'S STEP: *However dimly I comprehend it, a Higher Power is always with me.*

Day 24—SEVEN DEADLY SINS

"There are days when it takes all you've got just to keep up with the losers." ROBERT ORBEN

When we conscientiously practice humility, we're automatically getting rid of hurtful pride. When we develop our other positive talents and attributes, we're seeing to it that the other seven deadly sins bite the dust too.

As a result, it seems pretty logical that having asked God to remove our defects and shortcomings, we should concentrate on improving the attributes we *do* possess. When we dispel the negatives, the positives come to the fore.

Greed dissipates when we recognize it as a demand from our inner child to satisfy old unfulfilled needs for love and approval. Greed is finally erased when we learn to accept ourselves as worthwhile human beings who demonstrate self-love and self-approval, and covetousness disappears when we applaud the success of others.

Lust meets its nemesis when we accept our healthy sexual drive and no longer need to exploit or dominate our partners.

Patience and serenity diffuse anger. And our process helps us daily as we work to develop those qualities.

Gluttony—which can be equated with the craving for food, or power, alcohol, drugs or work—diminishes in intensity when we no longer need the cushion of excesses to define ourselves.

Envy is reduced to a normal desire for the good things in life as our ego demands lessen. We recognize that money, property and prestige are not the foundation for genuine self-approval.

And when sloth gives way to action we start "living our way into good thinking."

TODAY'S STEP: *I focus daily on improving the qualities of self-love and self-approval.*

Day 25—OUR ACT

"Nobody can be exactly like me. Sometimes even I have trouble doing it."　　　TALLULAH BANKHEAD

We've covered a lot of ground in these last few weeks. Interestingly, we find ourselves becoming more and more open-minded. We've rethought the value of clinging to characteristics that have brought pain to ourselves and others, and we've asked for help in getting rid of them.

However, we do not—and should not—seek perfection. We need to be satisfied with taking small steps toward recovery. We're beginning to stop sidestepping and evading responsibility for our actions. We're now convinced that only by honestly assessing and modifying our behavior can we restore any sort of balance in our lives.

"My whole personality," said an actress, "has been built around my caustic wit—my ability to squelch any kind of criticism. I've built a reputation on being brash, cynical and mouthy. If I suddenly started acting like a grown-up Shirley Temple, I'd probably never get another day's work. Is that what you expect me to do?"

No, certainly not. Many of us have developed an "act" that has served us well in our career or business. As long as that act isn't leading us around by the nose, and as long as it's not harmful to ourselves or others, it's perfectly appropriate for us to continue to use it. On the other hand, when it does cause us and others pain, we really need to think about letting it go.

TODAY'S STEP: *These days, I'm getting my act together by taking it off the road.*

Day 26—ACCEPTING THE UNACCEPTABLE

"Courage is simply the willingness to be afraid and act anyway." ANONYMOUS

Sometimes during the course of our lives we have to accept the unacceptable. This is particularly hard when we feel that we've been doing all the right things and don't deserve to be faced with unhappy circumstances. But life is never predictable. There are always twists of fate that leave us feeling helpless and abandoned.

These are the times when our resolve weakens; when we're tempted to backslide into behavior that used to bring us temporary relief. Despite all our hard-won gains, we feel totally impotent in the face of what is happening. This is when the three most threatening words in the recovery process spring to our lips: "What's the use?"

We didn't develop our problem overnight. And it won't disappear overnight. When we hit the hard places in life, we have to remember to be kind to ourselves. In recovery that means sticking to the program no matter what happens, and taking things one day at a time.

As Ken Keyes says in his book, *Prescriptions for Happiness:*

You'll have to learn to keep your fingers off that emergency button in your mind that keeps you wound up so tight inside. You'll have to tell your mind that what looks like a catastrophe just ain't so! There are many other people who are emotionally accepting what you're making yourself unhappy about. If they can accept the unacceptable, perhaps you can, too.

TODAY'S STEP: *When setbacks happen, I work even harder to accept the unacceptable.*

Step Seven

Day 27—A NEW SCRIPT

"An appeaser is one who feeds a crocodile—hoping it will eat him last." WINSTON CHURCHILL

Because of long-ingrained habit patterns, we tend to play old problems over and over. This happens almost automatically when we walk into familiar situations. Like actors in a play, we pick up our script and respond, as if on cue, to the drama that's being played out.

But by this point in the recovery process we're pretty familiar with our own predictable behavior patterns. We know how we tend to act and react. We need not be discouraged when an old script pops up. We simply need to write a new one that takes our new goal into account. And we need to practice it, even when we feel fearful about how others will react. Fear accompanies any change in attitude or behavior. But have we become so dependent on how others perceive us that we hesitate to make any changes in the old script? Considering where we are today, that doesn't seem likely any longer.

However, the sooner we can identify the signs that we're slipping back, the sooner we can start implementing our new script. We simply need to make sure we're more focused on self-acceptance than on trying to impress others. When these signals come up, we can call on our Higher Power once again for help in removing our shortcomings.

TODAY'S STEP: *Today I quickly recognize the signals of old patterns and I ask my Higher Power to help me take action against them.*

Step Seven

Day 28—FROM WORRIES TO MIRACLES

"Lead me not into temptation; I can find the way myself."
RITA MAE BROWN

When we humbly ask to have our defects and shortcomings removed, we feel as though we're standing alone on a windy hill stripped naked. An onrush of worries descends on us, for we have divested ourselves of many characteristics that used to be our coping mechanisms.

Typical of these worries are: How will I be able to face my coworkers? How will I get out of debt? Who's going to believe I've really turned over a new leaf? What if I can't handle sex comfortably? What if I've done permanent damage to myself? What if I can't form a decent relationship? What if I lose my job? What if my kids won't be able to forgive me? What if the Feds nail me on income tax evasion? What if I end up in jail? What if I lose my home? What if my traffic tickets catch up with me? What if I lose my driver's license?

How we wish there was some way to prove to you in advance that everything will turn out all right, provided you stay close to your program and the principles it entails. Although thousands of us have had just such experiences, it still doesn't seem logical that such miracles occur on a regular basis.

Today we can replace all our fears with faith. Since fear and faith cannot peacefully coexist we can choose to operate in a fashion that denies fear and encourages faith.

TODAY'S STEP: *God grants me the serenity to let go of my fears.*

Day 29—DON'T WORRY—BE HAPPY

"You have to believe in happiness or happiness never comes."
                                    DOUGLAS MALLOCH

One of the most popular songs of the late Eighties had the optimistic refrain: "Don't worry—be happy."

The message was that if we'd just follow this philosophy everything would turn out all right. That's very encouraging. But in the light of the mess we're cleaning up at the moment, this seems to be an idle promise.

Yet, yesterday, we said that thousands of us have experienced just such miracles. We don't want to imply that simply by surrendering to the Third Step, and by conscientiously applying the Sixth and Seventh Steps, that all our difficulties will evaporate and that we will walk in the sunshine of the spirit. It takes time and a lot of hard work on our part to get there.

We learned that we had to work through, and see through, all the roadblocks that stood in our way on the path to recovery. We had to face up to the havoc we had created. Slowly, sometimes painfully, we had to start our whole life anew, without any concrete evidence or assurance that the outcome would be favorable. We were like strangers in a strange land who were just beginning to get a glimmer of the customs and the language of our new environment. And yet, Bobby McFarin's musical advice still holds true.

TODAY'S STEP: *As I work Step Seven, I grow in my capacity to be happy.*

Day 30—BAD TURNS TO GOOD

"We possess only the happiness we are able to understand."　　　MAURICE MAETERLINCK

In this program—as in life—we've found that nothing in our past was a wasted effort. Over time, we realize that the seemingly bad frequently turn out to be a force for good. Our many negative memories have transformed themselves into guidelines pointing us toward a more positive approach to living.

Many among us have been faced with bankruptcy; with loss of spouse, children, or home; with loss of job; loss of car; loss of prestige and social standing in our community—even with imprisonment and confinement.

But despite these losses, *all* of us who have clung to our program, and whenever possible to our group, have found ourselves in a better position than we've ever occupied before. We've been able to clean the slate, write a new script and settle into a comfortable position in which we're able to love ourselves and to accept ourselves for all that we are.

We certainly do not discount the material possessions or positions of prominence that many of us enjoy. But we've learned that these things are not the top priorities on our list of happiness-producing factors.

TODAY'S STEP: *My life is being transformed by my Higher Power and me along with it.*

Step Seven

Day 31—MOVING RIGHT ALONG

"You know more than you think you do."
DR. BENJAMIN SPOCK

We've done it!

We've come through Steps Six and Seven with a real sense of accomplishment and no visible scars.

We've uncovered, discovered and discarded the character defects and shortcomings that have been our main obstacles to recovery. Now we're readying ourselves to further that process of recovery in our next two steps.

It's very encouraging to realize that we're more than halfway through our journey. And we're beginning to see our efforts bear fruit. We've examined some of our biases and prejudices and we've been able to discard many of them. Some we've elected to hold onto, for we feel they still serve our purpose. We need to keep reminding ourselves that no one else is going to grade our papers. Each of us makes that judgment individually.

Whether our sense of spirituality is rooted in a religious ethic or our own individual path, or whether we've simply complied with the suggestion that we turn our life and will over to some power greater than ourselves—the reality is that we *have* done it.

While it's still a little early for us to project what long-term benefits will accrue as a result of our work, we can certainly feel a renewed sense of self-approval.

TODAY'S STEP: *I am grateful for the removal of my shortcomings; I love myself for the progress I am making.*

Step Eight

STEP EIGHT

"Made a list of all persons we had harmed, and became willing to make amends to them all."

So starts the third phase of cleaning house. We've made our inventory, assessed our defects, shortcomings and wrongs. We've been ready to have them removed. We've humbled ourselves to ask for help in their removal.

Now comes another inventory of sorts. Not like the one in which we uncovered and discovered our own failings. Rather, this one is a list of those people in our lives who have been adversely affected by the chronic progression of our disease.

This list is not necessarily limited to the significant others in our lives. It also needs to include those people with whom we've had social or business dealings and who have suffered as a result of our actions.

It's important to include those whom we have defamed by gossip, and those we have cheated, humiliated, scorned and betrayed. We will be scrupulous in our appraisal, for the benefits we will derive as a result of this action are enormously rewarding.

Step Eight

Day 1—HOW TO BEGIN

"Intelligence is not to make no mistakes, but quickly to see how to make them good."

BERTOLT BRECHT

To get a toehold on how to proceed with this step, it is helpful to review Steps Four and Five. Our list of resentments clearly indicates that there are many people with whom we need to set the record straight. Despite the fact that we've admitted our wrongs to God, to ourselves and to another human being, this is the first time in our program that we're actively preparing to acknowledge to others the harm we've done.

The interpersonal difficulties we've had in the past were not necessarily all our fault. Nevertheless, in Step Eight, it's our own house that needs putting in order. Therefore, no matter what part others played in the situation, we need to focus only on ourselves and our own responsibility. We derive no value at all from clinging to the memory of personal slights. Nor can we afford such rationalizations as, "I would never have behaved that way if she hadn't started it," or, "He asked for it. He was so damned self-righteous!"

In this Step, we're trying to free ourselves from the wreckage of our own mistakes. Since we're also seeking forgiveness for the unkind, unfair and untrue things we've done in the past, our best bet is to clean up our side of the street.

TODAY'S STEP: *In reviewing my inventory, I acknowledge that I have harmed others.*

Day 2—TRANSFORMING OUR RESENTMENTS

"The Haves and the Have Nots can often be traced to the Dids and the Did Nots."

ANONYMOUS

In Step Eight we keep coming around full circle to our number one difficulty—resentment. Somehow it seems to recur with even greater intensity as we make our amends list. It's so hard to let go of the feelings that others deserve to be punished for their actions toward us. Getting to the point where *we're* willing to make amends to *them* is a real exercise in self-control.

The whole purpose of the steps that preceded Step Eight, as well as those that follow it, is to make us feel at one with ourselves. "Enlightened self-interest" is the name of the game of recovery, for until we put our own house in order, we won't be able to make any real progress.

This step doesn't suggest that we become meek, fawning or subservient. On the contrary, our strength and resolve grow enormously when we do not immediately react to negativity or even hostility from those we approach as we follow the dictates of Step Eight. It's not their mess that we're trying to clean up. It's ours. No matter how negatively they may respond to our efforts to set the record straight, we must remember that we're not setting out to seduce them into forgiveness or absolution. We're simply clearing away what we frequently refer to as "the wreckage of our past."

TODAY'S STEP: *Making amends increases my own sense of self-worth.*

Day 3—AMBIVALENCE

"The fundamental defect of fathers is that they want their children to be a credit to them."

BERTRAND RUSSELL

Often the most difficult task we face in Step Eight is making amends to a parent.

What mixed emotions we all have about this!

Many men will say they never seemed to be able to cut the mustard as far as their fathers were concerned. Nothing they ever did was good enough. And their fathers never really demonstrated their love for them.

Many women, on the other hand, experience difficulties with their mothers. Sometimes this difficulty stems from the mothers and daughters competing for the attention or affection of the husbands/fathers.

The normal process in growing up is to leave our parents' home and make our own way in the world. However, for some of us, the umbilical cord has never been severed. We continue to behave as if we were still under our parents' control and responsible to them for all we do.

Even if we've become successful in our own right, we continue to be deeply affected by their opinion of us, and we're constantly seeking their applause and approval. We vacillate between love and resentment for them because although we need them, we resent our dependency.

TODAY'S STEP: *I examine my relationships with my parents fearlessly and without blaming.*

Day 4—WRITING A LETTER

*"An ounce of blood is worth more than a pound of
friendship."*   SPANISH PROVERB

Step Eight tells us we must become willing to make amends
to the people on our list, and Step Nine brings us out of
the passive and into the active phase of our recovery process. But, for the moment, what we really need to do is
some soul-searching about why we need to make these
amends, and the possible benefits we may derive from
doing so.

Yesterday, we suggested parents as probable candidates
to head our list. However, many of us no longer have a
living father or mother, although we still carry an enormous
amount of guilt over how we behaved toward them.

A wonderful solution was shared by a member of a
self-help group who said: "The only way I could get rid of
all that residual guilt and anguish was to write a letter to my
dad, seal it and toss it into the fireplace. In it, I told him
how much I truly loved him, and how he had always been
there whenever I needed him. I also told him how sorry I
was for having lied to him, stolen from him and disparaged
him in front of my friends because he was not successful
enough to satisfy my ego needs.

"Then I promised him that I'd do some nice, helpful
things for older people whenever I could. I also promised
to do those things silently and in his name. Then I felt
better."

TODAY'S STEP: *Even if it is no longer possible to be in
touch, I find a way to express my amends to those I have
harmed.*

Step Eight

Day 5—HOW WE'VE HARMED OTHERS

"We act as though comfort and luxury were the chief requirements of life, when all we need to make us really happy is something to be enthusiastic about."
ANONYMOUS

Some of us had startling revelations when we did the exercise in which we evaluated the payoffs we experienced from our character defects. Now, if we look at those defects—this time to assess how they affected others—we'll find that our list of amends will start to grow.

For instance: How did our depressions affect our family, business associates, friends and neighbors? What impact did our lying have on them?

What about unfaithfulness, reckless handling of money, excesses of food and drink, being judgmental, unreasonable expectations, sexual demands? Indifference? Dependency? Secrecy? Procrastination? Neglecting health problems? Selfishness?

We've tried to convince ourselves that our attitudes and behavior really harmed no one but ourselves. But as we really begin to dig, we find that we've only looked at the tip of the iceberg. The more we probe, the more we realize we have to probe. Since no human being exists in a vacuum, it would be an impossibility not to affect others by our deeds, our moods and our demands.

TODAY'S STEP: *In honestly reviewing my character defects, I add to my list of amends.*

Day 6—MATTERS OF PROPERTY

"Income tax returns are the most imaginative fiction being written today."   HERMAN WOUK

Once we've covered all the financial areas where amends are called for, we need to see where matters of property have been affected. These can include places of employment, business and social activities, as well as the manner in which we treat both public and private facilities.

Have our actions caused damage or property loss to others when we have carelessly (or sometimes willfully) defaced or vandalized public buildings or real estate belonging to private parties?

Have we been responsible for automobile or recreational vehicle accidents in which others have been injured?

Whether we owned our own home or rented from others, have we allowed the place where we live to have become so unkempt or seedy that it reduced property values or became a health hazard to others?

Have we been careless with cigarettes and burned holes in furnishings or clothes? Have we failed to do an honest day's work, or have we collected sick-time pay when we were simply goofing off? Have we failed to follow through on a commitment that caused our company and/or others to suffer financial losses? Have we made promises to help or support a cause and then failed to fulfill our obligation to do so?

As we search our conscience, we will certainly find many more instances where we need to set the situation right: where we must do whatever is possible to make restitution.

TODAY'S STEP: *I honestly examine the ways I have caused material loss and/or harm to others.*

Day 7—MATTERS OF PRESTIGE

*"I have never seen a greater monster or miracle
than myself."*
MICHEL DE MONTAIGNE

Today we need to look more closely at how morality enters
into the blueprint for making amends. And this brings us
into the area of "omissions and commissions."

• Have we been unfaithful to the significant others in
our lives?

• Have we dealt in character assassination against someone we know?

• Have we been so self-obsessed that we've failed to
meet the needs of our spouse? Our lover? Our parents? Our
siblings? Our friends?

• Have we been a parent who has not been sensitive to
the needs of our children? Have we ruled them by emotional blackmail? Have we withheld love and approval?
Have we not been there for them when they needed us?

• Have we been so preoccupied in furthering our own
social or business careers that everyone else must take
second place on our priority list?

• Have we been demanding? Critical? Patronizing? Un-
truthful? Self-serving?

As we answer these questions on our written inventory
of amends (for it must be written—just like our Fourth
Step), we will probably discover even more incidences
where money, property and prestige were the motivating
factors for our old behavior.

TODAY'S STEP: *I uncover ways the need for prestige has led
me to wrongdoing.*

Day 8—THE COURAGE TO MAKE AMENDS

"Courage is to feel the daily daggers of relentless steel and keep on living." DOUGLAS MALLOCH

Someone once said that we come into this world like a clean sheet of paper, and that everyone we meet scribbles on us. This may well account for the part of us that feels victimized by circumstances beyond our control.

As we pursue Step Eight and write our own findings on paper, we become more and more aware of our own culpability. And yet, we also begin to realize that when we face up to our problems we can evoke skills and talents we didn't know we had. When we go deep inside ourselves, we find that we *do* possess the courage to face those to whom we have done harm. We also know, that having aligned ourselves with a power greater than ourselves, we have an ever-present support system to bolster our resolve.

As we progress, we can define more and more clearly how we were drawn into our dependency. With hindsight, we can identify the attitudes and actions that catapulted us into this downhill run. We can track how one act led to the next. One lie led to the next. One disaster led to the next. Until, at last, we were forced to realize that we were caught in a web of such tenacity that it was impossible to find a way out by ourselves.

The old adage "forewarned is forearmed" now becomes a vital tool in preventing us from falling back into old habit patterns.

TODAY'S STEP: *With the support of the group and my Higher Power, I face my amends with courage.*

Step Eight

Day 9—DEPRESSION

"The lowest ebb is the turn of the tide."

ANONYMOUS

As we resurrect past situations, and the people who were involved with us, many of us begin to reexperience old depressions.

But now, we can begin to look at our depressions in a different light. Not so much from the standpoint of who or what caused them, but rather what we gained from them. As we make our list of those we've harmed, we can also think about the payoffs we experienced by having depressions. There always has to be a payoff in any continuing behavior. True, it might be a negative payoff, but it does serve a purpose.

One woman reported that migraine headaches were her payoff. It took her a long time to figure out how something that painful could work to her advantage, but she finally got it. Whenever she had a migraine, she was forced to retire to a dark room where she was unable to tolerate any sounds, sights or smells. She might stay there for a day or more in complete seclusion until the pain and nausea had subsided enough for her to emerge.

The payoff was, of course, that during the headache episode no one could expect her to do anything. Hence, she was not only freed from responsibility, but no one had the heart to confront her when she was in such obvious pain.

TODAY'S STEP: *I see clearly the payoff in my depressions and other difficulties.*

Day 10—RISKING OURSELVES

*"It's O.K. to ask dumb questions. It's easier than
facing up to dumb mistakes."* ANONYMOUS

Very often we experience uneasiness and a sense of helplessness as we pursue our list of persons to whom we have
done harm. This is because it takes a great deal of courage
to face up to our own shortcomings.

A copy of a poem which appeared in a "Dear Abby"
column might be helpful at this point.

To laugh is to risk appearing the fool.
To weep is to risk appearing sentimental.
To reach for another is to risk involvement.
To expose your ideas, your dreams, before a crowd,
    is to risk their loss.
To love is to risk not being loved in return.
To live is to risk dying.
To believe is to risk failure.
But risks must be taken, because the greatest hazard
    in life is to risk nothing.
The people who risk nothing do nothing, have
    nothing, are nothing.
They may avoid suffering and sorrow, but they
    cannot learn, feel, change, grow, love, live.
Chained by their attitudes, they are slaves; they have
    forfeited their freedom.
Only a person who risks is free.

Our responsibility is to ourselves. By accepting the need
to end the qualms of conscience caused by our behavior
toward others, we can face ourselves with affection and
approval.

TODAY'S STEP: *The risks I take in making amends pay off
in terms of better relationships.*

Step Eight

Day 11—HURT FEELINGS

"Nature couldn't make us perfect, so she did the next best thing. She made us blind to our faults."

ANONYMOUS

One of the most difficult hurdles in Step Eight is to overlook the harm others have done to us in order to concentrate on our own responsibilities.

True, since we were very small, others have had the capability of hurting our feelings. And when we start making our list of those we've harmed, we understandably argue that they also did harm to us. We cite their superior or patronizing attitudes, their criticism, and—worst of all—their abandonment of us.

Of course it hurts to experience this kind of behavior from others. Yet it's often not so much their actions, as it is our reactions that account for our feelings.

Step Five had us talking about our defects of character, our shortcomings and the nature of our wrongs. When we did this, it became fairly obvious that those wrongs affected many persons in our lives.

So, despite our own hurts, we must admit—were the situations reversed and we were on the receiving end of some of those old scenarios—we would probably have reacted just as negatively as they did.

TODAY'S STEP: *I put myself in others' shoes and see my actions from their point of view.*

Day 12—OLD MEMORIES

"The doctor can bury his mistakes, but an architect can only advise his clients to plant vines."

FRANK LLOYD WRIGHT

Do you ever get a sinking feeling in the pit of your stomach when some episode—long forgotten—rises up and hits you right between the eyes?

Our "forgetter" is suddenly overpowered by the memory of a situation or an incident in which our performance was less than exemplary. When this happens, it usually triggers memories of a whole sequence of similar actions or occurrences.

And these memories, in turn, give rise to greater feelings of shame and hopelessness. This is when we need to be reminded that this is not a negative development; it's exactly the opposite.

The ability to feel shame is a clear indication that our finer nature is coming to the fore. It means that our present thinking and attitudes have developed to such an extent that we're highly unlikely to behave the way we used to in the past.

The whole intent of this step is to help us understand that the nature of our disorder made it impossible for us to behave in any other way than we did. But, we need never experience those negative feelings again—provided we adhere to our program and the principles it teaches us.

When we think of the mistakes we have made as stepping-stones to learn new ways to live, we can stop dwelling on the past and look forward to the future.

TODAY'S STEP: *I gain the courage to remember and to learn from my past.*

Day 13—THE HOME GROUP

"You only live once, but if you do it right—believe me, that's enough." FRED ALLEN

Personal stories give us greater insight not only into the personal meanings of each step, but also into the results that occur when we do them. The dynamic of sharing experience, strength and hope with others adds immeasurably to our own sense of belief and relief. These, and other benefits seem to multiply when we align ourselves with a "home group"—the self-help fellowship we attend on a regular basis, and in which we openly participate.

When we hear others admitting that they had to practice humility in order to make their list, we can more readily see why this is a requisite for us, too. When we are told by a group member we admire that this step shows courage and dedication, we feel more inclined to tackle it than when we felt it was demeaning and fawning. The more we hear others admitting their own reluctance, their fears, their unwillingness or their skepticism, the easier it becomes for us to proceed. Their stories reassure us that we are not lacking in commitment or character.

When someone who has been badly treated by a former spouse, or abused by a parent, or eased out of a business partnership tells us why they put those very people on their list to make amends to, we become a little more convinced that there is both power and purpose in this exercise.

TODAY'S STEP: *The candor and support of my home group gives me the courage to face my amends.*

Step Eight

Day 14—WORKING THE LIST

"From the cowardice that does not face new truths. From the laziness that is contented with half-truths. From the arrogance that thinks it knows all truth. Good Lord, deliver me." **KENYAN PRAYER**

Some of us began our list with five or six people who had been negatively affected by our actions in the past. Think about them for a minute. Did we choose these particular people because they were the ones with whom we were the least personally involved? Did this give us the chance to gradually work ourselves up to finally confronting the people with whom we have been the most intimate?

Others of us have felt that we wanted to tackle the hardest ones first, to clear the air with those whom we were most deeply involved. Once we have squared things with them, their support could prove to be of great help as we pursue the remainder of our list.

The ghosts of our past lurk on the periphery of our consciousness. The sooner we put all those old shameful and humiliating memories to rest, the better we will begin to feel about ourselves.

The practice of making amends doesn't simply mean we face the people on our list, make our apologies and consider the deed done. We need to give careful thought to how we approach each person and how we set things as right with them as we can.

TODAY'S STEP: *I give careful thought to the people on my amends list and how to approach them.*

Step Eight

Day 15—EXPANDING OUR LIST

"It is easier to do a job right than to explain why you didn't."   ANONYMOUS

We analyzed our defects of character in Steps Four, Five, Six and Seven. Now let's go back and take a look at them. As we think about each of those shortcomings, let's consider the effect they might have had on others.

This exercise allows us to define the exact nature of our wrongs more clearly. It also gives us a better sense of how we need to approach those persons.

For example, if we see procrastination as one of our character defects, we try to identify those who might have been negatively affected by this failing. It might be a co-worker, someone from whom we borrowed money, someone who depended upon us to fulfill an obligation.

As we review our previous step work, we begin to find people, long forgotten, creeping into our awareness. While we're not seeking out casual occurrences and chance encounters, or being overscrupulous, we are attempting to be as thorough as we can in identifying those to whom amends are due.

TODAY'S STEP: *I courageously reexamine each character defect to see how others might have been harmed by it.*

Day 16—AMENDS TO OUR CHILDREN

"Children have never been very good at listening to their elders, but they've never failed to imitate them." JAMES BALDWIN

Today it might be well for those of us who are parents to consider how our children have been affected by our addiction or compulsion. Much too often, we forget to put them on our list of persons to whom we owe amends. We rationalize that, after all, our behavior in recovery will certainly be amends enough.

If they're young, we say they're probably not old enough to comprehend what our disease is all about. If they're grown and away from home, we argue that they were simply on the periphery of all our troubles. We don't need to burden them with unnecessary emotional disclosures.

We have never been more mistaken. Children, regardless of their age, should be high on our list of amendees.

True, actions speak louder than words, and our actions have most certainly changed, but verbalization is an important component in fulfilling the intent of Step Eight. In all probability, one of the greatest legacies we can leave our children is the knowledge that their parents have been caught in the clutches of a serious disorder, but that they were able to face the challenge and overcome it. It tells our children that they too have it in their genes to turn failure into success.

TODAY'S STEP: *In making full amends to my children, I brighten their future and mine.*

Day 17—FINDING A NEW SOURCE OF APPROVAL

*"Forgiveness is the answer to the child's dream of
a miracle by which what is broken can be made
whole again, what is soiled is again made clean."*
                                      DAG HAMMARSKJÖLD

When we were very young, we learned by imitation. We
were most apt to be influenced by our peers and those
self-discovered idols whose approval we wanted more than
anything else in the world. When we grew up, we still
carried with us these same emotions. Our whole lives have
been shaped by the dictum: "What will people think?"

Now we're coming face-to-face with those same people
whose opinions we've valued so highly. It's a difficult challenge.

Although Steps Eight and Nine are incredibly difficult,
they have enormous power. Once we've cleared away the
wreckage of our past behavior, we find that we can walk in
dignity and freedom. Once we've wiped the slate clean, we
need never look over our shoulder to see if *they* are out to
get us. Our secrets are no longer lurking in the wings, ready
to be discovered and exposed.

Once done, Steps Eight and Nine open up a whole new
vista of comfort. We truly feel as if the weight of the world
had finally been taken from our puny shoulders. We get in
touch with our own self-acceptance. We experience self-
approval.

TODAY'S STEP: *I make amends to others, not for their
approval but for my own growth.*

Day 18—GENERATION GAP

"There was a time when we expected nothing from children but obedience, as opposed to the present, when we expect everything of them but obedience."

ANATOLE BROYARD

Making amends across the generation gap—in both directions—can be quite daunting. Because misunderstandings are so easy, we have to consider the other person's point of view very carefully before we begin.

People who were born before 1945 came into a world without nuclear weapons, credit cards, polio shots, frozen food, contact lenses, television sets, SSTs, radar, plastic, laser beams, pantyhose, electric blankets, ballpoint pens, clothes dryers, Xeroxes, or wash-and-wear clothes. Man had not yet walked on the moon, artificial hearts were unheard of and computers were only space-age projections. There were no sex changes, gay rights, desegregation, meaningful relationships, or house husbands, and society did not approve of liberated women. Coke was a soft drink, pot was something you cooked in, and AIDS were helpers in the principal's office.

These are but a few of the changes that have occurred with lightning rapidity in a few short decades. This explains, in part, the reason for the great divergence of attitudes and standards across the generations. Older people need to make allowances for the liberalization of traditional customs and ideas. And younger people need to understand the basis for some of the biases they see in older folks. This is why our list must take into consideration the attitudes and beliefs of those to whom we're attempting to make amends.

TODAY'S STEP: *In making amends, I put myself in the shoes of those older or younger than myself.*

Day 19—MAKING AMENDS

"I never did give anybody hell. I just told them the truth and they thought it was hell."

HARRY S TRUMAN

Our resistance to making amends decreases in direct proportion to our growing understanding and acceptance of the reason behind this step.

Certainly we want to set things right with others, but more important we want to set things right with *us*. The entire program has just such intent. To set things right with us.

Although Steps Eight and Nine were not designed to make others feel better, we know for a fact that in most cases they do. The true intent of these two steps is to create a very workable formula for us to apply as part of our overall recovery plan.

Our wishful thinking takes flight in hoping that once we have committed ourselves to recovery, our slate will be wiped clean. It is as if some benign force will make all those missteps of the past disappear. The bad news is that that will not be the case.

The very good news is that once we have swept away all this painful debris, we never have to contend with it in our life again. This is not to infer that we will emerge from our Twelve Step experience as whole and perfect human beings, immune to errors and missteps.

What it *does* mean is that having cleaned our slate, we can avoid that behavior in the future which created our past dilemma.

TODAY'S STEP: *My commitment to setting things right grows daily.*

Day 20—IT'S IN THE DOING

"There's no point in burying a hatchet if you're going to put up a marker on the site."

SYDNEY HARRIS

We cannot paint life by the numbers. There's no way to plot and plan in advance how people will react to our attempts to make amends. Which is just fine because the real issue here, is not how they will respond to us, but the absolute necessity of our going through with this exercise no matter how uncomfortable it may be.

Our experience tells us that when we're truly sincere about admitting our part in the difficulties we've had with others, they're generally most receptive to our willingness to try and repair the harm we have caused.

There are, of course, those who have been so deeply hurt by our past actions that they turn a deaf ear to us. It's a given that we may have to win back trust from others. They've been through many disappointments because of us. Often, they've been so deeply affected by our behavior that they have more faith in our disorder than they do in our ability to get well and stay well.

Despite our negativity and fear about how we think some of them may react, it really is essential to put them on our list. We must commit ourselves to be willing to make amends to them. It will do us little good to skip over certain people because of our personal dislike of them. Our list must be comprehensive.

TODAY'S STEP: *I make amends for my own sake and let go of others' responses.*

Step Eight

Day 21—OLD LIES

"One of the most striking differences between a cat and a lie is that a cat has only nine lives."

MARK TWAIN

Because of our disease, lying became so much a way of life for many of us, that sorting out what was real and what was fantasy can be a Herculean task. Part of the difficulty is that we convinced ourselves that many of the tales we told were really true. This honest self-deception becomes a real stumbling block when we're trying to sort out the people to whom we owe amends. We persist in seeing things as we fantasized them, rather than as they actually were.

Lying became an escape mechanism in our former lifestyle. It was a survival technique developed to protect us from the onslaught of criticism and abandonment. One falsehood would lead to the next and the next. Finally, we found ourselves so caught up in an inextricable net of lies, we—and others—were hard-pressed to discover where the truth really lay.

It takes great courage to be willing to face someone— and without any editorializing or explaining (other than to let them know of our desire to recover)—tell them, flat out, that we lied. Our natural tendency is to try to give them a plausible explanation about why we lied. But to work Step Eight the right way, we must reject that ploy and simply admit to the fact that we did lie.

TODAY'S STEP: *I am learning to admit when I have lied and I no longer make excuses.*

Day 22—LIVING THE TRUTH

*"Without wearing any mask we are conscious of,
we have a special face for each friend."*

OLIVER WENDELL HOLMES

Our relationships with the people on our list is a very important part of our considerations. Were we married? Romantically attached? Professionally connected? A simple friendship? We need to look at how we behaved in all these circumstances.

Did we carry on extramarital liaisons? Did we sleep around, engaging in casual encounters? Did we practice character assassination against our bosses? Did we cheat our partners out of their fair share, arguing that, after all, we were the ones who brought in most of the business? Did we allow others to gossip about our friends, and not stick up for them when they were being harshly judged?

Each of these instances call for amends, even if the parties in question have no idea they occurred.

Many of these people deserve our amends on more than one level. We must take care not to simply skim the surface of the difficulties in each case. We need to dig deep and expose the entire scenario so we can make a clean breast of it all. Once done, no matter what the response, we can be free of the fear that sooner or later we will be found out.

TODAY'S STEP: *I have the courage to come clean and face those harmed by the worst of my actions.*

Step Eight

Day 23—CRYING WOLF

"To win one's joy through struggle is better than to yield to melancholy."
ANDRÉ GIDE

Those of us whose problem has been chemical addiction often have great difficulty reestablishing relationships of trust with people. The nature of addiction creates a separation from the significant others in our lives that is hard to heal.

Alcoholism has aptly been called "the lonely disease." This is because, as the disease progresses, either the alcoholic pulls away from intimacy, unable to bear the increasing shame and helplessness, or the people close to him or her leave the alcoholic because they can not bear to live with the deterioration the disease is causing.

However, this withdrawal from intimacy doesn't mean that the alcoholic's love for family and friends has lessened. As a matter of fact, it simply demonstrates that he or she cares enough to leave, rather than cause increasing discomfort to others.

When the time comes to make amends, we need to know that our overtures may not be accorded much belief. After all, haven't we promised, over and over, to mend our ways and to never, never, never, touch the stuff again? Like the boy who cried wolf, we have run out of credibility.

TODAY'S STEP: *Making amends heals my separation from others.*

Step Eight

Day 24—JAY'S STORY:

"There can be no love in one who does not love himself, and one can only love himself if he has the compassion that grows out of the terrifying confrontation with one's own self."

WILLIAM IRWIN THOMPSON

"This was not a step that made much sense to me. I wasn't married, I'd moved to another state right after college, and wasn't close to my family at all. As a matter of fact, my parents were a lost cause as far as I was concerned. My father was a workaholic who didn't give a damn about anything or anybody except his corporation. And my mother paid great attention to nothing except her clothes and makeup. My family was upper–middle class but at the bottom of the barrel when it came to parenting and nurturing.

"Cocaine was the find of a lifetime, and I partied with the best of them. I could do no wrong in my business—I made money hand over fist. And I had good relationships with plenty of women.

"Eventually, my business went up my nose. The only people I could think of to put on my list after I recovered, were those I owed money to—and I owed a lot.

"But finally I realized that I'd never really given to my parents—only taken from them. I had let down every single person who ever worked for me. And I'd let a lot of women think we might make something permanent out of our relationship, when I had no intention of getting married.

"No list? I had a huge one!"

TODAY'S STEP: *I let go of self-justification and denial in order to make the list of those I harmed.*

Step Eight

Day 25—GOOD GUYS AND BAD GUYS

"Never get into a wrestling match with a skunk."
ANONYMOUS

Practicing Honesty, Open-mindedness and Willingness—the H.O.W. of our successful journey toward recovery—is a major part of every one of the Twelve Steps. And it is never more important than in Steps Eight and Nine.

We've been aware all along that writing out this list was just the beginning of making amends. Deep down, we knew we were eventually going to have to face up to *all* the people on our list and make a clean breast of our transgressions.

This is where willingness is often diluted by our personal antipathy toward those individuals whom we disliked and toward whom we behaved really badly. We may not feel guilt about what we did to them. As a matter of fact, we may feel they deserved what they got.

No one says we have to be fond of everybody on our list. Nevertheless, Step Eight clearly states: "all people we had harmed." This includes the bad guys along with the good guys.

Remember, we're not doing it for them. We're doing it for us. The whole purpose of our program is to clear away our own wreckage; to wipe the slate as clean as possible, to go about living our lives with no more ghosts to plague us.

TODAY'S STEP: *I make amends to others I've harmed, whether I like them or not.*

Day 26—BEING PREPARED

"People who fly into a rage always make a bad landing."   ANONYMOUS

Those of us who are used to being ruled by the "tyranny of the clock" usually want to get this phase of recovery over quickly. We're impatient to do everything in record time, and so we tend to rush through our list of persons we had harmed without referring to the inventory we compiled in Step Four.

But we're not playing "Beat the Clock" here; this is our future we're working toward. The more we cross-reference our defects and shortcomings, the more we will discover about our relationships with others.

When we first looked at our resentments, nearly every one of them was aimed at some significant person in our life who had caused us to feel fear, guilt, anger or suspicion. Now we need to take a look at the role we played in each of those instances. We need to see how our own actions precipitated others' behavior toward us.

Over and over we need to remind ourselves that it does not matter what they have done to us. In each instance, our mission is simply to take care of our own responsibility.

Because it's very possible that many of the persons on our list won't react favorably to our attempts, we need to prepare ourselves for their reactions. We need to know that we will not lash out, no matter how negatively they may respond to our overtures.

TODAY'S STEP: *I allow the process of making amends to unfold in its own proper time.*

Step Eight

Day 27—FORGIVING OURSELVES FIRST

"The worst of men are those who will not forgive."
THOMAS FULLER, M.D.

We need to be very clear about one thing in our minds as we compile our list of persons to whom we need to make amends. We are agreeing—in advance—to ask them for their forgiveness.

"Wait a minute," some of us say. "You mean that in addition to telling these people that we feel we need to make amends to them, we also have to ask them to forgive us? This smacks of overkill. Surely, the very act of admitting our faults to them should be enough. We don't fancy the servile, deflating task of begging their forgiveness."

Isn't there a familiar ring to this complaint? It's just such an attitude that's done us in before. Then, as now, we found it hard to let go of our pride and humble ourselves before others. But "humble" does not mean "humiliate." On the contrary, "asking humbly" demonstrates a great deal of courage and the strength of our resolve. More than that, it is an indication that we have enough faith in our new resolve to no longer be fearful of repeating any of those past performances.

Above all, before we set out to make our amends, we must first forgive ourselves. When we can do that, we reaffirm the commitment we made in the Third Step to put our trust in a power greater than ourselves.

TODAY'S STEP: *I forgive myself and in so doing, come to love myself again.*

Day 28—PREPARING TO MAKE AMENDS

"If we spend our time with regrets over yesterday, and worries over what might happen tomorrow, we have no today in which to live." ANONYMOUS

Pain is caused by problems. In the past we tried to alleviate or eliminate our pain with methods that often backfired, even though our intentions were good. This is what we mean when we say that our disorders were conceived in innocence. If we hadn't been caught up in our disorder, our actions would probably have been different. But trapped as we were, we could see no alternatives.

Because we don't live in a vacuum, other people are always affected by our behavior—good or bad. Although we had no intention of harming others, they often became victims of the fallout of our actions. Consequently, it does no good to insist we didn't mean to act that way. The fact is, we created the harm, whether by intent or not. And it's now up to us to make reparations.

Equally important is our resolve when we do approach these people. We have to tell them of the nature of our compulsion. We need to explain that this step is one of utmost importance to us: We're not expecting them to forgive us, although it would be a big bonus if they were to do so. And, finally, we need to explain that we're willing to make whatever restitution is needed, regardless of the consequences to ourselves.

TODAY'S STEP: *I am willing to do all that I can to make my amends.*

"The one thing worse than a quitter is the person who's afraid to begin."   ANONYMOUS

Our sense of pride makes it difficult for us to admit to past errors and omissions. However, we can turn that around and see how pride is very much a part of Steps Eight and Nine.

Not that boastful, crowing, arrogant, posturing that often covered our deep feelings of inadequacy and fear, but pride in the best sense of the word. The kind of pride that acknowledges our hard-won successes. The kind that starts as a glow in the pit of our stomachs when we feel ourselves winning a struggle against what seemed insurmountable forces. The kind that brings us a new confidence in ourselves.

This is the kind of pride we demonstrate when we have committed ourselves to a set of principles that make reparations absolutely necessary if we're to enjoy the fruits of a dignified existence. At this point, our list of persons to whom we're now ready to make amends becomes an opportunity rather than a punishment.

TODAY'S STEP: *As I release false pride, I face my amends with greater courage.*

Step Eight

Day 30—REVELATIONS

"If you have behaved badly, repent, make what amends you can and address yourself to the task of behaving better next time. On no account brood over your wrongdoing. Rolling in the muck is not the best way of getting clean." ALDOUS HUXLEY

We're now seeing clearly that it was our own mental habits and self-edited memories of how we perceived things that prevented us from living our lives in a more productive manner. We're beginning to understand how misplaced pride and phony models of prestige got in our way. How we used to cling to these mind-sets, intent on being right rather than being comfortable or happy.

When we began to uncover and discover these defects of character and shortcomings in Steps Four, Six and Seven, we experienced a whole new set of principles we could employ in our daily living. These discoveries were like revelations. They clarified so many of our past misconceptions, biases and prejudices that we felt we'd entered a whole new dimension.

These are precisely the feelings we want to take with us as we prepare to face those to whom we will make our amends. Our intent is to be simple, direct and specific. We're not going to editorialize, or to exaggerate or diminish the wrongs we feel we have done. As Sgt. Joe Friday of the old "Dragnet" TV series used to say: "Just the facts, Ma'am."

TODAY'S STEP: *The positive qualities I have developed in my recovery stand me in good stead as I face my amends.*

Day 31—FORGIVING OURSELVES

"If I had done everything I'm credited with, I'd be speaking to you from a laboratory jar at Harvard."
FRANK SINATRA

Great people across the ages have made it their life's task to heal and mend. Jesus Christ, St. Francis of Assisi, Buddha, Gandhi and Mother Teresa come to mind. Their philosophies have always taught that forgiveness is an essential part of the healing process, and that one of the most deserving people to forgive is ourself.

Most of us wouldn't hesitate to forgive a friend or someone else we love who had caused us heartache, the moment they asked us to. A parent is always ready to forgive a child who has committed some wrong. Yet somehow when it comes to self-forgiveness, we run into a blank wall.

We may try to rationalize, justify or explain ourselves at first. But once the evidence of our own guilt becomes indisputable, we find it almost impossible to be compassionate with ourselves. The dark side of our persona becomes so unacceptable in our eyes that we'd almost prefer to disappear than face ourselves.

Now is the time to toss out all those old self-judgments and to revel in the progress we're making. Now is the time to treat ourselves with the respect and approval we give so freely to those who are near and dear to us.

TODAY'S STEP: *With the love and support of my Higher Power, I release self-judgment and forgive myself.*

Step Nine

"Made direct amends to such people wherever possible, except when to do so would injure them or others."

Step Eight got us ready for the big event, but here's where we truly go into action.

This is the step where we take our courage in hand, and sally forth to do battle with all our old ghosts. We are armed with the knowledge that the ultimate aim of this step is to wipe our own slate clean. And we're prepared to meet some reactions that may be hostile and unforgiving.

Our objective is to be honest and straightforward enough to walk away from these encounters knowing that we have fulfilled our obligation to set matters as right as possible.

This sets the stage for us to be able to forgive ourselves regardless of whether those to whom we make amends are willing to forgive us. It is in self-forgiveness that we become truly convinced that lasting recovery is possible.

Nothing can match the relief we feel when there is nothing hanging over our heads any longer. Joy returns to our lives when we have divested ourselves of guilty secrets to the point where we're no longer fearful that at any moment our misdeeds will be exposed for all the world to see.

It's been said that we're as sick as our secrets. Step Nine helps us walk in our world in comfort and confidence.

Day 1—THE TWELVE STEPS

"He who hesitates is not only lost, but miles from the next exit."   ANONYMOUS

Interestingly enough, when the steps were first put together, they numbered only six: complete deflation; dependence and guidance from a Higher Power; moral inventory; confession; restitution; continued work with other alcoholics.

These were devised in the days when Alcoholics Anonymous was in its infancy and meetings were attended by only a few people in New York and Akron. The *Big Book of Alcoholics Anonymous* had not yet been written, so their message of recovery was being carried only by word of mouth.

How fortunate we Anonymous groups are today that, when the book was finally written, the steps after much forethought were expanded to twelve. They now proved to be comprehensive enough to be applied to a wide variety of ills, disorders, compulsions and addictions. Countless people in other kinds of self-help programs have been able to avail themselves of a gold mine of assistance by following this formula.

As you can see, early on, the need for restitution was a prime factor in the AA recovery program. We have also found this to be true in the recovery process of every addictive disorder we have encountered. The catharsis in facing those to whom we have done harm is so powerful a healing factor, that we doubt very much if those who do not practice it can achieve total recovery.

TODAY'S STEP: *I cherish the wisdom of the steps as they are written.*

Day 2—EFFORT AND RISK

"Resistance causes pain and lethargy. It is when we practice acceptance that new possibilities appear." ANONYMOUS

We know that Step Nine entails both effort and risk.

Effort is required because we must get into action. We must think about how to approach the person(s) to whom we wish to make amends. It's essential to plan our procedure thoughtfully, for we cannot achieve a satisfactory result with a hit-and-run encounter. For this reason, we need to arrange a place and time where we can honestly face those persons and explain to them what we're trying to do and why.

Step Nine also involves risk because it's conceivable that the hurt or harm we've done the people on our list is so grave that they cannot be forgiving. In fact, they may be downright uncivil to us.

It may feel unproductive to approach someone we suspect will make us feel guiltier than ever. And yet, taking this step offers us an opportunity to really get in touch with our deepest levels of honesty. If we're positive that, at our current stage of recovery, this encounter might work strongly to our disadvantage, then perhaps we can delay it until we feel we've reached a degree of self-acceptance that allows us to be totally candid with everyone.

Remember, we're not expecting a happy ending to all our encounters. But we are anxious to fulfill the task of taking care of our own responsibilities.

TODAY'S STEP: *I willingly take the risk and make the effort to make direct amends.*

Step Nine

Day 3—MAKING PEACE

"All men should strive to learn before they die what they are running from, and to, and why."
JAMES THURBER

Step Nine allows us to clean up our lives and get rid of the stumbling blocks that have prevented us from reaching our highest good. It allows us to make peace with ourselves by making peace with those we've caused pain and harm.

Even if they don't respond to us positively, we know we've done our share. We know we've tried to set the record straight—and that in itself is an enormous plus.

Like the ancient mariner, we've been carrying an albatross on our shoulders that's been weighing us down and feels like an impossible load to dump. But dump it we do. And in the doing, we find renewed respect for ourselves.

Certainly more than one of us has been fearful of making these amends. But in overcoming that fear we know we've strengthened our resolve to live free from these old feelings of impending doom.

When we have no more secrets, and nothing to hide, we can go about the daily business of living with renewed optimism. Free from the constraints of being afraid to face others, our own sense of self takes on a new and positive aspect.

TODAY'S STEP: *I lay down my burden of guilt gratefully as I make direct amends.*

Step Nine

Day 4—PLOYS

"It is difficult to live in the present, ridiculous to live in the future and impossible to live in the past."
                                                        JIM BISHOP

As we review the list we made in Step Eight, we can now attempt to sort out our prospective amendees. Step Nine makes it clear that we must make amends "except when to do so would injure them or others."

We need to carefully assess whether our making amends might affect not only the persons with whom we wish to clear the air, but also others associated with them. For instance, if we were involved in some unsavory business deal, we have to consider whether we might implicate others who were also involved. We must carefully weigh the value of clearing our own conscience against the difficulties our disclosures might cause them.

Frequently, our immediate thought is: "Great! This gets me off the hook with lots of folks, because making amends to some of them would create a domino effect." When we work Step Nine we have to be sure that we don't make it just another ploy in an attempt to avoid humiliating ourselves in front of others. The intent of Step Nine is not meant solely as a means of clearing our own conscience and relieving us of further responsibility. We *do* need to carefully consider the impact it may have on others. And we also need to resist the temptation to avoid as much personal discomfort as we can.

TODAY'S STEP: *I use discernment in making my amends.*

Step Nine

Day 5—FORGIVING OURSELVES

"Getting out of a rut is the highest mountain we have to climb."
ANONYMOUS

If we have thoroughly absorbed the message of guilt-innocence that we explored in an earlier step, then we've accepted the fact that if it hadn't been for our disease, we would have handled our lives and affairs very differently.

This being so, one of the first amends we need to make is to ourselves. We need to forgive ourselves for behaving in a manner that caused others disappointment and hurt. In order to do this, we need to remind ourselves that even when we were caught up in the progression of our disorder, we did the very best we could at the time. And further, at this phase of our recovery, there is no way we could or would behave in the same manner as we did then. Our finer nature, which was buried so long under the blanket of our addiction/compulsion, now comes to the fore. Today we know that we have sufficient positive attributes to act in an honest and acceptable manner.

We always evaluate ourselves in a much harsher manner than we would judge others who have committed similar offenses. This very attitude is a form of inverse pride.

TODAY'S STEP: *I make amends to myself by letting go of unrealistic guilt.*

Day 6—MATTERS OF MONEY

"I don't know the key to success but the key to failure is trying to please everybody."   BILL COSBY

Admittedly, many wrongs have been done to us by others. But it's not our purpose to set out, like Don Quixote, to right those wrongs. Ours is not a quest to bring our enemies to their knees; it is plainly and simply an exercise in self-examination and restitution.

If we seem to be belaboring this point, it's simply because this is one of the most common difficulties that has beset many of us. Somehow, it's difficult to comprehend why *we* have to take all the responsibility for the bad experiences we've had with others. We stubbornly cling to the notion that they should be held responsible for their part.

We do not take all the responsibility. We simply acknowledge where *we* were wrong. And we become willing to make amends for the part that was our doing.

We must look carefully at where we may have bilked or conned someone, or where we accepted payment for work that was haphazard or shoddy. We examine all our dealings with money—borrowing, overspending, cheating, withholding, wasting. We carefully assess each incident that has proved harmful to ourselves and others.

TODAY'S STEP: *I take responsibility for the wrongs I have done, and let God handle the ways I was wronged.*

Step Nine

Day 7—MAKING AMENDS

"You can fall many times, but you aren't a failure until you begin to blame someone else."

ANONYMOUS

There are people with whom it would not be wise for us to make certain amends. Although we might be willing, we have to weigh whether our admission would adversely affect their lives.

One of these people might be our spouse. To tell him or her that we carried on an affair with someone in our circle of friends serves no purpose other than to relieve our own conscience. It would pain our spouse and cause a rift in a friendship that has been mutually satisfactory. It might also cause problems in the family of our one-time lover and lead them or us to seek divorce as the only alternative.

Some of us have worked through this by admitting to our spouse that we engaged in an extramarital experience, that we take full responsibility for the affair, and are unwilling to implicate anyone else. When pressed, we have clung to our stand.

If we feel that our spouse could pressure us into a full confession, it might be to everyone's advantage for us to refrain from disclosing the matter at this time.

We're already making amends to friends and family by the change in our behavior, by following the principles the program has taught us, and by not falling back into destructive habit patterns.

TODAY'S STEP: *I am developing the wisdom to know when making amends might cause further harm.*

Day 8—THE POWER

"Mix a conviction with a man and something happens!"
ADAM CLAYTON POWELL

All of the Twelve Step programs have a spiritual base, but many of us continue to find it difficult to accept the message of Steps Two and Three. We've tried to follow the sequence of the steps, "acting as if" we do believe. Yet, deep within us, there remains this nagging doubt that we're being drawn into a religious ritual we can't honestly ascribe to.

Earlier we talked about making our group the power greater than ourselves, of believing that they believe, and following the path they keep assuring us has worked for them. We've also been told that many among us are agnostics and atheists who simply cannot swallow any spiritual concept that smacks of a Godhead.

Once again we'd like to state that religion is not our business. But spirituality is. Experience has shown us that those who cling to the belief that the universe is a hostile place that began in a void and will end in a void have a sense of hopelessness about continuing to follow this recovery formula.

In the Ninth Step, we discover that through the doing—not the thinking—we begin to experience a feeling that some power is working with us and through us for our ultimate good.

TODAY'S STEP: *A Higher Power lives through me when I take this step.*

Step Nine

Day 9—WRITING AN AMENDS

"Marriage is three parts love and seven parts forgiveness of sins." LANGDON MITCHELL

Once we've set up our priority list and identified those people to whom we must first make amends, our next step is to carefully review the way in which we plan to approach them.

If we're no longer living in the same area, we may have to write to them, outlining the "whys" of what we're doing, and assuring them that whatever their reaction may be, we're prepared to accept it.

Some people will simply not respond to our letters. They may still harbor resentments toward us, and we should be prepared for that outcome. Some will respond with forgiveness and encouragement. Still others may wish to close the book on any further contact.

Our experiences in writing amends have been as varied as the personalities of the writers. An example that comes to mind concerns a career army officer who wrote to his ex-wife:

From: U.S. Army Major L.L. Doe
To: Mrs. Mary Doe
Subject: Increase in child support.
This officer regrets the circumstances leading to the divorce of the above-named principals. Consequently, this officer has arranged for an increase in the child-support payments to the issue of the then-existing marriage between said principals, namely L.L. Doe, Jr.

> Signed,
> Major, U.S. Army L.L. Doe

TODAY'S STEP: *Writing an amends can lead me to greater honesty.*

Day 10—POINTS OF VIEW

"Our repentance is not so much regret for the evil we have done, as a fear of what might happen to us as a result of it." LA ROCHEFOUCAULD

Writing our amends as a long, narrative essay on cause and effect won't necessarily achieve the results we hope to accomplish. Wading through our tendency to be verbose and go into complicated explanations of the how and why of our actions can be a tedious chore for those to whom we send these letters.

Based on past experience, we believe that when we can be brief and to the point, the recipients of our letters are less suspicious of our intentions than when we get carried away with our own rhetoric. Nevertheless, there are times when a detailed and explanatory letter is called for. We have to decide for ourselves when this is appropriate.

There are times, too, when our recollection of a past incident may not agree with the memory of the person with whom we are attempting to set things straight. If they should reply to our letter, and question our version of the event(s), it may well be wiser to accept their perception, rather than engage in a debate that might lead to further misunderstandings.

Our intent is to clear up the wreckage of our past—not to argue that our point of view is correct.

TODAY'S STEP: *I keep my written amends brief, simple and honest.*

Step Nine

Day 11—WHAT AMENDS?

"The sky is not less blue because the blind man does not see it."
DANISH PROVERB

Ironically, there will be times when we discover that some people weren't even aware that we owed them any explanation or amends for our past performance. This can be a bit humiliating, for we had assumed that we were important or powerful enough to make a deep impact on everyone in our lives.

However, it's our own sense of guilt that needs to be assuaged, whether or not they remember. We've found it wise to explain what we're about and why we're trying to set things right with our universe. There's a great deal of comfort in knowing that we've been up front and candid with others, and that we no longer need to carry the burden of unresolved conflicts.

Many of us thought we knew exactly how others perceived the things we said and did. We've assumed that their perception of our relationship is thus and so. But when we face them, we may find that they have an entirely different point of view.

Therefore, a good approach is to begin by establishing the time, place and circumstances under which an incident took place. We can then ask them if they recall the situation, and what their thoughts about it were and are.

TODAY'S STEP: *I accept that others' perceptions of unfinished business may differ from mine.*

Step Nine

Day 12—THE PROMISES

"Suffering isn't ennobling, recovery is."
CHRISTIAAN N. BARNARD

There is a lovely section of The *Big Book of Alcoholics Anonymous* called "The Promises" that describes the benefits derived from working the Ninth Step. Now seems an appropriate time to quote it:

> If we have been painstaking about this phase of our development, we will be amazed before we are half-way through. We are going to know a new freedom and a new happiness. We will not regret the past nor wish to shut the door on it. We will comprehend the meaning of the word serenity and we will know peace. No matter how far down the scale we have gone, we will see how our experience can benefit others. That feeling of uselessness and self-pity will disappear. We will lose interest in selfish things and gain interest in our fellows. Self-seeking will slip away. Our whole attitude and outlook upon life will change. Fear of people and economic insecurity will leave us. We will intuitively know how to handle situations that used to baffle us. We will suddenly realize that God is doing for us what we could not do for ourselves.
>
> Are these rash promises? We think not. They are being fulfilled—sometimes quickly, sometimes slowly. They will always materialize if we work for them.

TODAY'S STEP: *As I work the steps on a daily basis, the promises of the program are mine.*

Day 13—RESPONSIBILITY

"The best angle to approach anything is the try-angle."   ANONYMOUS

It's easy to remember the wrongs we perceived others had done to us. They frequently crowd out our memories of the harm we had done to them and to ourselves. Sorting out our responsibility may be an extremely painful procedure, for our sense of what is equitable makes us think that as long as we are owed amends by others, it's not necessary for us to make the first move.

This kind of thinking leads to impotence. It completely arrests the development we've been experiencing by following the steps up to this point. The program is simple and direct. There is really no opportunity for complete recovery unless we're willing to follow it exactly as it is written.

Our job in Step Nine is not to judge what has been done to us, but what we have done to others. Our job is to make restitution for our part, despite the fact that the other person might be even more guilty than we.

Only when we've taken the action called for in this step, will its value become evident to us. Mulling over the pros and cons in our minds is of little value, for we're experts at devising all sorts of rationalizations and excuses about why it's not necessary to make amends to all those to whom we've done harm.

TODAY'S STEP: *Putting aside what others have done to me, I make amends so that I can grow.*

Day 14—WE AS "OTHERS"

"I dote on myself, there is that lot of me and all so luscious."
WALT WHITMAN

The *Big Book of Alcoholics Anonymous* was written by alcoholics for alcoholics and proved to be an incredible tool in the recovery of millions. However, when the Twelve Steps became the basis of the programs for a number of other anonymous self-help groups, the text did not necessarily lend itself to some of their problems. But, since it was the only text then available that dealt specifically with the "H.O.W." of recovery, many groups chose to use it as their guide. They felt that the nature of any dysfunction would be adequately covered in the message of the Twelve Steps, even though their problems might be something other than alcoholism.

This explains why for some disorders it might seem very difficult to accept the fact that we were at fault in all of our dysfunctional relationships. Under certain circumstances, more harm was done to us than we had done—in reality we were much more the victim than the aggressor. In such cases, we agree that approaching these people in order to make amends would not be necessary. Step Nine clearly states: "except when to do so would injure them or others." In this case, we are the "others."

TODAY'S STEP: *I clearly discern when making amends would harm me.*

Step Nine

Day 15—INDIRECT AMENDS

"It would be nice if we could forget our troubles as quickly as we forget our blessings." ANONYMOUS

There are cases where direct amends are not indicated. With some people we may be able to make only partial restitution, for to approach them directly could cause harm to them or others. The important thing is that we did identify them in Step Eight, and that we are willing to make amends to them. Sometimes it is possible, anonymously, to rectify some of the harm we have done.

Writing letters to those who have passed away has proven to be an effective tool to clear away regrets and repentance. When we follow this by doing something good for someone else in their family or circle of friends, we feel that we have followed the intent of Step Nine.

In the case of money matters, we might send a cashier's check to our prospective amendee. If our amends are related to the workplace, and others might be implicated, some of us have worked through a third party—often a professional—to set things right. Also, when someone has left the area, and we have lost contact with them, the willingness to make amends when our paths cross again is sufficient.

However, we have to avoid the tendency to rationalize away the need for amends—particularly with those we don't like. It's a perfectly normal facet of human nature to want to avoid things that are uncomfortable. But the rewards of Steps Eight and Nine are so freeing that they're well worth the struggle.

TODAY'S STEP: *I hold to the spirit of Step Nine even when it isn't possible to make amends directly.*

Day 16—A POSITIVE STEP

"Don't be afraid to take a big step if it is indicated. You can't leap a canyon in two small jumps."

ANONYMOUS

We want to approach those people to whom we wish to make amends with all the tact we can muster. This is not to suggest that we should pussyfoot around our issues, or be servile and cowering.

On the contrary, we need to approach them with dignity and consideration, knowing that, in the long run, what we are about will benefit both them and ourselves. Cringing servility and self-abasement are not in the spirit of our undertaking in this positive step toward recovery. We should be justifiably proud that the progress we have made has enabled us to regain enough self-esteem to undertake this challenge. We need to carry ourselves in a way that shows others we feel good about ourselves when we make our amends.

The challenge of the Fifth Step found us admitting to God, to ourselves and to another human being the exact nature of our wrongs. It proved to us the incredible catharsis of ridding ourselves of all our shameful secrets.

Now we're tackling the second most challenging step in our program. Just as in the completion of the Fifth Step, when we felt the weight of the world slide off our backs, so Step Nine affords us an incredible feeling of relief. It's as if our souls have had a wonderful cleansing beauty bath.

TODAY'S STEP: *I make my amends with dignity and tact.*

Day 17—IT'S NEVER TOO LATE

"Recovery sometimes comes in increments, although we want it all now." ANONYMOUS

Making amends to someone you've not seen in a number of years can sometimes be a very difficult undertaking.

A member of Narcotics Anonymous shared this story. She grew up in a healthy middle-American family, and went to a prestigious college, which is where she began using speed to keep her studies up and her weight down. In her senior year she married a graduate student. They had three children; her husband prospered, and they had an active social life.

But this is when she began to realize that she was now unable to function without her "medication." And as time went on, she became less and less capable of handling her role as wife and mother. Fed up, her husband ultimately divorced her, won custody of the children and remarried. She did not see her children for fifteen years, during which time she experienced many sad and degrading incidents.

A few years ago she stopped using drugs and became involved in a Twelve Step program where, in her early recovery, she felt too much shame to contact her children. Finally, she found the courage to write them, explaining her addiction and assuring them she had never stopped loving them.

"Today we are friends," she told us. "Their stepmother is a wonderful woman, and they love her. But they love me too! And that's what counts!"

TODAY'S STEP: *No matter how long it's been, I am ready and willing to make amends.*

Day 18—NO MATTER WHAT

"Sometimes when you look in his eyes, you get the feeling that someone else is driving."

DAVID LETTERMAN

It's amazing how much more clarity we gain from listening to others' struggles with Step Nine. Some of us believed we owed no amends to those who had harmed us; we felt justified in what we'd done to them.

However, this is not what the step tells us. We are charged with making amends to *all* persons we had harmed, regardless of who they were or what they did.

Just such a story was shared by a woman who told us that she had worked in the family business because she was so overweight she was ashamed to be seen in the normal working world. Over the years, she was frequently molested by her stepfather, although she told no one. She got back at him by syphoning off money from the daily proceeds.

After joining Overeaters Anonymous and successfully taking off and maintaining a weight loss of eighty-nine pounds, she got a different job. Freed of her stepfather at last, she saw no reason to make financial amends to him. But, as she worked through the steps one by one, she finally became convinced that it was necessary to clean up her own act, no matter what he had done. When she went to him, money in hand, he tore up the check and told her to let bygones be bygones.

It didn't matter whether he did it to salve his own conscience or not. She was free of her guilt and shame.

TODAY'S STEP: *By making honest amends, my soul is free of its burdens.*

Day 19—A NEW PERSONA

"I have always thought respectable people scoun-
drels, and I look anxiously at my face every morn-
ing for signs of my becoming a scoundrel."

BERTRAND RUSSELL

Very often just our new behavior alone is an amend. When
we consistently practice honesty, courtesy, dependability
and consideration, we rekindle the trust and affection that
has been lost to many of us.

In the Sixth and Seventh Steps we talked about "acting
as if," and living ourselves into good thinking. We can now
see how these actions really bear fruit as we become more
and more comfortable with our new persona.

A question we've found valuable to ask ourselves is: "If
you were told that you were going to live another fifty
years, and that you'd spend each day of those years doing
and saying exactly what you're doing and saying today—
how would you behave?"

Certainly, most of us would rather live in peace and
harmony than chaos and discomfort. We would almost
certainly agree that it's very difficult to remain serene when
we have unresolved relationship problems or feel that we
have failed to meet our financial obligations.

In thinking of those fifty years to come, or conversely,
in living this day as if it were our last, we might feel more
motivated to put our affairs and relationships in the best
possible order.

TODAY'S STEP: *My life, as I live it today, is an amend to
myself and others.*

Day 20—BOB'S STORY

"There are six requisites in every happy marriage. The first is faith and the remaining five are confidence."
ELBERT HUBBARD

Sometimes our attempt to make amends is not met with success. This story was told by a man who had had a severe sexual disorder and whose marriage had been destroyed as a result of it.

When he was seventeen, Bob had had an affair with a woman who played tennis with his mother. She had turned him on to sexual practices he never knew existed, and although he was careful of what he demanded from his current girlfriend, he became more and more obsessed and involved with "kinky" sex.

In his marriage, Bob played the role of the considerate lover, the perfect husband and father. However, magazines and personal columns put him in contact with every sexual practice and all the willing partners he wanted.

A nasty accident, where a girl died, brought everything to light, and Bob was nearly sent to prison. His wife sued for divorce and got a restraining order which prevented him from seeing his children.

His recovery program demanded that he make amends. But when Bob contacted his former wife, she was not willing to listen to his attempt at amends, nor would she permit him to contact his children.

Unfortunately, it is sometimes impossible for those on whom we've inflicted pain to forgive us. Our best recourse is to accept their refusal, get on with our new life and make our amends by helping others whenever possible.

TODAY'S STEP: *If my amends are not accepted, I let go of the need to be forgiven.*

Step Nine

Day 21—TRIAL & ERROR

"When all else fails, follow directions."

ANONYMOUS

When we hear people saying that we can make peace with our past, that all our misdeeds and misjudgments can serve us in positive ways, many of us have a hard time seeing how that could be possible. Yet, when we come to think about it, we realize that almost everything we learned came by trial and error.

As little children we learned how to tie our shoelaces by discovering how not to do it. We learned how to ride a bike by falling off. We learned golf by slicing and digging up divots. And we're learning how to live comfortably by being aware of the wrong turns and clouded decisions we have made during our former addictive/compulsive existence.

Gradually, with the help of others, we begin to understand the deeper meaning of Step Nine. As we work through it, we realize that we're starting to let go of our feelings of shame, resentment, guilt, fear and a host of other negative feelings. The way this happens is through our growing acceptance of the nature of addiction. Now is when we truly begin to comprehend that it is a form of illness, just like diabetes or cancer.

No longer guilty! Wow! But we are *responsible* for trying to repair the damage our disease has done to ourselves and others. We want to get well, and in order to do so we have to retrace our steps and wipe out all we can of the harm we've caused others.

TODAY'S STEP: *As I make my amends, I free myself of fear, guilt and shame.*

Day 22—ADULT CHILDREN OF ALCOHOLICS

"Parentage is a very important profession; but no test of fitness for it is ever imposed in the interest of the children." GEORGE BERNARD SHAW

Adult children of alcoholics who have experienced physical and/or emotional damage at the hands of their parents often attribute their own addictive/compulsive behavior to the childhood traumas they had suffered during their formative years.

We would never downplay the harm that can be done to children in a family where one or more of the parents is alcoholic. However, we must also look at the possibility that the tendency to shift blame from our shoulders onto theirs can be a severe impediment to our recovery.

When we make our amends list, it is important that we look at our own role in the family dynamics. We need to recognize that we might have done things calculated to make them feel guilty or acutely uncomfortable.

By admitting that our own disease rendered us incapable of behaving in a rational manner, we come to realize that perhaps our alcoholic parents weren't able to act in any other way than they did. Therefore, for the purposes of our own recovery, we need to make what amends we can without editorializing on the harm done to us. Many of us can attest to the value of just such action.

TODAY'S STEP: *Recognizing that my parents were sick people too, I can release my judgments of them.*

Step Nine

Day 23—LEANERS AND LEANEES

"The best reformers are those who start with them-selves."   ANONYMOUS

The "leaner-leanee" phenomenon exists in every dysfunctional relationship. And when either one changes, the other is deeply affected.

We need to understand that there was both safety and balance in a situation of this sort. Because human beings are the most adaptable of any species, we quickly learn to cope with all sorts of unhealthy and unproductive relationships and circumstances, simply in order to survive.

Often in the early stages of recovery, our significant others, whether leaner or leanee, are threatened by the changes they see in us. And they actually try to sabotage our progress.

In making amends, we cannot be critical of their reactions. We simply need to own up to our own role in the relationship and admit our own pathological behavior. We must patiently try to reassure them that we are not discounting the important role they have played in our lives.

Sometimes, for our sake and theirs, we have to decide to end a relationship. But that in itself can constitute an amend—both to ourselves and to the other person once we realize that neither of us can benefit from continuing to stay together.

TODAY'S STEP: *I establish an honest relationship with those who were with me during my addiction.*

Day 24—THE PATH

"Why you do something is more important than how you do it." ANONYMOUS

Self-searching taught us many things about ourselves that we'd really never examined before. Happily, not all of the discoveries we made were negative ones. And this helped us begin to envision a life relatively free of oppressive memories of the wreckage of our past—after we had set things right with the persons who had been hurt by our addictive/compulsive behavior.

It's remarkable how, once we'd convinced ourselves of this, we experienced relatively little difficulty transmitting our optimism to those with whom we made our peace.

When people who are currently working apply for a different job, they exude a certain balance and confidence to their prospective employer. Unfortunately, this is rarely evident in those who are unemployed and desperate to find work. The new employers feel those positive "vibes" and are predisposed to hire the confident applicants rather than the ones whose anxiety transmits an aura of uncertainty.

When we approach those on our list with an inner sense of assurance, we have prepared ourselves for any outcome. We naturally feel a certain amount of pain and discomfort if someone refuses our amends, but this in no way diminishes the value of making the attempt. Because we have been true to ourselves, and true to the principles we've come to believe in, our own sense of self-esteem remains intact.

TODAY'S STEP: *Making amends heals my self-esteem.*

Step Nine

Day 25—THE PAIN OF OTHERS

"Make up your mind that you can't, and you're always right."
ANONYMOUS

Initially, we may have felt that a casual apology would suffice with our prospective amendees. But as time went on we began to see that such action might produce a very negative result.

When other people have been deeply affected by our past actions and attitudes, it can be an insult to their sensitivities to brush the incidents off as minor, as a mere lapse of good manners.

We need to be scrupulous in owning up to the fact that if they had behaved toward us as we did toward them, we would be gravely wounded. It is very important to acknowledge the severity of the damage we may have inflicted on them and to assure them of our concern for their feelings.

A good rule of thumb is to follow the Golden Rule. We must do unto them what we would have wanted them to do unto us had our positions been reversed.

At first glance, it may appear to us that this is not entirely fair, especially if their behavior toward us was less than admirable. But we must remember that our intent has been, and will continue to be, the cleaning up of our own side of the street.

TODAY'S STEP: *My apologies come from the depths of my being.*

Step Nine

Day 26—JOHN'S STORY

"It is hard to pay for bread that has been eaten."
DANISH PROVERB

John, a member of Debtors Anonymous tells of the difficulty he had in making amends to his father-in-law.

"There's a saying that 'swallowing pride never choked anyone,' " said John. "But I darned near proved that wasn't true.

"It's difficult to explain how I got so deeply in debt. Credit card roulette is probably the best explanation I can give you.

"I was a pretty good stockbroker. But I had been living higher and higher on the hog for some time, robbing Peter to pay Paul, and skating on thin ice. I married this girl whose dad had megabucks, and gave her whole family the impression that I was right up there with them.

"Her dad footed the bill for a lavish wedding and treated us to a honeymoon in the Caribbean, where I continued to spend like there was no tomorrow.

"When the you-know-what hit the fan, my wife promised to stand by me if I joined Debtors Anonymous. I did. But God, it was hard to face her old man. My group pushed me into leveling with him, and he was pretty angry and unforgiving for what I'd done to 'his little girl.' I almost lost my temper more than once. But, in the end, I managed to keep my cool, and my wife and I are working on paying back all the money I owe. If her dad wants to keep on hating me, that's not my problem. I've done what I *could* do, and I have to accept his response."

TODAY'S STEP: *I can stay centered, even when the response to my amends is negative.*

Day 27—TRUST

*"God promises a safe landing but not a problem-
free flight."*   ANONYMOUS

Some of us have had so many advantages in our lifetime,
we're hard put to explain to others how we fell into such
a prolonged state of unproductive behavior. Consequently,
some people to whom we wish to make amends will find
it difficult to credit us with being truly sorry for the distress
we caused.

They do not trust us because they feel we have some
irreparable flaw in our makeup; that we're simply playing
the game of making restitution without any true commitment to setting our lives in order. They're suspicious that
this is simply another ruse to be readmitted into their good
graces. They see us as "the boy who cried wolf." In such
cases, it may seem to us that trying to convince them of our
sincerity is a losing battle.

Even though we have changed and grown, we have to
respect their opinion. We must be patient, believing that,
although it may take quite some time, our actions will
eventually convince them of our sincerity.

We will not dwell on this unhappy situation. Nor will we
insistently try to convince them of our good intentions. We
will simply get on with our lives knowing that a power
greater than ourselves is working for our ultimate good.

TODAY'S STEP: *I make amends through changed behavior
as well as with words.*

Step Nine

Day 28—BLACKOUTS

"We are judged by our actions—not our intentions. We may have a heart of gold, but so does a hard-boiled egg." ANONYMOUS

AA members who experienced blackouts say they've had some difficulty doing this step because they simply didn't remember doing the things people told them they'd done. They reported feeling helpless because they could neither defend nor explain themselves. Although they couldn't imagine behaving in the manner that their prospective amendees described, they were forced to give credence to what they were told about themselves.

A blackout, for those not familiar with this phenomenon, does not mean that someone has passed out. Rather, it's like a short in an electrical connection—the memory center does not register an event or events in which the person has participated. Although to all outward appearances that individual is functioning in a normal manner, he or she is simply not recording the proceedings.

And yet, every one of them said that, until they had tackled this most difficult step, they could not shake the monkey of guilt off their backs. They felt humiliated about what they learned about themselves. But, at the same time, they felt immense relief that they would never have to deal with such shame again as long as they were able to remain clean and sober.

TODAY'S STEP: *Even when my memory of the situation is cloudy, I can accept the truth and sincerely make amends.*

Step Nine

Day 29—RESPONSIBILITY

"It's a funny thing, if you refuse to accept anything but the best, you very often will get it."

SOMERSET MAUGHAM

Sometimes we feel so elated after making a few amends that we rush to clear up all past misunderstandings and interpersonal problems.

Prudence is the key word here. We want to weigh carefully the effect this will have on both ourselves and others. We may feel such a sense of exhilaration with our early success that we want to shoulder the entire blame for everything that's gone wrong in our relationships up to this point.

This is not only foolhardy, it's unrealistic. We are no more responsible for everything that has gone wrong in our lives than we are capable of having caused it all. Our inventory and our Eighth Step list have highlighted our defects, wrongs, and shortcomings. And although we can now see that they were certainly a prime factor in our relationships, the others are also responsible for their share in the interaction.

We must weigh our words carefully. On the one hand, we need to be careful not to lay the blame on anyone else. But, on the other hand, we need to limit our amends to the part that was our responsibility.

Shouldering the blame for more than is our due can backfire. It can create even harsher judgments on the part of those to whom we are making amends and lead to an uncomfortable aftermath.

TODAY'S STEP: *I accept responsibility for my share of the problem, but no more than my share.*

Day 30—REBALANCING RELATIONSHIPS

"The past cannot be changed, but the future is in your power."   ANONYMOUS

When we have been in relationships that simply limp along from year to year, we experience frustration and anger. We want to have a life that is fruitful and vital. When it isn't, we often blame the other person for causing our unhappiness. All too often that other person begins to accept that accusation, and takes on the responsibility for our aberrant behavior.

When it comes time to clean our personal house and make amends to those persons, it's not unusual for them to continue to exhibit the same lack of self-esteem that made them accept our indictment of them in the first place. In a relationship where there is a leaner and a leanee, both have adapted to their roles. When one steps out of character, the other feels off balance and confused.

We need to employ patience and tact, and above all, rigorous honesty when dealing with those "enablers" who felt that what they were doing was in our best interests. It is painful for them to realize that they were doing all the wrong things for what they thought were the right reasons. Gentleness and reassurance are the prime ingredients in making amends.

TODAY'S STEP: *I make amends to my enablers with honesty, gentleness and love.*

Day 31—ASSETS

"Nothing succeeds like success."   ANONYMOUS

We've done it! We've worked through all the negative factors that have plagued us up to this point in our recovery. We've cleaned the slate. Now we can create a lifestyle that is both productive and rewarding.

It's like throwing out all our old worn-out clothes, taking a long cleansing shower, stepping out into a new room, and putting on a whole new wardrobe.

What better time to take another look at our list of assets, attributes and talents and to begin making them a part of our daily lives.

If we've forgotten the list, or disposed of it, all we need to do is make another one, using the alphabet as our guideline. Remember? On Day 24 of Step Four we listed the letters of the alphabet down the left-hand margin of a legal-sized tablet. Then we wrote out our talents, assets and strengths, starting with each letter, for instance, A—Attentive, B—Brave, C—Considerate.

How about adding: A—Action-oriented, B—Benevolent, C—Confident. We do possess these attributes, after all. By doing these steps, we've proved it—even to ourselves.

TODAY'S STEP: *By making my amends, I've learned to embrace my assets and strengths.*

Step Ten

> *"Continued to take personal inventory and when we were wrong promptly admitted it."*

People who have had great success with Step Ten, tell us that this process constitutes an ever-renewable lease on their personal recovery program. Many of them report that the practice they find the most effective is to take a daily inventory to determine whether they're still on target.

When we think of our program as a contract that periodically comes up for renewal, we will not fall into the trap of becoming smug about our progress. Recovery is not an event. It is a process, and an ongoing process at that.

Some folks have told us they skipped from the Third Step to the Tenth so that they would not add any more wrongs, defects or shortcomings to their inventory until they finally got up the courage to face Step Four. They felt if they took a daily inventory they might even be ahead of the game by the time they sat down to list the nature of their wrongs.

In the next thirty-one days, we will examine the intent and the power of Step Ten. By the end of the month we will surely begin to reap some of its benefits.

Step Ten

Day 1—BLUEPRINT FOR LIVING

"A man cannot be comfortable without his own approval."
MARK TWAIN

For those of us who keep a journal, the Tenth Step has really been in effect for some time. Perhaps we haven't pinpointed our errors and omissions in quite the same manner as we're now prepared to do, but in all probability we've gained a sense of when and how we slip up.

In essence, this step is a blueprint for living one day at a time. Although each of the Twelve Steps are designed for that precise objective, Step Ten really brings this technique into focus.

When we were little, most of us had fantasies about an ideal existence in which we were rich, successful, healthy, and brave. Our heroes were those who overcame seemingly insurmountable obstacles against evil forces or tragic circumstances and emerged victorious and heroic in the eyes of others. We wanted to be like them.

Today, as we overcome seemingly insurmountable obstacles against the malignant progression of our disorders, we are our own heroes and heroines. We are emerging victorious over the defects and shortcomings of our past. Those close to us are looking at us with new respect. And, above all, we are beginning to like and trust ourselves.

TODAY'S STEP: *In my daily inventory, I find a blueprint for living.*

Step Ten

Day 2—SAME OLD SONG

*"Cast your bread on the waters and you get but-
tered toast."*   ANONYMOUS

In Step Ten we want to pay special attention to those who
have been dominated by our past disorders. We need to
demonstrate a great deal of patience and understanding
with them.

In Step Nine we spoke of the leaners and the leanees
and how that kind of enabling relationship affected our
personal lives. As we continue to take our daily inventory,
we want to look at how we behave toward those people
right now. Are we still being demanding? Impatient? Condescending? Critical?

Old habits are very hard to break. Once we've established a pattern of interaction with others, it's extremely
easy to fall back into that old, familiar routine. Sometimes all it takes is a sight, a sound, a smell, a remembered phrase from a song or even a familiar gesture to
trigger our reaction. And there we are, behaving in that
old familiar manner. Like Pavlov's dog, we've been conditioned to responses which we developed as protection
against criticism during the progression of our disorders,
but which are now totally inappropriate.

In the past we might have convinced others that they
were responsible for our irresponsible behavior. Now we
want to be sure that we're not continuing this same type
of emotional blackmail.

TODAY'S STEP: *My daily inventory reminds me to change
my old relationship patterns.*

Day 3—ADMIT IT

"We have more ability than willpower, and it is often an excuse to ourselves that we imagine things are impossible."
LA ROCHEFOUCAULD

We felt a great deal of relief and very likely, a feeling of pride, when we made amends to those persons we had harmed in the past. Step Nine gave us some experience in how to make amends, and we can continue to call upon that experience today to promptly admit our wrongs.

No one we know enjoys admitting that he or she goofed. This leads to a tendency to procrastinate when it comes to admitting our mistakes. But we will learn, in time, that the term "promptly" has great merit. Cleaning up today's wreckage today means we don't have to go through needless agonizing or loss of sleep trying to summon up courage to do so.

As a matter of fact, it usually seems much more difficult when we think about it than when we do it. We always make mountains out of molehills in our minds when we worry about how our admission of wrongness will be received by others. We need to remind ourselves that all these steps were created as tools, and that our program is one of enlightened self-interest. When we're O.K. with ourselves, we're generally O.K. with others too.

TODAY'S STEP: *When I am wrong, I promptly admit it.*

Day 4—CALIPH ABDUL

"Men are much more unwilling to have their weaknesses and their imperfections known than their crimes."   LORD CHESTERFIELD

Isn't it strange how some of the things that weigh most heavily on us are the tacky, embarrassing, childish things we've done rather than those really serious behaviors and missteps which occurred in the past?

This reminds me of a tale told in an unexpurgated version of the Arabian Nights:

There was once a Caliph who was holding a very large audience in his palace. Suddenly, he broke wind with an extremely audible outburst. He was so humiliated that he fled the royal city and went into hiding for years, certain that everyone was discussing his embarrassing performance.

Finally, after a number of years had passed, he decided that the incident had probably been forgotten, and he made his way back to his city. Just as he was approaching the palace, he passed a woman in the marketplace explaining to her little boy that he had been born on the day that Caliph Abdul broke wind. The poor man turned around and headed back into the desert, where he became a hermit for the rest of his life.

An outrageous example, perhaps, but how often have we acted like the Caliph, and allowed our own fear of embarrassment to prevent us from taking the necessary steps to free us from isolation and shame.

TODAY'S STEP: *I keep my past behavior in perspective, without overdramatizing it.*

Step Ten

Day 5—PAINSTAKING

*"All I want is the best of everything, and there's
very little of that left."*
                                            LUCIUS BEEBE

As we review "The Promises" we discussed in Step Nine,
certain words stand out that merit a closer look. For example, "If we have been painstaking about this phase of our
development . . ."

As we worked Step Nine, were we entirely willing to
make complete amends to others? Or have we held back to
some degree—telling the truth, but not necessarily the
whole truth?

Have we refrained from placing blame on others? Or
have we, by innuendo, given them the message that they
are also guilty?

Have we freely admitted to manipulating situations so
that we could salve our own conscience, whether it caused
discomfort to others or not?

Have we admitted our wrongs to others in a cold and
dispassionate manner, giving them the impression that
we're condescending and superior?

If we fault ourselves on any of the above ploys, Step Ten
gives us an opportunity to rectify it before we compound
any more half-measures or evasions that will come back to
haunt us.

TODAY'S STEP: *I reconsider whether I have been painstaking enough in making my amends.*

Day 6—NEW FREEDOM

"Never bend your head. Hold it high. Look the world straight in the eye." **HELEN KELLER**

If we're doing a spot-check inventory, we must remember to: credit ourselves with the progress we have made, and the ghosts we have exorcised; accept and acknowledge our assets as we put them into action, and practice the technique of "acting as if" that we learned in the Sixth and Seventh Steps as an aid to rising above our shortcomings. For example: If we're afraid, we ask ourselves: "How would I 'act as if' I weren't afraid?" That's it! We act as if we're not afraid.

Once we've laid certain issues to rest, and we know they will no longer come back to haunt us, we experience a surge of freedom and satisfaction with ourselves. We know we have accomplished something major. We begin to feel more confident that we can move freely among our peers without the fear that any minute they will discover our guilty secrets.

Many of us have been in such a blue funk about ourselves for such a long time that we hardly recognize happiness when it's right in front of us. Freedom is certainly a major component of happiness, and we're beginning to experience that feeling more and more.

TODAY'S STEP: *In my daily assessment, I have the freedom to acknowledge my accomplishments.*

Step Ten

Day 7—THE PAST

"Judgment comes from experience, and great judgment comes from bad experience." BOB PACKWOOD

As we develop the ability to put our past difficulties, performances and biases into perspective, we begin to understand that we hold in our hands a valuable tool for survival. Although our past brought us to the state where we felt helpless and useless and created harm and chaos in our lives and those of others; although it seemed to push us to the point of no return, the opposite is true.

Slowly we are beginning to understand that every misstep in our past lives was part of the dynamic which led us to our present state of recovery.

With the blueprint of all past errors clearly defined, we can work Step Ten with confidence. We can see that had we not committed every one of those past actions that led to our cry for help, we would not have been desparate or needy enough to reach out.

We recognize that it was our finer instincts that took over in our struggle for survival and made us willing to humble ourselves enough to seek help. We could not have reached that point without experiencing every negative moment that marked the progression of our disease. Therefore, we now need to look at all those unkind, unhealthy, unproductive, antisocial actions as milestones that were necessary to bring us to our present state of recovery.

TODAY'S STEP: *Remembering my past mistakes helps me avoid today's pitfalls.*

Day 8—PAST EXPERIENCES

"It is no easy thing for a principle to become a man's own unless each day he maintain it and work it out in his life." EPICTETUS

Our physician friend has a wonderful way to describe the phenomenon of releasing regrets of our past performances. He uses an analogy of the Eiffel Tower. Like the Tower, our lives would have toppled if anything had been taken away or added in the construction phase. It took every bit of material, assembled in precisely the right pattern, to create the Tower and to bring us to the point where we found ourselves ready to seek and accept help.

When we think of the architect who designed that incredible edifice, we can remember our own architect—our Higher Power—who has brought us to the threshold of a new and productive existence.

Unlike the Eiffel Tower, though, we're not a finished product. We accept the fact that we are truly the sum of our past experiences. But, we also know that we will be changing as new and positive experiences happen to us in our continuing recovery program.

It is useless to live in past regrets or be fearful of what tomorrow may bring. Our goal is to live in the now, extracting all its benefits to strengthen us in the days to come. With one eye on yesterday and one eye on tomorrow—as the saying goes—we'll be cockeyed today. By taking a daily inventory, we keep the focus on today and on our recovery.

TODAY'S STEP: *My daily inventory plants my feet firmly in the present.*

Day 9—SACKCLOTH AND ASHES

"We have to learn to be our own best friends because we fall too easily into the trap of being our worst enemies."
RODERICK THORP

As recovering people, our self-images have taken such a beating that we sometimes wonder whether we'll ever feel totally O.K. about ourselves again. We tend to doubt that our feelings of uselessness and self-pity will ever go away.

We call this the "sackcloth and ashes" caper. Surely by now we've inventoried enough assets and strengths to know that we're not only productive and useful, but also, with our newfound strength and resolve, no longer pitiful.

Recovery is victory. And victory does not produce feelings of worthlessness. On the contrary, there is a dawning realization that we're now shaping a whole new existence for ourselves, an existence free of the nagging fear that we're weak-willed and useless.

Not too many people have a second chance to do life right when they've failed. But we do. If we can see our recovery as a rebirth, we can discard the shell of the old entity and make a fresh new start. By continuing to take our personal inventory, our past mistakes become useful guideposts to keep us on the right track.

TODAY'S STEP: *A daily inventory is the foundation of my second chance at life.*

Day 10—CONFIDENCE

"You have freedom when you're easy in your harness."
ROBERT FROST

We've already experienced the tremendous relief that came from cleaning up our side of the street by making amends to those we had harmed. We no longer feel that cloud of impending doom hovering over us, threatening to expose us to everyone as a sham and a charlatan.

With a clear conscience we can now go about our business secure in the knowledge that we no longer need to hide from anything or anybody. We have succeeded in our task of making restitution for past behavior. We have cleared up our financial responsibilities, or at least made partial payment of our outstanding debts. We have shouldered the blame for shattered relationships. We have gone back to our workplace and put in overtime, without pay, to make up for those hours when we shirked our responsibilities, or took time off that was not appropriate. In addition, we have been demonstrating our sincerity by our actions and our dependability in all our affairs.

With growing self-acceptance and self-approval, we can now face others with confidence. We can look anyone straight in the eye without flinching in fear that they will greet us with contempt or disdain. We no longer find it necessary to avoid certain people, places or things. We're finally secure enough in ourselves to feel comfortable with others.

TODAY'S STEP: *As I take my daily inventory, I can face people with confidence and self-respect.*

Step Ten

Day 11—THE COMMITTEE

"Getting out of bed in the morning is an act of false confidence."
JULES FEIFFER

In recovery many people feel they're in constant inner dialogue with themselves. They call this the committee in their heads. Some of them say that, when they wake up in the morning, the committee is in full session, and they are assailed with doubts and confusion about how they're going to face their day.

There's a whole squirrel cage of "what-ifs" spinning around in their minds. What if my wife is in a bad mood this morning? What if my husband complains about breakfast? What if I'm late to work? What if I don't get a raise? What if I lose my job? What if I win the lottery? What if I don't win the lottery? What if the plane I'm taking crashes? What if I can't send my kids to college? What if my boyfriend is cheating on me? What if my girlfriend dumps me? What if I get AIDS? What if I have an accident?

A handy rejoinder shared with us by a fellow "inner dialoguer" was to say to his committee: "Thanks for sharing!"

Then he was able to go about the daily business of living with some degree of detachment. He said that whenever he found himself pointing the finger at someone or something he felt was responsible for his feelings of fear and insecurity, that three were pointing back at him.

When we adjourn the committee in our heads we can take an honest personal inventory.

TODAY'S STEP: *I can put aside my inner chatter and get on with living today.*

Step Ten

Day 12—RESENTMENTS

"Nothing on earth consumes a man more quickly than the passion of resentment."

FRIEDRICH NIETZSCHE

We need to continually examine our feelings to see if the recurring theme of resentments enter into our daily stock-taking. Resentments are, without doubt, the most dangerous threat to our continuing recovery program. Time after time, people have reported that their inability to let go of resentments led to a relapse into their former addictive/compulsive lifestyle.

Although Steps One through Nine have alleviated much of our pain and discomfort, we're not totally home free when we arrive at Step Ten. This is because the illusion of total recovery is exactly that—an illusion. We spent many years developing the problem that brought us to our knees. All of its side effects cannot be cured in a short period of time, no matter how assiduously we apply ourselves to working the steps.

Sometimes we begin to feel sorry for ourselves. We think the burden of responsibility rests entirely on our shoulders, and that others are not doing their share. This leads to our digging around in the past and deciding they have always acted like that. That maybe the way we behaved back then was not so much our fault as theirs. That we were foolish to shoulder all the blame when we made amends. That anyone would have done the same things we did under such circumstances.

This is why holding on to resentments can be so dangerous to our recovery.

TODAY'S STEP: *My daily inventory helps me to release old resentments.*

Step Ten

Day 13—NOTHING TO LOSE

"Committing yourself is a way of finding out who you are. A man finds his identity by identifying. A man's identity is not best thought of as the way in which he is separated from his fellows, but the way in which he is united with them."

ROBERT TERWILLIGER

Yesterday we talked of recurring resentments and the danger of falling back into what is called the "stinking thinking" pattern.

This might be a good time to try another experiment to point up the pitfalls of relapse.

Take a large sheet of paper, fold it and tear it in half. Now tear the two sheets in half. Next tear the four sheets in half so that you have eight small pieces of paper. Now write on each piece of paper a description of eight separate things that you feel are, or would be, the most important or necessary things you need to make your life happy and fulfilled. Number them in order of their importance.

Now look at number eight, think deeply about it and then crumple it up and throw it away. Do the same with seven, six, five, four, three and two. Now look at number one. Really concentrate on how important it is to you. What your life would be like without it. Now, crumple it up too and throw it away.

How does that make you feel? Suppose you could take only one back? Would it be the same number one? Or would you choose another as the most important?

If recovery was not your number one priority, this might be a good time to rethink whether you have truly committed yourself to following the way of life outlined in these steps.

TODAY'S STEP: *Today, and every day, recovery is my number one priority.*

Day 14—THE PICKLE REVISITED

"Do not measure another's coat on your own body."
MALAY PROVERB

Remember the pickle? We had no trouble accepting the reality that once a cucumber had become a pickle, it could never go back to being a cucumber again. So it is with us. We can never return to who or what we were before our disorder took over. But we can accept our present "pickleness" as positive rather than negative.

After doing our Fourth and Fifth Steps, we recognized that had we not been caught up in the chronic progression of our disorders, we would never have acted out those antisocial, unproductive behaviors that propelled us into our search for recovery. Those behaviors did change us though, and we need to be aware that the conditioning we underwent takes a long time to be erased from our subconscious. Some of us believe that it is always there. And this is why we must be vigilant in determining whether we're reacting out of an old negative idea, or we're rethinking the situation and acting out of our newfound knowledge and positive resolve.

If we think of ourselves as one of the "twice born," we can be less nostalgic about what we were and more excited about what we're becoming. As one seventy-year-old man said in response to a brash youngster who had criticized his progress, "Listen, sonny, God isn't finished with me yet!"

TODAY'S STEP: *Whenever I get into a pickle, I promptly admit my mistakes.*

Step Ten

Day 15—FORGIVING FREELY

"The welfare of each is bound up in the welfare of all."
                                                    HELEN KELLER

Sometimes we get the idea that Step Ten's function is to be a stern parent who observes and criticizes our every move. This is certainly not the intent of this step. Quite the opposite. Rather, it is a protective device that helps us to understand how easily the old ghosts of the past can reassert themselves and become stumbling blocks to our recovery process.

It is of no value whatsoever to cling to the memory of wrongs done to us. We have cleared up our own wrongdoings to the best of our ability, and we have tried to rectify our past mistakes. It is imperative that we learn to forgive ourselves. And in that same spirit we also want to forgive others.

Once we've learned to forgive others spontaneously and freely, we will realize that we've overcome another obstacle in the way of our recovery process. When our feelings are hurt, we will learn not to retaliate in kind—although we certainly do not intend to act as a doormat to anyone. We will be assertive—but not aggressive—when it comes to being treated unfairly, for we've come to the realization that we deserve the same kind of courtesy and consideration that we are now giving others.

TODAY'S STEP: *I recognize the freedom of forgiveness.*

Day 16—RIGHT ACTION

"There is no failure except in no longer trying."
ELBERT HUBBARD

Fairness and truth are an essential part of this step. Fairness, not only toward others, but also toward ourselves. Truth, because we're now operating in an arena where people have begun to trust us again, and we want to be worthy of that trust. When we practice courtesy, we find that people are courteous to us. And when we're kind, we experience kindness being displayed from unexpected sources.

Whether we spot-check our inventories daily or periodically, they enable us to keep a running tab on our assets and strengths. And they offer a technique for measuring our progress in understandable terms. They help us to be more alert in identifying old behavior patterns, and to practice living up to our full potential.

When we find ourselves in challenging situations, we can rely on our growing intuition to help us through. We remember the prayer that says: "God, I offer myself to Thee to build with me and do with me as Thou wilt. Relieve me of the bondage of self." Even if we are agnostics or atheists we can put this thought out into the universe. Almost invariably, we will choose the right action.

TODAY'S STEP: *My daily inventory guides me into unexpected sources and right action.*

Day 17—POSITIVE MONITORING

"If you think you have no faults, that makes one more."   ANONYMOUS

If we have been keeping a daily journal or have kept a copy of our Fourth Step written inventory, we can keep reviewing the nature of the wrongs we discovered about ourselves and spot-check to see if we're repeating any of those old behavioral patterns.

Old habits die very hard. They are automatic knee-jerk responses to years of conditioning and often reassert themselves without conscious thought on our part. Frequently, it's only after the fact that we become aware of the full impact of what we've said or done. But the temptation to sweep those behaviors under the rug is an old idea. It's not in keeping with the intent of the Tenth Step.

Stockpiling our lapses creates anxiety, for we know that we're eventually going to have to come to terms with whatever it is that we've said or done.

However, when we can promptly admit we're wrong, we instantly clear our conscience of that nagging voice that continually reminds us we've fouled up again. It's like keeping up with the housekeeping everyday, rather than allowing things to get to the stage where we're overpowered at the thought of the job. We can simply tackle the issue at hand and get on with more productive endeavors.

By viewing our daily monitoring as positive rather than punitive, we will soon find ourselves more comfortable with ourselves and others.

TODAY'S STEP: *It's becoming easier to promptly admit when I am wrong.*

Day 18—SELF-FULFILLING PROPHECY

"When you encounter opposition in your life you can look at it as a means to keep you from slipping." ANONYMOUS

There is a phenomenon called a "self-fulfilling prophecy." The way it seems to work is that if we have a belief about ourselves—for instance that we'll fail at something we want to do—we will fail. That negative belief brings a foregone conclusion. And almost automatically we start manifesting the behavior that will bring about a negative result.

Life is often unfair, but it is reciprocal. When we sow seeds of deprivation, failure and helplessness, we reap the harvest of just such negative projections.

On the other hand, when we cheerfully accept challenges, we feel that even if we don't win, we've profited by the experience. And we create an atmosphere of optimism for ourselves and others that inevitably leads to good results we had not foreseen. It is rather like learning a new game. We try to master it, but are realistic about the fact that we may not immediately succeed. We keep on trying, however, because we've learned what doesn't work.

We can use our daily inventory to keep tabs on negative attitudes like these that can become self-fulfilling prophecies.

TODAY'S STEP: *If I'm going to create self-fulfilling prophecies, I'll now make certain that they're positive.*

Day 19—TAKING RISKS

"Today I accept the abundance of life. I live greatly, think creatively, and love openly."

DR. PEGGY BASSETT

As we continue the practice of daily inventory-taking, it's helpful to examine those situations in which we have hesitated to voice our opinion for fear of being rejected or misunderstood.

Surely, by now we should be aware that honesty (like love) sometimes has to play an unappealing role, and that when our beliefs are being challenged by others, it is our responsibility to stand up for our principles.

We might be fearful that in disagreeing, we risk the friendship or approval of others, but it is necessary for us to take just such risks if we are to continue the principle of being true to ourselves.

There are those times, too, when we are hesitant to reach out to someone who is hurting for fear that they will view us as meddlesome or presumptuous. Again, the risk is well worth taking if we remember our own silent cries for help and the wish that someone, somehow, could sense our pain and could hold out a helping hand.

Because we have come so far on our own journey of recovery, and because our daily inventory helps us to see our own weaknesses and shortcomings, we develop a much greater understanding of the difficulties of others, and are able to reach out to them with honesty and empathy.

TODAY'S STEP: *Today I dare to take risks that will enhance my life.*

Step Ten

Day 20—CHECKING OUR INVENTORY

"Learn as if you were going to live forever. Live as if you were going to die tomorrow." ANONYMOUS

In Step Four we did an inventory that had many of us digging into our past to determine what our shortcomings, wrongs and defects had been and still were. Then we listed our strengths and attributes to see which of those would be powerful enough to extinguish our unproductive behavior patterns.

In Step Ten we want to concentrate on the *now*. We need to check our daily inventory to see whether we're still harboring resentments, indulging in self-pity or defeatism, procrastinating, acting grandiose, behaving selfishly, or feeling jealous.

These are but a few of the red alerts that help us understand why we might not be feeling comfortable at the moment. Each one of us can probably think of many more.

If this sounds as though we must spend all our waking hours examining and reexamining ourselves for flaws, this is not the case. The personal inventory is simply a useful tool to help us when we're experiencing uncomfortable feelings with ourselves or others. It's at these moments that we need to mentally review our memories of past behaviors. This allows us to identify the negative emotion that is presently being stimulated. Once we can identify the cause, we know how to rectify it.

TODAY'S STEP: *When I take stock every day, I can recognize and correct my character defects.*

Step Ten

Day 21—RED ALERT

"With faith, nothing is impossible."   ANONYMOUS

Some folks have told us that their inventory keeps them centered in the decision they made in the Third Step—to turn their will and their lives over to the care of God as they understood Him.

It is so easy to fall back into old patterns of self-sufficiency, and to say in effect, "Thanks, Higher Power, for taking me this far. But now that I know the ropes, I can manage my life from here on in."

Red alert! Red alert! Red alert!

The entire recovery program is established on a spiritual base. Without believing and committing ourselves to some power or force greater than ourselves, self-will will take over and start to govern our lives again. Haven't we been convinced time and again that it was self-will and self-determination that found us floundering and brought us to our knees?

Our best intentions, our best intelligence, our best efforts couldn't prevent us from being caught up in our addictive behavior. It still happened, despite every effort we put forth to prevent it.

So, it is wise to heed that red alert, and to use it to rededicate ourselves to the commitment we made in our Third Step.

TODAY'S STEP: *My daily inventory helps me to turn my will over to my Higher Power.*

Step Ten

Day 22—JENNY'S STORY

*"If you want to read about love and marriage,
you've got to buy two separate books."* ALAN KING

Despite taking our original inventory, and trying to do the
Eighth and Ninth Steps to the best of our ability, certain
behavior patterns still take a long time to make themselves
known.

Jenny shared that her final divorce papers had a devastat-
ing effect on her. She truly felt she'd spent her entire
married life trying to be the perfect wife and mother.

"How could he have left me?" said Jenny. "Wasn't I
always there for him? Didn't I practice discipline and morality? Didn't I keep the house spotless, the children well
cared for? Didn't I put his needs above everyone else's?
After all I did for him, how could he leave me for an
empty-headed aerobics instructor?"

Although Jenny had identified her outrageous perfectionism in her Fourth Step, she had not been able to see
how that characteristic could drive someone away.

It was not until she had been taking a daily inventory
that Jenny was able to see how her rigidity was immobiliz-
ing her—and how it was affecting her relationship with her
children. The Tenth Step enabled Jenny to shed self-pity
and to risk taking the chance of developing a new and
healthy relationship.

TODAY'S STEP: *Each day, I gain greater self-awareness
through my inventory.*

Step Ten

Day 23—SUSAN'S STORY

"Think twice before you speak, especially if you're going to say what you think." ANONYMOUS

The value of taking a daily inventory cannot be overemphasized. It's invaluable in helping us maintain our sense of accomplishment and well-being. It's so easy to slip back into old habit patterns without some form of restraint. And this step provides just that protection.

Although—on the surface—Step Ten may not appear to be as powerful as the preceding steps, it is our greatest insurance against relapse.

We have to guard against inflicting emotional blackmail on those closest to us by sending out the message that *their* behavior might cause us to fall back into our old addictive ways. We also have to guard against trying to convince ourselves that their faults and shortcomings were and are the cause of our downfall. This is where the power of Step Ten really comes into play.

Susan, a recovering bulimic, was forced to use this step when her family finally rebelled against her "Mother Hubbard–Bare Cupboard" complex. They reminded Susan that the eating disorder was not theirs, they had a right to bring their snacks, potato chips, desserts and sodas into the house, and it was up to her to cope in a world where food abounds. The world wasn't going to change for her: Susan was going to have to do the changing.

TODAY'S STEP: My *daily inventory reminds me not to blame others for my shortcomings.*

*"One day I shall burst my bud of serenity and
blossom into full-blown hysteria."*   ANONYMOUS

Steps Ten, Eleven and Twelve are tools that help us maintain what we've already gained. They also further our ability
to develop the spiritual and ethical values that will open up
unlimited possibilities for us to enjoy a very rewarding and
comfortable lifestyle.

In Step Ten, we learn to read the warning signs of
negativity, irritability, fear and frustration. Gradually, we
become adept at identifying the defect or shortcoming
that's causing these feelings. That's when it becomes possible to readjust our thinking and to release those unhealthy
reactions.

As time passes, we become more and more adept at
this practice. We learn to catch ourselves before negative
thoughts and actions start to take hold.

We also learn to use the cautionary phrase, "H.A.L.T.":
"Don't get too hungry, too angry, too lonely, too tired."
In the recovery process we've discovered that those conditions are responsible for many a relapse. Therefore we try
to be vigilant about avoiding them. This is where the
spot-check inventory comes in. It's the most valuable tool
we have to abort negative emotions before they become
full-blown.

TODAY'S STEP: *My daily inventory helps me quickly spot
any signs of relapse.*

Day 25—DAILY INVENTORY

"Courage is fear that has said its prayers."

ANONYMOUS

Some fans of the daily inventory tell us they meditate first thing in the morning and pray for guidance during the day. Then at night they review the day's activities to determine whether there are any amends they need to make. However, they also review the positive aspects of their day and give themselves credit for all their accomplishments.

When it's possible to do so, they contact the people to whom amends are due and clear the air. If those persons are unavailable, they put that activity on their priority list for the next day, and persist in their attempts until they have fulfilled this obligation.

Just as in Step Nine, we make amends primarily to get right with ourselves. True, we also wish to set the record straight with those we might have offended or hurt. But the most important thing is to set the record right with ourselves.

We clearly remember how it felt to live with a guilty conscience in the past, and we no longer want to operate under such a cloud. Step Ten allows us to start each day with a clean slate and a clear conscience. It makes it easier and easier to face everyone we meet with assurance and dignity.

TODAY'S STEP: *When I make immediate amends I keep a clean slate.*

Day 26—LOUISE'S STORY

"It is much easier to keep up than to catch up."
ANONYMOUS

We never know what's going to shake us up and make us take a good hard look at ourselves. Sometimes it's a chance remark; something we've witnessed; sometimes something we've read.

A case in point was a graphic newspaper report about Louise, a young woman who was found dead in her apartment—a suicide. Neighbors had called the police when they noticed that grocery bags and newspapers had piled up at her door for a number of days.

Although Louise had lived in that neighborhood for some time, no one had ever seen her. The owner of the market she patronized said she always had her groceries delivered and she paid by check. They assumed she was feeding a family of three or four because of the size of her orders. Some of the kids in the neighborhood made up stories about Louise being a witch who kept her children prisoners.

When the police broke in, they discovered that the kitchen had literally become a garbage dump. They found Louise huddled by the open refrigerator, a leviathan who weighed almost four hundred pounds.

In her suicide note Louise said she couldn't bear to have anyone see how repulsive she had become. She had simply run out of funds and was too ashamed to ask for help.

The value of keeping a running tab on our inventory is pretty clearly illustrated by this story.

TODAY'S STEP: *My daily inventory alerts me when I'm getting in over my head, so I can ask for help.*

Day 27—THE HALLWAY

"Some luck lies in getting not what you thought you wanted, but getting what you have, which once you have got it, you may be smart enough to see it is what you wanted had you known."

GARRISON KEILLOR

There are times when we have difficulty believing in the expression: "When one door closes, another opens." When we look back on the work we've done, and the work we're doing now to apply the steps to our daily lives, we don't seem to see any visible proof that our current dilemma is being resolved. In fact, we often become very disillusioned about our progress.

This is when we have to remember that our situation did not occur overnight. Time is a necessary factor in resolving all the fallout it created.

In closing the door on our addiction, we sometimes have to wait in the hallway until the other door opens. Impatient by nature, we rebel at any delay, wanting what we want when we want it. Our tolerance for frustration is in short supply.

This is an excellent example of when the spot-check inventory is a very valuable tool. How? First, it helps us identify impatience as the defect involved here. We can then remind ourselves that when we uncovered the same character defect in our Sixth and Seventh Steps, we asked ourselves, "How would I act if I weren't impatient?" And that's the way we act now.

TODAY'S STEP: *I have faith that this daily work on myself will take me down the hallway to the next open door.*

Day 28—ELIMINATING THE "NOTS"

What You Think of Me Is None of My Business
TITLE OF A BOOK BY TERRY COLE WHITTAKER

When we come to terms with the fact that fear is self-created, we're in a far better position to tackle admitting our missteps to others than we were in the past. We remind ourselves that no matter how much we dreaded taking the Ninth Step, once it was done we felt considerably better.

However, we had trouble enough with our original amends step and we remember how our accumulated guilt and shame tied us even more tightly into our destructive behavior. We don't want to accumulate a whole new set of unresolved issues.

We sometimes try to convince ourselves that we're *not* strong enough to face up to others. That we're *not* articulate enough to explain our behavior. That we're *not* ready to admit our culpability. That we're *not* brave enough to make amends to those who intimidate us.

This is why eliminating the "nots" is of primary importance at this stage of recovery. We remember that "acting as if" has been useful to us in the past, so we use that device to push all these "nots" out of our way.

We've come so far by the time we get to Step Ten, now is *not* the time to backslide.

TODAY'S STEP: *By admitting promptly when I'm "not-ted" up I stay free of shame and guilt.*

Day 29—"TO DO" LISTS

"When you get to the end of your rope, tie a knot and hang on." **ANONYMOUS**

In Step Ten we're truly taking things out of the realm of theory and putting them into action on a daily basis.

We've always known that it's easier to take care of what's at hand rather than procrastinating. Nevertheless, we still persist in putting things off until tomorrow.

Most successful businesspeople start each day by making a "to do" list, which gives them the incentive to use their valuable time in an orderly fashion. By the end of their day, the things that were not attended to are given top priority on the list for the next day.

We can use this technique as a helpful tool in our own lives, when we do a daily check of our ups and downs. We can resolve to put those things we feel we handled badly at the top of our list of "to do's" for the next day.

Now is also a good time to remember that we're not only making amends to others. We're making them to ourselves by rectifying those actions that have made us disappointed in us. Forgiving ourselves is equally as important as clearing the air with others. Too often we let perfectionism stand in the way of progress.

TODAY'S STEP: *My daily inventory helps me stay organized and productive.*

Day 30—SHIFTS

"It is easier to get forgiveness than permission."
ANONYMOUS

As we're winding up the Tenth Step, this might be an opportune time to review the exercise we did on Day 13, when we took eight small pieces of paper and wrote down the people and things most important in our lives.

Let's do that same exercise today, and compare it with our original. Think about the priorities you had then and see if they're still the same. Experience has taught us that the healthier we get, the more likely we are to change our minds about what is of primary importance to us.

As we grow and change, we discover that tangible things become less important; they somehow give way to things of a more spiritual nature. Agnostic, atheist or believer, the evidence is certainly clear by now that some power greater than ourselves has been at work in our lives, bringing about remarkable shifts in attitudes, behaviors and beliefs.

Clearly, our perspective is quite different now than it was when we were first introduced to Step One. As our awareness has expanded, we have found ourselves becoming more sensitive, more discerning, more judicious and more intuitive. It becomes easier and easier for us to start with a clean slate each day and—with a minimal amount of effort—to keep it that way.

TODAY'S STEP: *My daily inventory keeps my priorities straight.*

Day 31—EXPECT A MIRACLE

"The harder one works, the more luck one seems to have."   ANONYMOUS

Despite our tendency to minimize the degree of progress we've made in our program, this is the moment when we need to be awed at how much we've accomplished. How often have we downplayed and discounted our progress? We're still assailed with self-doubts, and this makes us question the depths of our commitment. We're afraid we might simply have been giving lip-service to something we're not all that sure we really believe in.

Don't be discouraged. Many of us hit this stage in our recovery. We spent so much time in the past in bondage to our addiction, that an enormous measure of our self-confidence evaporated. We were left with the fear that we had no power to extricate ourselves from the mess we found ourselves in. We thought that only a miracle could free us.

Recovery, as we've said many times before, is not an event. It is a process. Recovery is not a destination. It is an ongoing journey. But it is always a miracle. A miracle that our own diligence and hard work—no matter how much we downplay it—had brought about. This is why, at this very important stage, we *are* ready for Steps Eleven and Twelve.

TODAY'S STEP: *When I take stock of myself day by day, my progress is clear.*

Step Eleven

STEP ELEVEN

"Sought through prayer and meditation to improve our conscious contact with God as we understood Him, praying only for knowledge of His will for us and the power to carry that out."

By the time we arrive at Step Eleven, most of us have become comfortable with the concept of spirituality. We feel that the phrase "God, as we understood Him," tells us clearly that, whatever our belief is, some spiritual contact is essential to our recovery program.

Those of us who have been fortunate enough to find a support group—and have participated in our own recovery by being an active member of that group—have come to know the comfort of being a "part of" rather than feeling pain and loneliness because we don't seem to fit in anywhere. This camaraderie has given us the benefit of hearing how others learned to pray and meditate.

Many people have said that of all the steps, they felt this one was the most healing. It reenforced their commitment to a power greater than themselves. And it gave them a more definitive sense of being on the right path at last.

For those of us who are loners, or whose circumstances preclude involvement with others, Step Eleven is like a beacon light. Its focus on meditation in addition to prayer teaches us how to create calm in the face of chaos. It also familiarizes us with the effective value of guided imagery, which we can use when we do not have someone with whom we can share.

Day 1—I VS. WE

"Example is not the main thing in influencing others. It is the only thing."   ALBERT SCHWEITZER

Step Ten taught us to continue to take our personal inventory. By practicing this step, we were able to recognize when we started moving away from dependence on a Higher Power and began to take back our own self-will.

It is essential for us to understand the message of Steps Ten and Eleven fully. They not only emphasize the need to follow their guidelines for our personal recovery, they also reflect the universality of their principles as they apply to others.

The Steps say: "Continued to take personal inventory, and when *we* (not 'I') were wrong promptly admitted it." And, "Sought through prayer and meditation to improve *our* (not 'my') conscious contact with God as *we* (not 'I') understood him." We are in no way attempting to diminish the impact of our own personal use of the steps. But we need to keep in mind that the Twelve Step process has been around for some time. It has been tested over and over. And when it is followed with care, it seems to be almost infallible.

A message to remember is: "We can do what I can't do." It is precisely because these steps have worked for so many thousands before us that we can be assured of their effectiveness. It is by listening to our predecessors and following their path that we can walk in dignity once more.

TODAY'S STEP: *The thousands who go with me and before me on this path make it easier to follow.*

Day 2—TALKING WITH GOD

"No one who has had a unique experience with prayer has a right to withhold it from others."
SOONG MEI-LING

Step Three had us making a decision to turn our lives and will over to the care of God as we understood Him. At this stage of recovery, Step Eleven has us actively engaged in dialogue with the God-concept we have adopted for ourselves—whatever that may be. In any case, most of us would be hard-pressed to give an adequate description of the form that entity takes on for us. Our belief may well be a highly personal and private one that we are reluctant to define.

Some of us have had no difficulty in integrating our religious beliefs into this spiritual program. We're quite comfortable with the God of our childhood. Still others have borrowed another phrase from the Twelve Traditions of AA, and think of their Higher Power as "a loving God as He may express Himself in our group conscience."

Whatever choice we have made, Step Eleven offers us the opportunity to practice talking to that power, whether by inner dialogue or by getting down on our knees to pray. Many of the agnostics on this path have admitted that although they have no real belief in God, they follow the ritual of praying because they've heard so many success stories from others who have done so with remarkable results.

TODAY'S STEP: *I engage in daily dialogue with God as I understand Him.*

Step Eleven

Day 3—UNIVERSAL TRUTHS

"Faith is believing what you know ain't so."

MARK TWAIN

The childhood prayer most familiar to many of us is:

Now I lay me down to sleep
I pray thee, Lord, my soul to keep
If I should die before I wake
I pray thee, Lord, my soul to take.

This prayer struck fear into the heart of many a child because of what that last line implied.

To "die before I wake" might well have been the reason many of us developed erratic sleep patterns. When we were children, grown-ups frequently told us that if we weren't good, God would be peeved with us, and we'd never get to heaven. We certainly didn't want to be taken before we had a chance to clean up whatever God was angry about.

One friend reported that when she had her own children, she changed that last line to: "and may God watch me through the night, until the morning's early light." Strangely enough, although she professed no real belief in God, she discovered that she was saying that same prayer to herself each night before she fell asleep.

When it was pointed out that she *had* made it through all the nights in her life to date, she admitted that there may indeed have been something helping her through her desperate times. She preferred, however, to continue equating her Higher Power with what she termed "Universal Truths."

TODAY'S STEP: *I can find comfort and help in old, familiar prayers.*

Day 4—PRAYER OF ST. FRANCIS

"Destiny is not a matter of choice. It is not something to be waited for; but, rather something to be achieved." **WILLIAM JENNINGS BRYANT**

Perhaps one of the best-known prayers in the world is that of St. Francis of Assisi. It is almost universal in its usage, for despite our own individual beliefs, few of us take issue with its message:

Lord, make me an instrument of Thy peace,
that where there is hatred, let me sow love,
that where there is injury, I may bring pardon,
that where there is despair, I may bring hope,
that where there is error, I may bring truth,
that where there is doubt, I may bring faith,
that where there is sadness, I may bring joy.
Lord, grant that I may seek rather to comfort
than to be comforted,
to understand, than to be understood,
to love, than to be loved.
For it is by giving that we receive.
It is by forgiving that we are forgiven.
It is by dying that we awaken to eternal life.

Everything we have been striving to accomplish thus far in our program is epitomized in the prayer of St. Francis. Over the next few days, we will examine portions of this prayer to determine how it both reminds us of the steps we have already taken and furthers our recovery.

TODAY'S STEP: *I pray earnestly to be an instrument of God's will.*

Day 5—PEACE AND SERENITY

*"Behind peaceful tranquillity lies conquered chal-
lenges."*
ANONYMOUS

Steps One, Two and Three open us up to an awareness that
we have lost the power to manage and control our lives,
that we have been caught in a downward spiral that will
destroy us unless some power or force intercedes on our
behalf.

In Step One, we admitted the unmanageability of our
lives. We realized we could no longer keep up the pretense
that somehow we were capable of setting things right. That
admission created a small opening in our wall of resistance.

In Step Two, we conceded that our behavior, attitudes
and reactions were certainly not very sane; that many of the
things we had said and done were not those of a rational
human being. This is when we admitted the irrationality of
our behavior, and began to concede that a power greater
than ourselves just might be able to help us recover. The
opening widened to a narrow channel.

Then, in Step Three, we decided—not without skepticism—that in order to find peace and to share it with
others, it was necessary to risk that gigantic leap into faith.
And we placed our will and our lives in the hands of
whoever or whatever that power was.

The channel became wider and wider as our resistance
lessened. At last we were able to see that peace and serenity
might be possible for us to achieve.

Step Eleven now reinforces all that our first three steps
taught us. We are truly convinced that life is worth living
on the right track.

TODAY'S STEP: *I recognize my Higher Power as the source
of peace and serenity.*

Day 6—PARDON

"Life is an adventure in forgiveness."

NORMAN COUSINS

In Step Four we did our inventory. And in Step Five, we shared the exact nature of our wrongs with God, ourselves and another human being.

Having identified our defects and shortcomings in those two steps, we were then ready to take Steps Six and Seven—to be ready and willing to have our Higher Power help us to remove as many of them as possible. Although we were well aware that this process would be a lengthy one, we did our best to eliminate as many as we were capable of doing at the time.

In Steps Eight and Nine we identified the people to whom we owed amends and set about doing what we could to make reparations. We forgave them for any hurt they might have inflicted on us and hoped we would be forgiven for our actions toward them. We tried, to the best of our ability, to clear up financial obligations and to repair what business or personal havoc we had created. Where we were not able to reach each of them in person, we wrote or telephoned, whenever doing so would not bring them further harm.

Of equal importance was the necessity to forgive ourselves. Until we were free from self-recrimination and self-pity, our chance for continuing progress was greatly diminished.

We realize now that had it not been for the work we did in Steps Eight and Nine, we would not have been ready to embrace the challenge and the opportunity that Step Eleven presents to us.

TODAY'S STEP: *With my Higher Power's help, I pray to forgive and be forgiven.*

Day 7—PRAYERS

"No one is as capable of gratitude as one who has emerged from the kingdom of the night."

ST. FRANCIS OF ASSISI

In Step Eleven it is helpful to review a portion of the prayer of St. Francis, and understand how aptly it reflects what we learned in the preceding steps:

"Where There is Error, I May Bring Truth"

Step Nine taught us that the very act of making amends to others involved an honest admission of our evasions and untruths. Now in working Step Eleven we ask for the power to carry out those principles which are more in keeping with God's will for us.

"Where There is Doubt, I May Bring Faith"

Step Three was the crucial turning point for us to release self-will and trust that there *was* a power greater than ourselves. Step Eleven reinforces this trust as we willingly let that Higher Power guide us through the maze of recovery.

"Where There is Despair, I May Bring Hope"

Each of the steps we have taken has reduced our feelings of unworthiness and shame. We had despaired of ever being right with our world again. But we found that as we admitted and accepted our problem; released self-will; trusted our Higher Power; made reparation for misdeeds; continued to monitor our progress and sincerely adopted the practice of prayer and meditation, we had entered into the very essence of Step Eleven.

TODAY'S STEP: *My prayers act as guidelines that allow me to be of help to others.*

"Do the truth you know, and you shall learn the truth you need to know." ANONYMOUS

Another helpful prayer is one which has appeared many times in a "Dear Abby" column and which, for all its simplicity, is not as easy to do as one would think. Excerpts from it have proven useful to many of us.

> Just for today, I will try to live through this day only, and not tackle my whole life problem at once. I can do something for twelve hours that would appall me if I felt I had to keep it up for a lifetime. Just for today I will be happy. This assumes to be true what Abraham Lincoln said, that "Most folks are as happy as they make up their minds to be."
>
> Just for today, I will adjust myself to what is and not try to adjust everything to my own desires. I will take my "luck" as it comes, and fit myself to it.
>
> Just for today I will exercise my soul in three ways. I will do somebody a good turn, and not get found out; if anybody knows of it, it will not count. I will do at least two things I don't want to do—just for exercise. I will not show anyone that my feelings are hurt; they may be hurt, but today I will not show it.

It's amazing to learn that our need for approval is so great that when we try anonymously to do someone a good turn, we're hard-pressed not to tell anyone else of our achievement. Try it!

TODAY'S STEP: *My prayers help me to live in the now.*

Step Eleven

Day 9—RIGHT WHERE WE SHOULD BE

"The value of consistent prayer is not that He will hear us, but that we will hear Him."

WILLIAM McGILL

Recovery is not an instantaneous process. It comes in increments and not everyone progresses at the same pace.

Much like children in school, some of us master math easily; others have no trouble with English; and some develop muscular and physical strength long before their peers. And there are some of us who become discouraged when we don't seem to be "getting it" as quickly as others.

This is where much of the power of Step Eleven lies. When we combine the knowledge about ourselves we acquired in our self-evaluation steps with the meditation and prayer called for by this step, we create a strong foundation for growth and self-acceptance.

This foundation stabilizes our purpose and resolve by telling us that we are exactly who we should be today, and where we should be today. By practicing principles that the past ten steps have taught us, we're well on the path to the kind of life we've yearned for. As long as we continue to seek guidance through prayer, and heed the inner voice that will manifest itself as we listen in meditation, then we're progressing at exactly the appropriate pace for us.

TODAY'S STEP: *Day by day, my Higher Power is leading me on the road to recovery.*

Day 10—GUIDANCE

*"When you feel you can't stand on ~~~~
longer, try a bended knee."*

Volumes have been written about the techn~~~~
tation throughout both Oriental and Occidental philosophies. They range from the teachings of mystics to sensory
deprivation and guided imagery.

Transcendental Meditation became a rage in the Sixties.
People followed the teachings of Maharishi Mahesh Yogi,
received their mantras, and once or twice a day, for twenty
minutes, went off by themselves to practice his techniques.

There are religious meditations that are devotional exercises, and there are other forms of active meditation in
which one simply ponders a question or follows the flow of
the breath.

Some of us have studied, and continue to practice, the
type of meditation that falls into the devotional category.
Others have found that, for them, prayer means talking to
their Higher Power, and meditation is listening to their
inner selves for guidance.

We believe that meditation is vital in developing our
instincts for making beneficial decisions for ourselves. As
we practice listening to our inner voices, we begin to sense
a feeling of divine guidance.

TODAY'S STEP: *I explore meditation techniques and find
the one that suits me.*

Step Eleven

Day 11—IMAGERY MEDITATION

"The man who has done nothing but wait for his ship to come in has already missed the boat."
ANONYMOUS

Guided imagery is relatively easy to master. At first, you may need quiet and seclusion. But those who are proficient in it tell us they are able to practice it whatever their surroundings may be.

To begin: Sit someplace comfortable, with both feet on the floor—or tailor fashion if you prefer. Now close your eyes. Relax. Inhale deeply and gently, filling the stomach like a balloon, and then the lungs. Then exhale slowly, pushing out the air gently with your stomach muscles. Repeat this procedure five or six times, focusing your attention on the rhythmic flow of your breathing.

Now, in your imagination, think of a setting where you feel happy, comfortable and safe. Perhaps by the ocean, a lake, a sunny meadow, a mountaintop, on a ship, in a vacation home, a fondly remembered room, or even an imaginary setting. Visualize yourself in that place. No one is with you. You feel warm and secure in your surroundings.

Now you're becoming aware that there is another presence with you. A benign and nonthreatening presence that you somehow understand is there to be of service to you. Choose whatever form you wish that presence to take. Now ask the presence for solutions to problems that disturb you, or advice on decisions you need to make, and then, quietly listen for answers.

More than one of us have been amazed at the insights we've gained by doing this exercise. We don't hesitate to recommend it to those who are searching for some form of meditation.

TODAY'S STEP: *Whatever the technique, meditation offers new images to explore.*

Day 12—CONTEMPLATION

"There are times when nothing a man can say is nearly so powerful as saying nothing."

ANONYMOUS

Contemplation is an exercise in which we reflect on, or ponder, an issue. When we do not want to act too hastily or rashly, we take time out to think the issue through and determine what will be the best one for all concerned.

Back when our compulsive behavior neared the point of doing us in, our low tolerance for frustration had reached such a volatile stage that we reacted rashly and sometimes violently to whatever seemed to pose a threat to us. Our best defense—we thought—was an aggressive offense. And we rarely gave considered thought to what the consequences of our actions would be.

Now, recognizing that we still have Pavlovian reactions to familiar stimuli, we want to take time to really think through the issues confronting us. Although contemplation might not appear to be a bona fide meditation, it is one of the classic forms meditation takes.

Listening to inspiring music can also put us in a meditative state, as can watching a spectacular sunrise or sunset, observing the rhythmic break of waves on the shore, or just plain daydreaming.

TODAY'S STEP: *In quiet contemplation, I gain the clarity to resolve my difficulties.*

Day 13—OPEN MEDITATIONS

"Nowhere can man find a quieter or more untroubled retreat than in his own soul."

MARCUS AURELIUS

There are countless books offering all sorts of meditations and exercises. Some of us have studied and implemented these teachings in our daily lives. And, as we've become more open to our intuitive responses, we've recognized that we're in touch with our own higher consciousness on a much deeper level.

We have become aware that it lies within our power to regulate our thinking and to establish order and balance in our emotions. We've found that we can release mental stress and physical tension. And this helps us focus on what is valuable and important in our lives.

If you, like many others, feel that you've simply not been able to get the hang of meditation, don't be concerned. The very act of talking to your Higher Power and listening for answers will suffice. Ritualistic practices are not a requisite for meditation.

Meditation is multifaceted. It can encompass concentrating on how to achieve our projected goals; musing over a passage in a book we're reading; focusing our attention on inspirational messages; even fantasizing or quietly letting our minds find their own focus. All these are forms of meditation.

TODAY'S STEP: *Meditation and contemplation restore my balance, each and every day.*

Step Eleven

Day 14—DEAF EARS

"Success is failure turned inside out." ANONYMOUS

An anonymous poem about the results of prayer has helped many of us understand the frustration we've felt when it seemed our prayers of petition had fallen on deaf ears. It gives us insight into the realization that a power greater than ourselves is far more capable of directing our lives than we are.

> I asked God for strength that I might achieve,
> I was made weak that I might learn humbly to obey.
> I asked for health that I might do greater things,
> I was given infirmity, that I might do better things.
> I asked for riches that I might be happy,
> I was given poverty, that I might be wise.
> I asked for power that I might have the praise of
>   men,
> I was given weakness, that I might feel the need of
>   God.
> I asked for all things that I might enjoy life,
> I was given life, that I might enjoy all things.
> I got nothing that I asked for, but everything that I
>   hoped for.
> Almost despite myself, my unspoken prayers were
>   answered.
> I am among all humankind, most richly blessed.

It seems to us that this prayer reflects our lives as they were before we made the decision to seek help. It also lets us know that when we turn our lives over to God, when we practice prayer and meditation, and when we follow the principles of the Twelve Steps, our lives can be far better than we had dreamed.

TODAY'S STEP: *In God's answers to my prayers, I understand His will for me.*

Day 15—THE SILENCE

"I just assumed that God was hearing me and answering my prayers."
MYRTLE FILLMORE

Today I choose to pray for others. But how shall I impart to them the gift of peace and love if my own heart is still unloving, and I have no peace of mind myself?

So I start with my heart. I hold before the God of my understanding each feeling of resentment, anger and bitterness that may still be lurking there, asking that His grace will make it yield to love someday, if not right now.

Then I seek peace. I list the worries that disturb my peace of mind and imagine that I place them in God's hands in the hope that this will bring me respite from anxiety, at least during this time of prayer.

Then I seek the depth that silence brings, for prayer that springs from silence is powerful and effective. So I listen to the sounds around me, or become aware of the feelings and sensations in my body, or my breathing in and out.

This prayer reflects the essence of the steps we have covered to date. It reminds us that we do not live in a vacuum; that when we carry old resentments and anger, we will be unable to maintain healthy relationships; that God can and will remove anxiety, and that, by meditating, we are guided in a new direction.

TODAY'S STEP: *Prayer is my tool for removing character defects and gaining peace.*

"Physical strength can never permanently with-stand the impact of spiritual force."

FRANKLIN DELANO ROOSEVELT

"Uncover—Discover—Discard" has been a recurring theme during our journey through these steps. But now we want to change "Discard" to "Recover." We are able to do this now because in Steps Four, Five, Six, Seven, Eight and Nine we identified our unproductive behavior patterns and began to rid ourselves of our defects and shortcomings. Although we will always find old attitudes and reactions cropping up in our daily lives, we now have the Tenth Step as a tool to take care of them.

The recover phase actually began in Step One and has been an integral part of all the succeeding steps. But now we want to look at it with even greater emphasis.

"Seeking only knowledge of His will for us and the power to carry that out" is a tall order indeed. We might assume now that, having put this much effort and dedication into working the previous ten steps, we should certainly have arrived at the point where we were ready for self-government. Surely, "turning our will and our lives over to the care of God" in the Third Step was simply a temporary measure?

Not so. The foundations of our program are deeply spiritual. They are based on the belief that if we want our lives to be productive and happy, then guidance from some source outside of ourselves is a prime necessity for the rest of our lives.

TODAY'S STEP: *Through prayer, I am gaining knowledge of God's will for me and the power to carry it out.*

Day 17—OPEN MIND, OPEN HEART

"The reason that we have two ears and only one mouth is that we may listen the more and talk the less."   ZENO OF CITIUM

It's important to listen to ourselves, as well as to our Higher Power, about our hopes and fears, our relationships with others, our dreams, our jobs, our wants and our needs. So once we've finished talking or praying to our Higher Power, we take time to listen to the inner insights that have come to us concerning these issues.

Recovery depends largely upon recognizing our continuing need for guidance. By developing our listening capabilities even further, we find that our intuition is becoming increasingly accurate.

When we exercise the muscles of our bodies, we develop physical strength and flexibility. When we exercise our powers of inner contemplation, we develop an inner strength and flexibility that allows us to better understand and deal with the issues that arise each day.

We are truly listening with an open mind and an open heart when we listen without prejudice to the stories of those who have gone before us; when we try to identify with what they have to say, rather than continually comparing the differences between them and ourselves; when we are courteous and attentive even to those persons who seem to have nothing to offer. Then, we are truly beginning to understand and speak the language of the heart.

TODAY'S STEP: *My prayers teach me to speak the language of the heart.*

Step Eleven

Day 18—SARAH'S STORY

"The secret of success is constancy to its purpose."
BENJAMIN DISRAELI

Sarah reported that this step, better than any other technique she had ever used, was her "counting to ten" step. She said she'd been cursed with a hair-trigger temper and a sharp tongue, and that all her life she'd practiced everything within her power to prevent herself from exploding at others.

However, she discovered that when she repeated the words of Step Eleven over to herself slowly and deliberately, they would shift her thinking from her own outrage to the recognition that God's will for her was not to take on the role of judge and executioner. Sarah found that even if she wasn't completely successful at reacting with dignity, she could at least, modify her responses.

We asked others in what way Step Eleven had proven of value to them and their responses were as varied as their personalities. Still, most of them reported that it was a step they found themselves relying on with increasing success.

We doubt whether any of us are capable of constantly keeping in mind and practicing the intent of all the steps all of the time. But many of us have learned to think of them in a form of shorthand. For instance, when we make a mistake, we say we'll "Tenth Step it;" or caught up in a dilemma we'll say we need to "Eleventh Step it."

TODAY'S STEP: *Constant contact with God helps me correct my character defects.*

Step Eleven

Day 19—REMORSE

"If we had our whole life to live over again, we might not have the strength."   ANONYMOUS

Letting go of remorse, even after we have identified and made our amends to those people we have harmed, still plagues many of us. Remorse is really anger directed against ourselves, and it only deflects us from our growing understanding of unconditional love that flows from our Higher Power.

For those of us whose religious affiliations are based on biblical teachings, we can relate our difficulties with remorse to the parable of the Prodigal Son. Like him, we hoped that once we'd seen the error of our ways and repented our actions, we'd be forgiven and welcomed back into the fold.

And now that we have been forgiven by many of the significant persons in our lives, and our Higher Power, we need to remember the third part of the equation—forgiving ourselves.

Those of us who are agnostics or atheists take a different view of absolution from remorse. On the one hand, we reject the notion of some deity's erasing our guilt. However, on the other hand, once we have adequately made amends to others, we can reassess our past actions. And now we can see them as the result of our compulsive addiction rather than as our true nature.

Therefore, knowing that we need never act that way again, we can release our remorse, and our feelings of guilt and shame.

TODAY'S STEP: *Constant contact with a loving, forgiving God helps me love and forgive myself.*

Day 20—CONFLICTING NEEDS

"Some things have to be believed to be seen."
RALPH HODGSON

Every human being has needs, some positive and healthy, some negative and unhealthy. All of these come together when we try to put the Eleventh Step into action.

"Seeking only knowledge of His will for us and the power to carry that out" can be very confusing, for sometimes those conflicting needs wage a civil war within us.

For example, we have the need for approval, yet at the same time we have the need to dominate and control. We have a need for acceptance, yet we also have the need to criticize, to humiliate, or to punish those who do not march to our drumbeat. We have the need to be loved, and yet we withhold love. We have the need to communicate, while at the same time we tend to be unwilling to voice any controversial opinion.

To answer these conflicts, we asked those who'd experienced success in overcoming these challenges how they'd done it.

"Slowly," they told us. "Slowly, and with much trial and error."

They said that the lessons about "acting as if" that they'd learned in the Sixth and Seventh Steps enabled them to ask themselves when they feel critical: "How would I act if I did not feel critical?" and then to act in a noncritical manner. This practice holds true in approaching each conflicting need.

TODAY'S STEP: *As I seek His will for me, I find it easier to let go of mine.*

Day 21—EMOTIONAL BALANCE

"Talking about God is not at all the same thing as experiencing God, or acting out God through our lives."
PHILLIP HEWETT

Step Eleven enables us to achieve a higher level of emotional balance than we've enjoyed in a good long while. Certainly, during the dark days that led to our final decision to avail ourselves of this program, we were emotional "basket cases."

The more we involve ourselves with the intent of this step, and the more we practice the forms of prayer and meditation that are comfortable for us, the deeper our sense of emotional stability becomes.

With self-will relegated to the back burner, we begin to experience a new, much more comfortable attitude about ourselves. We become increasingly aware that our lives are following a much more rewarding pattern than we've ever known before. We experience ourselves as more relaxed, more intuitive, more satisfied and more optimistic. We realize that we are no longer plagued with free-floating anxiety, and that somehow that cloud of impending doom has evaporated from our horizons.

TODAY'S STEP: *Prayer and meditation offer me peace and serenity.*

Day 22—PROGRESS

"Fear is the mind-talk that drowns out the positive messages from your intuition." ANONYMOUS

Now is an opportune time to pull out our Fourth Step inventory and review all the negative things we unearthed about ourselves; or to go back into our journal and reread how we felt when we were listing our defects and short-comings. It's difficult not to be pleased at the progress we've made when we see how many of our old defects and shortcomings are no longer a part of our persona.

Checking with people who are significant in our life is another way of measuring our progress, particularly if we've not kept any written history of our journey through this program.

In practicing our daily prayer and meditations, we've found it valuable to thank the powers-that-be that our progress has been so truly satisfactory. Despite our tendency to downgrade any of our accomplishments, acknowledging and taking pride in them is a positive factor in our continuing success. This is the kind of pride that cures, rather than destroys. It gives us a much clearer perspective of how we have changed negatives to positives.

Simply by doing these steps we've improved our conscious contact with the God of our understanding. Now it becomes increasingly clear that by working the steps, the steps begin silently to work us!

TODAY'S STEP: *I give thanks for the progress I have made.*

Day 23—THE GOLDEN RULE

"Spirituality is daily bread. Not cake served only on special occasions." ANONYMOUS

Spirituality is about developing a deep sense of unity with all the things of earth: nature, people and principles. Spirituality is what grows within us as we practice the intent of the Eleventh Step.

Once we've finally seen ourselves in the right perspective, we lose any hostility we may have had toward those with whom we work because we've chosen to be a worker among workers. This is not to imply that we imagine ourselves operating in the company of angels; it simply means that our attitude toward others becomes one of "live and let live," rather than "dog-eat-dog." Regardless of how high or lowly a position we hold, of how affluent or deprived we are, of what social strata we inhabit, we've become more comfortable with ourselves and thus with others as well. We're now more outgoing, and more self-assured.

In seeking contact with the God of our understanding, we become increasingly conscious that our goal is truly described by the Golden Rule, which advises us to do unto others as we would have them do unto us. This precludes resentments, hostility, animosity, criticism, and condemnation. More and more we sense that God's will for us is to love and be loved—uncritically, unreservedly and unconditionally.

TODAY'S STEP: *With the help of a Higher Power, I live in harmony with others.*

Day 24—THE TERRIBLE TWOS

"The difficulties of life are intended to make us better not bitter." ANONYMOUS

It is generally accepted that as children grow and develop, the "terrible twos" stage is one of the most taxing parents endure. This is when children, who are now talking and extremely curious and active, start asserting their own mind. This is when they discover the wonderful word, "no."

Those of us who have had our emotional growth arrested when we first began practicing our obsessive behavior, are very much like those two-year-olds. We're experiencing the freedom of being released from the burden of our addiction. We've mastered some of the "in" language of recovery. And, like a two-year-old child, we're sure that we're now quite capable of making our own decisions, and that we now have the power to regulate our own lives.

We balk at being told what to do or when to do it. We question whether a power outside of ourselves can truly understand our unique needs; whether it has the wisdom to dictate the path we should follow. Like the two-year-old, we say "No, no, no! I want to do it myself. No mommies or daddies, please. *I'll* choose the way I want to go."

RED ALERT! RED ALERT! RED ALERT!

When our self-will takes over again, when we delude ourselves into the belief that we have the personal power to manage our lives, we're reverting to the irrational thinking that caused all our troubles in the first place.

It is precisely at these times when self-will threatens to undermine all we have gained, that praying to know God's will for us is most crucial.

TODAY'S STEP: *I pray to let go of self-will and seek to follow God's will.*

Step Eleven

Day 25—CONSTANT CONTACT

"That's why people listen to music or look at paintings. To get in touch with that wholeness."

CORITA KENT

Newcomers have asked us what we mean by "a conscious contact." Perhaps the best explanation of what we mean by "contact" is the process by which we touch or hear someone or something that awakens a response in us. A "contact" can also be defined as a person who might be a connection.

In the Fifth Step, we admitted to God the exact nature of our wrongs. In the Seventh Step we humbly asked Him to remove our shortcomings. Now, in the Eleventh Step, we're simply asked to strengthen and improve the contacts we've already made. To do this, we must strengthen our connection with our higher contact.

This is something like making an electrical "connection." We know that when we flip on a light switch, electricity courses through the wires and gives us the desired illumination. In just this way, when we contact the God of our understanding, we sense a purpose and a power flowing into us that is not of our own making.

When we seek to improve this contact that we've already established, all we need to do is continue to talk to this power through prayer, and listen to the messages and guidance that comes through to us with increasing clarity in our meditations.

TODAY'S STEP: *Through prayer and meditation, my contact with God becomes constant and comforting.*

Day 26—IF ONLY

"Hell is made up of yearnings. The wicked don't roast on beds of nails; they sit on comfortable chairs and are tortured with yearnings."

ISAAC BASHEVIS SINGER

How often we have heard people say: "Everything would be O.K. if only I could get my wife (job, lover, family) back." "If only I had more money (a nicer car, a nicer house, a better education)." "If only I didn't have so many problems." "If only I were younger (older, smarter, healthier)." "If only the world could cease warfare, eliminate hunger, protect the environment." "If only." "If only." "If only."

Our program tells us that our lives will take a turn for the better when we learn to accept the *now*. We can fully expect that as a result of relinquishing self-will, our path will become a more fulfilling and productive one, and that our priorities will be rearranged in such a way that we can release the fear of what the future holds in store.

When we seek the knowledge of God's will for us, we can abdicate responsibility for what happens in the world at large. We understand that our first priority is to put our own house in order.

To some degree, we affect the lives of everyone with whom we come in contact. And like the concentric ripples in a pond when a pebble is tossed into it, our positive attitude has a far stronger effect than we can imagine.

TODAY'S STEP: *In relinquishing self-will, I discover that God's plans for me are good.*

Day 27—A SECOND CHANCE

"What is true is what I can't help believing."
OLIVER WENDELL HOLMES, JR.

Philosophers from time immemorial have spoken of the soul of man. The soul is that part of our beingness that reaches out for love and approval; that yearns for some concrete evidence that life is worth living and death is not the final chapter of existence. Fear of death, and the nothingness it telegraphs to many of us, makes us distrust the concept of a Godhead and an afterlife.

Most of us have not involved ourselves in this debate. We prefer to accept the *now* as the single most important factor in our existence. Because Twelve Steppers are not a religious body, we have no quarrel with any of the beliefs or nonbeliefs held by those who journey with us. We simply feel that, having been offered a second chance at life, we're content to put our trust and dependence in those who have preceded us. We're comfortable with our own individual concept of a Higher Power.

Fortunately, Step Eleven repeats the phrase "God, as we understand Him." And this frees each of us to choose a person, place, thing, concept or deity in which to put our faith. Many of us consider the group consciousness as an expression of a Higher Power, and we use it to further our progress.

TODAY'S STEP: *I am free to develop my own personal understanding of God.*

Day 28—MIRACLES

"After all is said and done, more is said than done." ANONYMOUS

Perhaps by now we've come to understand that spirituality is an earthly—rather than unearthly—way of life. Many of us have reported coincidences and events that seemed to materialize out of thin air. As one man put it: "Do I believe in miracles? You bet I do. I depend upon them!"

Somehow, things that looked like insurmountable hurdles have straightened themselves out with no conscious effort on our part. It's as if the problems for which we could see no solution and so turned over to our Higher Power have simply dematerialized. Our paths are now open to a level of freedom we thought impossible.

How often have we reminded ourselves: "You can't *think* your way into right living, but you can *live* your way into right thinking."

It is by action—that magic word—that we begin to reap the benefits of our new way of life. We have gained so much experience from doing the steps leading up to this one that almost without knowing it, our actions and reactions have become a complete reversal of the way we behaved before we asked for help.

TODAY'S STEP: *God works in amazing ways in my life.*

Step Eleven

Day 29—SUPPORT GROUPS

"If life gives you lemons, make lemonade."

ANONYMOUS

Aligning ourselves with a support group is one of the most healing of all aspects of recovery. It is so enriching to have people share their own frailties with us. And it is a consummate relief to realize that they speak from personal knowledge of some of the secrets we have kept locked inside ourselves.

At the instant of sharing, those persons are demonstrating more power than we may possess at the moment. For they are in the process of recovering from what is still our most desperate dilemma.

Support groups are a way of life today. Their aim is to create a nonjudgmental atmosphere where people with similar problems can come and share their experiences, their fears, their solutions, their strengths and their hopes.

As a result of participating in a recovery group, a woman who survived cancer decided to open a shop that served the needs of mastectomy patients. Her frustration in going from department stores to medical supply houses, beauty shops and health food stores to meet her needs during chemotherapy prompted her to design a one-stop facility for other women going through this experience. It was also her hope to provide a drop-in place where women could come for support and encouragement.

She shared with her group that it was the Eleventh Step's meditation that brought this vision to her, and it was her group's loving support that gave her the courage to make her dream a reality.

TODAY'S STEP: *God's presence is felt through the groups I attend.*

Step Eleven

Day 30—A NEW DAY

"You can't measure time in days the way you can money in dollars, because each day is different."
PHILLIP HEWETT

A practice many of us have developed is of starting our day off with some sort of prayer, meditation or affirmation. Many of us do all three! We ask the God of our understanding to guide us through the day and to help us continue to follow those principles and directions that the preceding steps have taught us.

In Step Ten, we developed the practice of taking a daily inventory, and this has given us a clue we can use to our advantage as we pursue our recovery program. It is simply that when we find ourselves falling short in our determination, we don't have to write our day off as a failure. We can simply admit where we're at fault, and then start our day over at that point.

"Oh, ho!" you say. "So that's how you've tricked us into accepting the one day at a time dictum."

Tricked? No. But accepting? Yes. For if we pledge ourselves to do something for the next twenty-four hours beginning at, say, 9 A.M., and something goes awry at noon, we can correct that condition and repledge our twenty-four hours to start at 12 P.M.

TODAY'S STEP: *My daily prayers alert me to my shortcomings, and God helps me remove them.*

Step Eleven

Day 31—MORE MIRACLES

"You can have anything you want, if you will give up the belief that you can't have it."

ROBERT ANTHONY

We have now successfully covered 11/12ths of our Twelve Step program, and in the process we've discovered a great deal about ourselves—as well as other significant people in our lives—that we simply were not aware of before.

Most of us have unearthed a sensitivity we'd kept under wraps for years, for we didn't want others to know how vulnerable we were. But now we're becoming less afraid to talk about our feelings of inadequacy, our fears, our likes and dislikes. We're far more sensitive to the feelings of others, and we're now sure enough of ourselves to release the need to control anybody or anything.

We've seen and experienced some amazing turns of events and "coincidences," which some of us call "miracles." And we've shared the kinds of experiences with others that gave us a sense of spiritual kinship with our fellow human beings.

These are true spiritual experiences. Perhaps they weren't spectacular illuminations. But every bit as wondrous is the slow, dawning realization that we like ourselves, our lives and other people.

TODAY'S STEP: *God's presence and will is apparent to me in the many miracles of my recovery.*

Step Twelve

STEP TWELVE

"Having had a spiritual awakening as a result of these Steps, we tried to carry this message to alcoholics (others), and to practice these principles in all our affairs."

We have now arrived at the grandaddy of all the steps. This is the greatest challenge of all.

We've come a long way. And we still have a long way to go. But what a way! The freedom we now enjoy will be triply enhanced when we have finished Step Twelve—the ultimate step in decisiveness and resolve—for its benefits are without number.

Our growing sense of self-worth is propelling us into the awakening that Step Twelve promises. By now, of course, we understand that there is no uniformity in the awakening process. Some of us experience a spiritual conversion that dispels all doubt. Others benefit by an educational process that allows us to view spirituality in a new and comfortable light. But no matter how it comes to us, the experience is so profound that it releases us from the bondage of self.

Step Twelve

Day 1—SUPERWOMAN AND SUPERMAN

"People ought to listen more slowly."

JEAN SPARKS DUCEY

By now we probably feel we're ready to take on the whole world. Like converts, we want to gather up all of those who have experienced the same problems we have, bring them into the fold, and heal them. We fancy ourselves like the Good Shepherd, rescuing the little lamb who has strayed from the fold. We're suffused with love for our fellow-sufferers, and feel that if they'd only talk with us for a while, we could convince them that we have the solution for their problems.

Poor Pitiful Pearl has metamorphosed into Superwoman: and Poor Pitiful Paul has become Superman. And they're proud of their new identities, as well they should be.

We're ready to explain in detail just exactly how we succeeded in losing the obsession that bound us in its grip for such a long time. We could talk for hours about our struggles and our ultimate victory. We're sure that if our identified prospects will just follow our dictates to the letter, they too will recover.

However, noble as these sentiments are, they need to be carefully evaluated. We need to remember very clearly how we, ourselves, felt when the program was first presented to us.

TODAY'S STEP: *My enthusiasm for spreading the word is balanced by my sensitivity to others.*

Step Twelve

Day 2—WISDOM

"The reward of a thing well done is to have done it."
RALPH WALDO EMERSON

It is slowly dawning on us that the preceding Eleven Steps are part of an ongoing process. We realize that just because we've been through them once doesn't mean we can pack them away in mothballs. Step Twelve clearly demonstrates that we could not have arrived at our present state of balance were it not for Steps One through Eleven. It also tells us that, in preparing to undertake the threefold message of this step, we're committing ourselves to a way of life that is a complete departure from the attitudes and behavior of our addictive lifestyle.

As problems continue to arise in our everyday life, we're able to take each one of them in turn, and work through the entire Twelve Steps with them. We can do this with skewered relationships, with money and employment problems, with emotional hang-ups and with any other situation that may be causing us confusion and discomfort.

Remember the old Latin adage: "Repetition is the mother of wisdom"? It is by repeatedly applying the steps in all our affairs that we reap the benefits of our new way of life. We also need to remember H.O.W.—Honesty, Open-mindedness and Willingness—that we learned in our early days of recovery. The power of this advice will become increasingly obvious as we enjoy the fruits of our labors.

TODAY'S STEP: *I continue to practice the principles of this program in all my affairs.*

Day 3—DAVE'S STORY

"Back of every achievement is a proud wife and a surprised mother-in-law."   BROOKS HAYS

Despite what some people have reported, spiritual awakenings don't tend to be all that dramatic. A typical one was shared by Dave.

"I didn't see fireworks in the sky, or feel I was in the presence of some celestial being," Dave recalled. "I certainly couldn't identify with anything as airy-fairy as blinding flashes of light, or some of the other phenomena some people talked about.

"It was simply that one day I realized my attitude and sense of value had undergone an enormous change. My identity was no longer reflected by the clothes I wore, nor the car I drove, nor the house I lived in, nor my yearly income.

"My family and friends began to take on much more importance to me than all those *things* that we usually equate with success. That didn't mean I was ready to chuck my position and take up farming so I could lead a more simple life. What it did mean was that issues of money, property and prestige were no longer my begin-all and end-all goals.

"As far as I'm concerned," said Dave contentedly, "you couldn't ask for a better spiritual awakening than that!"

TODAY'S STEP: *My day-to-day recovery is evidence of a spiritual awakening.*

Step Twelve

Day 4—HIGHWAY TO FREEDOM

"One of the greatest pleasures in life is doing what people say you can't do." ANONYMOUS

We had been caught up for so long in turmoil and confusion that we saw no alternatives to any other way of life. We despaired of ever understanding ourselves or of being understood by others. But the program offered us a highway to freedom.

Now our perspective has changed. Having examined and admitted our shortcomings and defects, we went about the business of making amends to those we had harmed. This done, we were able to reorganize our lives into a new healthy and optimistic pattern. We excised the skeletons in our closet with the Eighth and Ninth Steps. We learned the power of prayer, and practiced—to the best of our ability—a form of meditation that allowed us to maintain a reasonable balance in our lives. We learned that by releasing self-will and accepting the concept of a power greater than ourselves, our lives were proceeding in a much more satisfactory manner than ever before.

As we look back on our journey to the Twelfth Step, we realize we have been through a spiritual awakening. We have stepped out of a bad dream into a safe and sane world.

TODAY'S STEP: *My spiritual awakening is the result of working the previous steps.*

Day 5—EVERYDAY SPIRITUALITY

"Your goals don't start in your brain, they start in your heart." ANONYMOUS

Spirituality is all-encompassing. It's as much the ability to accept love as it is the capacity for loving. It's the sensation of having connected with another person on a meaningful level. It's the willingness to share of ourselves when we feel that someone else will benefit from that sharing. It's giving and forgetting the gift. It's being true because we've earned the trust of others.

Spirituality is a lack of self-pity—the willingness to release self-will. It's accepting who we are, knowing that we're becoming whom we hope to be. It's doing our very best and leaving the results in the hands of a power greater than ourselves. It's meeting challenges and not fearing failure.

The more we think about the deeper meaning of our path as we arrive at Step Twelve, the more we realize that we've just skimmed the surface of the meaning of spirituality in our lives. Perhaps it means that all the power in the universe is working to maintain health and balance in our lives; that we can now accept the past and not dwell in the future, and that we've developed the ability to keep ourselves in the here and now.

TODAY'S STEP: *I am able to practice the spiritual principles I have learned in all my affairs.*

Step Twelve

Day 6—THE ROSE

"Life is not a cup to be drained, but a measure to be filled." ANONYMOUS

In *The Inner Game of Tennis*, author Timothy Galway offers a comforting analogy to help us through the feeling that our spiritual awakening isn't as deep or profound as we would have hoped—now that we've reached the Twelfth Step.

When we plant a rose seed in the earth, we notice that it is small, but we don't criticize it as rootless and stemless. We treat it as a seed, giving it the water and nourishment it requires. When it first shoots up out of the earth, we don't condemn it as immature and underdeveloped; nor do we criticize the buds for not being open. We stand in wonder at the process taking place and give the plant the care it needs at each stage of its development. The rose is a rose from the time it is a seed until it dies. Within it, at all times, it contains its whole potential. It seems to be constantly in the process of change; yet at each stage, at each moment, it is perfectly all right as it is.

So it is with us. We're perfectly all right as we are. As we grow, we're deepening our sense of spirituality and our capacity to share with those in earlier stages. This helps our continuing search for even greater commitment and stability.

TODAY'S STEP: *I rejoice in my spiritual growth from the earliest seeds of my recovery.*

Step Twelve

Day 7—SPIRITUALITY

"No one gets lost on a straight path."

ANONYMOUS

While spirituality can be fueled by religion, it can also exist without it. It is important to know that we perform many spiritual actions every day of our lives. It is not necessary for us to get down on our knees to be spiritual. Spirituality is as ordinary a condition as it is esoteric.

Many people have said they feel a lot more spiritual looking at a newborn baby than by listening to a sermon.

Each time we do something unselfish, that's spiritual. When we make amends to those we have offended or harmed, that's spiritual. When we meditate, seeking knowledge of God's will for us, that's spiritual. When we speak well of another, or give someone a helping hand, that's spiritual. When we observe the beauty of a landscape or listen to inspiring music, that's spiritual.

It's not necessary to see visions or blinding lights to have a spiritual awakening. Rather, by following these steps, we become aware of altered perceptions and modified actions.

TODAY'S STEP: *In the simplest of things, I discover spirituality at work.*

Day 8—CARRYING THE MESSAGE

"Behold the turtle. He makes progress only when he sticks his neck out."   ANONYMOUS

Whether or not we've been aware of it, we've been carrying the message of recovery to everyone in our life today. As they've watched the changes in us since we first began to practice the principles of our program, they've seen a great metamorphosis taking place.

We've also influenced newer acquaintances, simply by our candor and lack of artifice. After we've finally discarded the burden of obsessive/compulsive behavior, we tend to be far less guarded and secretive. We no longer fear being "found out" because we have nothing to hide. What a blessing that is!

The support groups that have been so beneficial to our recovery have been another area in our lives where we've carried the message. We've done this just by showing up on a continuing basis; by participating in our own recovery by sharing our experiences, strengths and hopes with others; by being willing to discuss our past with someone who is wrestling with a similar problem. This is how we're demonstrating love and service to others and fulfilling this requirement of continuing recovery.

For "loners," a pen pal relationship is a marvelous way to carry the message. Computer networks and fax machines can also create a support system almost as good as being there in person.

TODAY'S STEP: *My daily practice of the Twelve Steps enables me to carry the message of recovery.*

Day 9—REBUILDING RELATIONSHIPS

*"When we admit we were wrong, we are wiser
today than we were yesterday."*   ANONYMOUS

Since we were very small, most of us have heard the adage:
"Actions speak louder than words." We think this is a very
appropriate guideline for our continuing recovery program.

We can think of no better way for us to carry the
message of recovery than to maintain good relationships
with those around us and to continue to work on problems
left over from our past.

Many of us have experienced family difficulties caused
by our diseases. Because of this we need to understand that
although our spouse or children may forgive us, sometimes
it's hard for them to trust again. As one husband sadly
remarked about his recovering wife, "I'm afraid I have
more trust in the disease than I do in her recovery."

Their feelings are authentic and need to be respected. It
takes time to heal old wounds. We want to guard against
petulance and resentment, against our own feeling that
they aren't giving us credit for being totally well and totally
responsible. As a matter of fact, we often try to manipulate
others by using our past disorder as a cop-out to avoid
facing an unpleasant situation, saying it would be a threat
to our recovery. But whenever we do this, we're actually
reinforcing their fears that our recovery might, indeed, be
a transitory thing.

TODAY'S STEP: *I practice the principles of recovery daily
and take the time to heal old wounds.*

Step Twelve

Day 10—SPIRITUAL PROGRESS

"I sought my soul, but my soul I could not see. I sought my God but my God eluded me. I sought my brother and I found all three."   ANONYMOUS

These words from the *Big Book of Alcoholics Anonymous* reassure and help us:

> Do not be discouraged. No one among us has been able to practice perfect adherence to these principles. We are not saints. The point is, that we are willing to grow along spiritual lines. The principles we have set down are guides to progress. We claim spiritual progress, rather than spiritual perfection.

We don't want to belabor the question of spirituality's relationship with religion but we have come to understand that spirituality is not in conflict with any denomination, philosophy or faith. We have found that it is a universal force, embodied in whatever form or manifestation we perceive, that allows us to live in love and respect of other people.

So, whether our awakening is dramatic or quietly emerging, whether it is an intellectual observation, or as embryonic as the tiny mustard seed, it *is* a bonafide awakening and will serve us well.

TODAY'S STEP: *I trust my own perceptions of God, be they religious or spiritual.*

Step Twelve

Day 11—ACCEPTANCE

"What you are is God's gift to you; what you make of yourself is your gift to God."

ANTHONY DALLA VILLA

Perhaps one of the greatest awarenesses that these Twelve Steps brings us is that there truly is such a thing as unconditional love.

Many of us have felt there have always been provisional price tags on love. Love was given conditionally, provided we lived up to the expectations of those who claimed to love us. As children we learned—very painfully—that certain behaviors were unacceptable and punishable. Whatever the intent of this punishment, it made us feel that we were bad, and that *they* didn't love us anymore.

When we first fell in love, we discovered that there were strings attached to our relationship. We were loved if we did and said all the things the object of our affections wanted us to do and say. When we failed to come up to their expectations, they withdrew love or abandoned us.

Because of our spiritual awakening to the unconditional love of the God of our understanding, now we have entered a dimension in which we are accepted as we are, both bright and dark sides exposed, and we are welcomed without criticism or judgment.

TODAY'S STEP: *My reward for practicing these principles in all my affairs is the gift of acceptance.*

Step Twelve

Day 12—"FIXED FRAME MENTALITY"

"I had a very simple technique of behavior. I was always jumping up in your lap to be petted, and if you didn't pet me, I jumped off of your lap and bit you."
ALLEN REID McGINNIS

A "fixed frame mentality" has plagued many of us. This is where we form a fixed opinion and image of ourselves and others. We stuff that picture into a frame where there is no space for any other interpretation. We tell ourselves, "That's the way we (they) are and that's the way we (they) always were and that's the way we (they) will always be!"

Happily, this begins to disappear as we work our way through the steps, and we now look at ourselves and others with a new perspective. We've not only proven to ourselves that we are capable of major change, but working the steps has given us an entirely new look at the persons most intimately associated with us. We understand how our actions have caused reactions from others and, conversely, how others' actions have caused us to react. We see that in any dysfunction, illness or addiction, everyone associated with the impaired person is affected by that disorder. Actually, some of them become even sicker or more neurotic than the one who is temporarily impaired.

Sometimes it is awkward to reverse an opinion or a bias we may have formed in relationship to other people, but we *know* that we have changed and we will continue to change. Our Ninth Step taught us that when we approached others with honesty and openness, their reaction to us was quite different than it had been in the past.

TODAY'S STEP: *My fixed approach to life is transformed by practicing these principles in all my affairs.*

Day 13—HEALING THROUGH SHARING

"No one can escape from prison without the help of those who have escaped before."   G.I. GURDJIEFF

Practical experience in Alcoholics Anonymous has proven that the most positive insurance against relapse is to work with others who have the same affliction. By watching others work the Twelve Steps, people in recovery reexperience graphically how mixed-up they had been in the past and how hard they have struggled to reach their current state of balance. They come to understand that they are more capable of helping those people than anyone else. Simply by sharing their own experiences, they are able to gain the trust of newcomers and help guide them through the now familiar and well-practiced Twelve Steps.

Some helpful hints from those recovering alcoholics are: Be careful not to overpower newcomers with too strong an approach, and try to remember your own hesitancy and fears about accepting this way of life—especially the difficulty you had in turning over your life and will to an unknown force.

When we see that our newcomers are dubious about the spiritual aspects of the Twelve Steps—which they perceive as religious—we need to reassure them, as we were reassured, that in the early stages of recovery, the choice of a power greater than themselves can simply be their sponsors or the group.

TODAY'S STEP: *In sharing with newcomers, I carry the program's message.*

Step Twelve

Day 14—WORKING WITH OTHERS

"Men seldom give pleasure when they are not pleased themselves." SAMUEL JOHNSON

Sometimes we get so carried away with enthusiasm about our own recovery, that we approach newcomers with a fervor they find threatening. We need to back off if they show any reluctance to pursue the path we have taken. But we also need to let them know that we will be available at any time, should they ask for help.

Remember those fellow-travelers also seeking recovery who helped guide us. Experience, that infallible teacher, has taught us that continuing involvement with others and attendance at self-help group meetings are very supportive factors in maintaining our new way of life.

In early 1990, *Newsweek* magazine published an article about the number of support groups that have sprung up around the country, most of which are patterned after AA.

Despite poking mild fun at some of the more unusual groupings, they admitted that where the best minds in medicine, philosophy, psychology and religion had failed, these self-help groups had established the value of working together, and were having great success.

TODAY'S STEP: *I carry the message, yet I don't get carried away.*

Step Twelve

Day 15—HEALING LAUGHTER

"Grief can take care of itself, but to get the full value of joy, you must have somebody to divide it with."
MARK TWAIN

A very helpful adjunct of recovery is attending self-help groups. For those of us who have felt like outsiders, the sense of belonging they offer is tremendously rewarding. When we regularly attend a "home group" where laughter and optimism prevail, we both share and receive the benefits of experience, strength and hope.

Visitors unfamiliar with the dynamic that allows participants to tell horrendous stories about their past, only to have their listeners respond with uproarious laughter, are sometimes appalled that anyone could find humor in those tragic stories.

This laughter is healing, not derogatory. It speaks to their feelings of blessed relief that, like the speaker, their dark days are behind them. Those things, which were once tragedies, have become stepping-stones for success. The candor with which people talk, the courage they show in telling their stories, and the wisdom they share can be a revelation to the uninitiated.

TODAY'S STEP: *In sharing my story with my group, I carry the message.*

Day 16—RECOVERY COMICS

"Everything is funny as long as it is happening to somebody else."
                                                    WILL ROGERS

What are people laughing at in fellowship meetings? Here are a few examples:

Joe: "I sleep in the buff. Every morning I get up, play the theme from 'Rocky,' put on a cowboy hat and jump on my trampoline in front of a mirror. There is no way I can take myself or the world too seriously when I have started off the day being the butt of my own joke."

Kathy: "I tried to drown my sorrows in drink, but I just taught the little rascals how to swim."

Stu: "What I would do is, I would buy ten or twelve dollars' worth of candy bars at a time. Some of them I'd put in a plastic bag and stash in the toilet tank. Others, I'd arrange behind the books on our bookshelf. The rest I'd hide in the chandelier in our dining room. When we had company and ate in the dining room, I'd have one helluva time getting them out before anyone saw them, or they melted."

Virginia: "I'd get a prescription from my doctor, empty the bottle, drop it in the john until the label was smeary. I'd bring the bottle back to the drugstore, explain my 'accident,' get a new supply, and make out-of-town rounds until I had enough to hold me until the next time I could legitimately ask my doctor for a refill."

For many of us, it was this kind of self-deprecating humor that enabled us to hear the message of recovery.

TODAY'S STEP: *My sense of humor helps me to carry—and to get—the message.*

Step Twelve

Day 17—TO BE HAPPY, JOYOUS AND FREE

"If you have one eye on yesterday, and one eye on tomorrow, you're going to be cockeyed today."
ANONYMOUS

If the outcome of recovery is to live a humorless, stodgy, monastic existence, few of us would bother.

By sharing experience, hope and strength we learn that our goal is to be happy, joyous and free. We will experience greater and greater intuitive powers. Fears that used to plague us will dissipate and we will walk in dignity among our fellows.

We learn the blessed virtue of laughing at ourselves, which helps us put things in their proper perspective.

As Jack put it in a self-help meeting: "I noticed the last time I was at a funeral that all the headstones, simple or monumental, had one thing in common. That was the date of the person's birth and the date of death. Those dates were separated by a matter of only a few inches. And I thought, Gee! Those couple of inches represent someone's entire life. So it seems to me that if life is so short, we'd better learn to enjoy the *now*. We'd better make our now as happy, loving and productive as we can."

TODAY'S STEP: *Through practicing these principles, I learn to laugh and to be joyful.*

Step Twelve

Day 18—SPIRITUAL AWAKENINGS

"Keep hanging around the barber shop, and sooner or later you're going to get a haircut."

ANONYMOUS

Whether we know it or not, we've undergone a number of spiritual experiences as we worked the previous Eleven Steps. These have all led to the spiritual awakening promised by Step Twelve.

Although many of us do not feel we've truly arrived at this stage, the promise of the step is at work within us. It might not happen right this moment, but the seeds have been planted and are germinating in our subconscious. For those of us who are discouraged by a lack of concrete evidence, we suggest reaffirming the Third Step commitment to turn our lives and wills over to the Higher Power we've chosen as our guide.

Even though we now have irrefutable evidence of the dramatic changes in our lives, we may still find it difficult to dismiss those old ideas of doom and gloom and believe it's possible to rid ourselves of the negative conditions we have created. Some of us find it hard to believe that having screwed up so badly, we're truly on the right track at last.

But, believe it we must, for by applying the lessons of the Twelfth Step, we become not only increasingly comfortable with ourselves but also with our fellows.

TODAY'S STEP: *A spiritual awakening is evident in the major changes in my life.*

Day 19—PEER HEALING

"In the country of the blind, the one-eyed man is king."
MICHAEL APOSTOLIUS

Perhaps we think ourselves inadequate to carry the message to others, believing that our own recovery is so tenuous that we don't feel we have enough to offer someone who is just exploring a recovery program.

Nothing could be farther from the truth.

The minute we take the first step—admitting our personal powerlessness—we can offer a ray of hope to people who have come to the end of their rope in trying to overcome their own addiction. We need no more information than our trust that this program is—at long last—the vehicle that will help us to recover.

People talking to people, without prejudice and without being judgmental, is the most effective way to reach those who are suffering shame and remorse.

When faced with professional help, many people feel "less than"—even though this attitude is unrealistic. And yet, the word of someone who is struggling with a dilemma similar to theirs gives them hope and encouragement. They feel that if a peer can do it, then maybe it's also possible for them to do it.

TODAY'S STEP: *Even as I struggle, my experience is of value to others who still suffer.*

Day 20—BELIEF AND TRUST

*"No matter what may be your lot in life, build
something on it."*   ANONYMOUS

What is meant by a "spiritual experience" differs widely
among those of us in recovery.

Whether religious or nonreligious, the experiences that
recovering persons have shared with us all seem to agree
with the key words in the Twelfth Step: "Having had a
spiritual awakening as a result of these Steps." There is clear
recognition that some benign power is guiding them.

Granted, those of us who are religious might already
have a strong belief that God, as we know Him, has been
a prime mover in our recovery from the very start. We
believe this to be true, but we also believe that others will
soon recognize that, as a result of the steps, their belief has
been deepened.

The terms "spiritual experience" and "spiritual awakening" have been used many times in our discussions. Those
of us who are nonbelievers and have used the group as our
Higher Power, have gradually come to accept that the
personality change we have experienced as part of our
recovery is one of the most significant spiritual awakenings
we may ever know.

TODAY'S STEP: *My path of recovery is a progressive spiritual awakening.*

Day 21—REACHING OUT

"Don't wait for your ship to come in. Swim out to it."   ANONYMOUS

Perhaps one of the most conclusive pieces of evidence that we have achieved a spiritual awakening occurs when we try to help someone whose disorder is much like our own. In communicating with a newcomer, we often find ourselves verbalizing beliefs and assurances we sometimes didn't know we possessed.

AA members frequently advise newcomers: "When all else fails, work with others." This advice becomes a vital guideline to keep us on our chosen path. As we share what we used to be like, what happened and what we're like now, our own doubts diminish. The therapeutic value of such action not only touches the newcomer but also reinforces our own resolve to cling to the principles we're pursuing. And the amazing thing about action of this kind is that, whether or not our prospect is receptive, we have intensified our own commitment to a far greater degree.

However, we must keep in mind that there is a vast difference between compliance and surrender. Some of us may suspect that we have complied with the advice to reach out simply to reassure others. That's why we need to question whether or not our surrender has been a total one. Remember, the very act of reaching out to someone else is good living; in time, good thinking will follow.

TODAY'S STEP: *The service I give to others strengthens my own understanding of these principles.*

Step Twelve

Day 22—SUPPORTING OTHERS

"You're a good man, Charlie Brown."

CHARLES SCHULZ

When we observe the attitudes of newcomers change from fear, anger, resentment and despair, to hope and a semblance of confidence; when they begin to trust and confide in us; when we see a new light in their eyes and a spring in their step; when tension lines leave their faces and they begin to hold their heads high then, perhaps for the first time, we get a sense of spirituality in action.

Even if it's been difficult to measure our own progress adequately, working with others gives us indisputable evidence of the power these principles generate in the lives of others. We can concede, without question, that our own lives are better than they have been in a very long time. We can also admit that we're invested in supporting those who share this journey with us, and even with those who have not yet found the path to recovery. For many of us, this is a dramatic change from our self-serving and self-centered past.

In a sense, we are our brother's keepers. And they are ours. And this exchange contains much of the magic of recovery.

TODAY'S STEP: *In giving support to newcomers, I reexperience the miracle of recovery.*

Day 23—PRACTICING THE PRINCIPLES

"Singing lessons are like bodybuilding for your lar-
ynx."
                                    BERNADETTE PETERS

The next move we're asked to make in Step Twelve is to carry that same feeling of good fellowship we feel toward our fellow-travelers into every area of our lives. "What an order!" we cry. "I can't go through with it. Lord knows I've struggled long and hard just to be able to communicate and cooperate with people pursuing this same path. And now you ask us to go out into this dog-eat-dog world and practice the same tolerance, trust, honesty and unconditional love with everyone? Impossible!"

No, it's not impossible.

As a matter of fact, when we see the results of putting these principles into practice in the outside world, we're in for even more amazing revelations than we've already experienced. Since we haven't yet tried our new wings in that larger arena of chaos and confusion, we have no idea how powerful they have become. What a surprise we have in store when we discover they're quite capable of carrying us through all the challenges life presents.

One man shared that when he returned to the business he'd practically ruined, he began practicing the principle of, as he phrased it: "Helping God's little kids help themselves."

His colleagues were so confused by his business tactics that they were sure he had some diabolical takeover plan up his sleeve. However, when business boomed and the profits rolled in, they were only too happy to follow his lead.

TODAY'S STEP: *What I've gained in the program, I now apply to every area of my life.*

Step Twelve

Day 24—SAYING "YES" TO LIFE

"Dear God—help me to get up. I can fall down by myself."   ANONYMOUS

A pervading guideline in most recovery fellowships is letting go of all our old ideas.

This injunction doesn't mean just those ideas we perceived as being detrimental to our health and well-being. What we're talking about is *all* our old ideas.

We can now see that, as our addictive/compulsive disorder progressed, our entire thinking process underwent a change. This change was necessary to allow us to justify our thoughts and actions. It was as if some sort of virus had altered and redirected our thought processes and we lost the ability to think and act in an acceptable and rational manner.

Now we can say "No" to all those old ideas, and "Yes" to a new way of life. We think of ourselves as "the twice born," and check every instinctive reaction to see if it fits into the H.O.W. mode—Honesty, Open-mindedness and Willingness—that we put in place when we took the Fourth and Eleventh Steps.

We say "Yes" to surrender, "Yes" to responsibilities, "Yes" to purpose, "Yes" to commitment, "Yes" to cooperation, "Yes" to a trust in a power greater than ourselves, "Yes" to love and "Yes" to service.

TODAY'S STEP: *Through practicing the principles I have embraced new ideas; I now approach all my affairs differently.*

Step Twelve

Day 25—OUT OF THE ASHES

"Yes, Virginia. There IS a Santa Claus."
TITLE OF NEWSPAPER STORY

December 25th is the day when scores of people throughout the world celebrate the birth of the Christ child. Christmas, in the United States and many other countries, creates an aura of loving and giving, and demonstrations of goodwill.

But the spirit of Christmas can be celebrated every day of the year, and sometimes it helps to bring that spirit into our present-day lives.

In Charles Dickens' story "A Christmas Carol," Ebenezer Scrooge—in one night—experiences the phenomenon of rebirth. As the result of these steps, we, too, can expect that same amazing experience. Our old entity, damaged and wounded, is put to rest. Now we can begin to experience the happiness, joy and freedom that has been promised by those who have gone before us.

Scrooge saw what he used to be like and why, and this helped him to realize that he now had the opportunity to be very different. He began to realize that a loving, caring, giving person lived within him, and almost immediately began to feel a positive response from all those around him.

So it is with us. By scrupulous adherence to the Fourth, Fifth, Sixth, Seventh, Eighth and Ninth Steps, we saw what *we* were like. We took action to rid ourselves of the load we were carrying and began to trust in the process of recovery. We put all our old negative judgments behind us. And we rose out of the ashes of despair to enjoy a positive, joyous view of the future.

TODAY'S STEP: *As a result of these steps, I lay the ghosts of Christmas past to rest.*

Day 26—RECOVERY IS A PROCESS

"Moving fast is not the same thing as going some-where." ANONYMOUS

Indifference and complacency are two of the most danger-ous pitfalls we can encounter at this stage of our program. We must continually remind ourselves that *recovery is not an event, it is a process.*

Despite the fact that we've successfully completed al-most all of the Twelve Steps, we have yet to arrive at a destination. We're still on a journey. "Completing" the steps simply means that we've successfully charted a road-map that gives us direction for our journey in this new way of life.

Many of us feel that, having done the steps, we're no longer in need of any further guidelines. "Thanks for shar-ing," we say, "but we can handle it from here on out." Or, "Look, it's been a very interesting trip. But since my case is different, I certainly don't need anyone to monitor me or give any more advice."

This is exactly the point where we need to reread the last line in this step: "to practice these principles in all our affairs." Surely the message could not be any clearer than that? And surely it means that now that we've discovered the formula, we need to keep putting it into practice on an ongoing basis in our daily lives.

TODAY'S STEP: *I continue to practice these principles in all my affairs and to share them with others.*

Day 27—PROGRESS, NOT PERFECTION

"We are continually faced by great opportunities brilliantly disguised as problems."   ANONYMOUS

There's no doubt that our value systems have undergone considerable change. We've seen many things that seemed of primary importance become much less significant. What we once thought absolutely necessary for our mental, emotional, physical and financial security has undergone a profound change.

Learning to live in the *now* has helped erase the fears and uncertainties that immobilized us in the past. When we've truly forgiven ourselves for our past behavior, we find that we're able to function with a renewed sense of purpose and confidence.

It would be wonderful if, consistently, in every aspect of our daily lives, we were able to practice the Honesty, Open-mindedness and Willingness the steps describe—if we could accord to everyone the same courtesy, compassion and tolerance that is a pervading theme of our program.

To our dismay, this is not always the case.

But succeeding in this to any degree is all that is necessary today. Just as our addiction was progressive, so is our recovery. Remember, we seek progress rather than perfection. Slowly but surely the results will become more and more evident—even to us.

TODAY'S STEP: *I no longer aim for perfection, but I cherish my progress.*

Step Twelve

Day 28—THE LIGHTER SIDE

"Obstacles are things you see when you take your eyes off the goal." ANONYMOUS

Participants in discussion groups often share wonderfully simple one-liners that not only elicit laughter, but also help us deal with those seemingly insurmountable problems that life has a habit of dealing out. We remember them because they are humorous and because they debunk complex, fear-provoking analytical processes that many of us persist in using as the only way to find a solution to our problems.

"If it works, don't fix it."

"Compared to what?"

"When all else fails—follow directions."

"What step are you working today?"

"Inch by inch, it's a cinch. By the yard, it's very hard."

"No pain—no gain."

Reducing our problems to the simplest equation possible and being willing to see that every dark and oppressing situation has a humorous side immediately reduces the size and importance of the problem. One of the surest signs of progress is the capacity to laugh at ourselves and to recognize that what we see as problems are really opportunities for growth.

TODAY'S STEP: *Laughter is often the medium of my message.*

Step Twelve

Day 29—WALKING THE WALK

"An atheist is a man who has no invisible means of support." ANONYMOUS

We no longer cling to the belief that we're not capable or that we don't have the strength to be the kind of person we've always wanted to be. We've finally stopped denigrating ourselves. No more sackcloth and ashes for us.

Now we're aware of the possibilities, rather than the impossibilities, of achieving our goals. We find ourselves willing and eager to share these positive feelings with newcomers who have just started on our path.

Even though some of us have not yet experienced a "spiritual awakening," we cannot deny that there have been profound changes in our lives and in our attitudes. We also find that we get a lift when we're able to reach out a helping hand and, every once in a while, with no conscious thought, we find that we're "walking the walk and talking the talk."

The steps themselves have become so much a part of our doing and thinking processes that we almost automatically react in a healthy manner to circumstances and stimuli that used to distress or anger us.

TODAY'S STEP: *Almost without conscious thought I am beginning to practice the principles in all my affairs.*

Step Twelve

Day 30—"H.O.W." WE GOT WHERE WE ARE

"I once wanted to become an atheist, but I gave up—they have no holidays." HENNY YOUNGMAN

Step One—*Honesty:* We admitted our powerlessness—an act that found us beginning to understand the strength of humility and the curative power of surrender.

Step Two—*Open-mindedness:* We recognized that our behavior lacked sanity and balance and conceded that there might be some power—somewhere—that could do for us what we could not do for ourselves.

Step Three—*Willingness:* In Step One, we *admitted* our powerlessness. We now *accepted* that fact and demonstrated our acceptance by becoming willing to turn our will and lives over to a power greater than ourselves.

Step Four—*Honesty, Willingness:* We tackled this step accepting the shame and pain of self-assessment and were scrupulously honest about detailing all the wrongs we had committed.

Step Five—*Honesty, Open-mindedness, Willingness:* We strengthened the commitment we had made in Step Three by admitting to the God of our understanding, to ourselves and to another person everything we had discovered about ourselves in Step Four.

TODAY'S STEP: *In reviewing the steps, my spiritual awakening becomes clear.*

Day 31—HOW WE GOT TO WHERE WE ARE

"The world is so full of a number of things, I'm sure we should all be as happy as kings."
ROBERT LOUIS STEVENSON

Steps Six and Seven—*Honesty, Open-mindedness, Willingness:* These were our clarifying steps. They made us even more aware of the havoc that our addictive/compulsive behavior had created in our own lives and in other people's lives. Once again, we turned to our Higher Power to help us rid ourselves of those defects and shortcomings.

Steps Eight and Nine—*Honesty, Willingness:* We listed all those who had suffered as a result of our behavior and with courage and determination we set about making whatever restitution was possible.

Step Ten—*Honesty, Open-mindedness, Willingness:* We took stock of our behavior each day. We checked to see where we were in error and promptly admitted it so we could keep our own house in order.

Step Eleven—*Uncover, Discover, Discard:* We took the essence of each preceding step and brought it into play in this step of reaffirmation and rededication.

Step Twelve—*Uncover, Discover, Recover:* We reviewed our progress and found it good. We released the need for perfection. We accepted these steps as a blueprint for our life to come, and were content that we had finally reached our safe harbor.

TODAY'S STEP: *I am firm in my resolve to share the joy of recovering with all who will listen.*

INDEX